Judas
at the
Jockey
Club

Judas at the Jockey Club

and Other
Episodes
of Porfirian
Mexico

William H. Beezley

University
of
Nebraska
Press
Lincoln
and
London

Library of Congress
Cataloging
in Publication Data
Beezley, William H.
Judas at the Jockey
Club and other
episodes of Porfir-
ian Mexico.
Bibliography: p.
Includes index
1. Mexico – Social
life and customs.
2. Mexico – History –
1867–1910.
3. Social classes –
Mexico.
I. Title.
F1233.5.B44   1987
972.08   86-11320
ISBN 0-8032-1195-3
alkaline paper

To Blue

Contents

Illustrations

page 2

Preface

The episodes comprised in this volume result from my attempt to understand the lives of everyday Mexicans in the heyday of progress. Obviously the approach and the techniques are not original with me; I owe a great deal to the scholars and writers cited in the notes. Michael Meyer, Luis González, Rhys Isaac, Fernand Braudel, and Carlo Ginzburg have had an influence on my thinking, although of course they cannot be faulted for the twists I have given to their words and ideas. Several colleagues have tried to get the kinks out of my interpretations. At one time or another, Dirk Raat, John Hart, Joe Hobbs, Mark T. R. Gilderhus, Eric Van Young, Paul Vanderwood, Ray Sadler, Charles Harris, Mike Novak, Rich Slatta, Judy Ewell, and Susan Deeds have all tried. Encounters between persuasion and obstinacy are often pleasurable and I enjoyed their efforts, however futile. Special thanks to Annette Thomlinson and Amy Hosokawa for typing this manuscript. I also owe a debt to Kurt Vonnegut for two of my prevailing notions about history. In *Palm Sunday,* he recounts the story of the Hungarian physician named Semmelweis, who discovered that the mortality rate in maternity wards could be greatly reduced if the attending medical students would wash their hands with soap and water. When the number of deaths declined, the jealousy and ignorance of the physician's colleagues caused him to be fired; hand washing stopped and the mortality rate once again began to climb. The lesson, Vonnegut tells us is that "vanity rather than wisdom determines how the world is run." This is a conclusion that I accept for much of the Porfirian dictatorship. In another novel, Vonnegut created the King of Michigan, who pronounced on the value of history that it can only prepare us to be surprised again.[1] My trek through modern Mexico's past was a journey filled with surprises, some delightful, others not. I hope the reader will be surprised and, thus prepared, will enjoy the unexpected.[2]

This is not a volume in social history, psychohistory, historical anthropology, nor even ethnohistory. I hope it is history—that is, an effort to reconstruct some pieces of Mexico's experience, following where the evidence, an idea or some characters, not the methodology, leads—sometimes, but not necessarily, even reaching a conclusion. I have relied to a great extent on foreign travelers' accounts because these outsiders did not take for granted Mexico's everyday activities, food, clothing, work habits, family arrangements, and housing. They described them faithfully and in detail as curiosities for their readers back home. Travelers' accounts must be used cautiously, but several historians, most notably Rhys Isaac in his Pulitzer Prize–winning *The Transformation of Virginia*,[3] have demonstrated the great value of the observations by these visitors. In choosing this source material I have ignored census information and for the most part other statistical compilations. The Mexican government until the twentieth century collected only statistics of convenience, for example those to lure more foreign investors. I leave it to someone else to evaluate their reliability and their utility. Moreover, I have a strong aversion to the theoretical approach that attempts to study the everyday person by reducing him or her to a cipher. As a historian, I find most interesting the extremes, those individuals who skew the curves, distort the charts, and create bumps in the projections. It has been necessary on a few occasions to bite my lip and use numbers, but for the most part I have ignored them and examined the more ordinary aspects of life in Mexico from other sources. Especially useful have been the brief "anecdotes," as Braudel would say, that can be pieced together in such a way that they form a mosaic that reveals the patterns and habits of the lives of those on both sides of the bullring and of those who gathered on Holy Saturday for Judas burnings.

Judas
at the
Jockey
Club

590. Cock fighting. Mexico.

Traditional and modern Mexicans
watch an 1890s cockfight. Courtesy of
the Archivo General de la Nación.

Introduction

Judas burnings on the day before Easter have long been a part of the Spanish tradition in Mexico and constitute a form of social parody in Mexican life. The Jockey Club (organized in 1881) took up this people's ritual and began burning these effigies outside its clubhouse in the late 1880s. The spectacular destruction of several Judases in 1893 proved to be the last of the club's sponsored burnings because of tremendous pressure brought against this elite social club through the newspapers and the city council. This 1893 event, Judas at the Jockey Club, provides a window on both elite and everyday society of Mexico when the dictatorship of Porfirio Díaz stood at high tide.

These Judas burnings began at some unknown time in the colonial period. Perhaps they started in imitation of the inquisition's practice of burning dead heretics in effigy, or perhaps the impetus came from the even older example of pagan celebrations running back to the Roman Saturnalia that burned parodical figures at the spring equinox. Whatever the origin, the inspiration was biblical. The New Testament book of Acts describes Judas's remorse following his betrayal of Jesus and his suicide by hanging. After Iscariot hanged himself, the body exploded, spewing intestines in all directions. Mexico's Judas effigies, filled with gunpower, likewise exploded, sending burning papier-maché limbs in all directions.[1] By the time of Mexican independence in 1821, the burning of

Judas had become a folk tradition with well-understood customs; it was the secular complement to Easter Saturday's Gloria Mass, marking the resurrection of Christ. Effigies rarely resembled the biblical Judas with flaming red hair; rather they parodied some local bureaucrat, some wayward cleric, some pompous dude, or some nabob with up-turned nose.

Exploding these surrogates of authority, fashion, and manners, like other folk celebrations, acquired informal regulations. The first principle of this event was that it extended equality to the celebrants, relaxing or reversing all rules and prerogatives of the hierarchy. This freedom has often been described as turning the world upside down, because it offered a time of license, a time of conviviality, and a time of critical parody of the establishment. This harmless, humorous safety valve released hostility without disrupting society. The Jockey Clubmen in 1893 presented a Judas burning that served as a sarcastic look at themselves and at the popular classes; other burnings the same year continued the tradition of folk handicrafts that mocked the elite. These burnings will be examined in detail, then placed in the context of other Judas burnings throughout the Porfirian regime; reflecting public concerns and folk interests, they serve as one measure of the mind of the everyday Mexican. Fears of the railroad and of Chinese coolie competition for jobs, to cite only two examples, were projected onto Judases, who were adorned to represent these threats and then were exploded.

Porfirio Díaz's government attempted to regulate these Judas burnings because the celebrations threatened disorder, mocked the establishment, and above all waved traditional Mexico in the face of bureaucrats dedicated to their particular notion of order and progress. Tracing the Judas burnings reveals the conflicts in Mexico City between traditional society, constantly reinforced with immigrants from the countryside, and the modernizers, regularly encouraged by the increasing foreign investors. The struggle to shunt aside the old Mexico or to preserve it has been described most often in terms of political centralization and economic expansion; this conflict had its social side that became apparent in the Judas celebrations.

Appreciation of the conflict between tradition and progress in the 1890s requires a discussion of society's arrangement. A photograph in the Centro de Información Gráfica of the Archivo General de la Nación, Mexico City, triggered the recognition that Mexicans split their people into two major segments. C. W. Waite took the picture of a cockfight in about 1900 on an unidentified village street; he captured representatives of Mexican society: the owners of the cocks, one dressed in a tailor-made, western-cut suit with a homburg and the other in a tight-fitting charro suit with a felt sombrero; the elderly, powerful landowner looking on, supervising and sanctioning the contest; and the spectators, half in store-bought clothes standing in the shade and half in hand-woven cotton blouses in the sun. The sharp division between those in the cool shade and the hot sun followed the social distinction apparent in the fashions; it recalled the seating arrangement in the bullring. Here was a clue that the seats in the sun and in the shade revealed more than the difference in the price of tickets; it represented the basic division in Mexican society.

The bullfight becomes a metaphor for Mexican society. It has done so since the Spanish first introduced it into their colony shortly after the conquest of the Aztecs. The corrida de toros, whether it occurs in one of the permanent rings built for that purpose or in one of the rickety temporary structures slapped together for some local fiesta, remains consistent in its seating arrangements, order of events, participants, and ritual motifs. This event offers the most obvious expression of the social arrangement in the stands; the sunny and the shady sides of the ring reflect the basic division within Mexican culture. From the 1500s until the present, this society, although arranged into different classes, occupational and professional strata, regional groups, and ethnic divisions, recognizes essentially two parts. Bullfight aficionados came from all walks of life; anyone of these persons might insist on a complex description of Mexico that included rural-urban, fieldhand-landlord, owner-worker, upper-lower, and traditional-modern occupational and status distinctions, but once they arrived at the bullring they knew without hesitation that they belonged on one side or the other of the arena, either in the shade or in the sun. Los de arriba (the topcats) had no trouble separating themselves from los de abajo (the underdogs); the gente decente have a sense of identity as strong as those who belong to the pueblo. The poor, the lower class, the workers, the campesinos, and the peónes watch in the sun; the owners, the upper class, the wealthy, the foreigners, the managers, the politicians, and the churchmen sit in the shade. On both sides of the arena, these groups arranged themselves according to standards of wealth, family, status, or class and had no interest or concern for the group assembled on the other side of the sand.

The following essays examine those people in the shade and those in the sun. This analysis does not ignore the importance of class or family name or occupational stratification, but puts emphasis on the dichotomy in the society whereby a Mexican from any of these groups when he went to the bullring did not forget his position in society but nevertheless recognized the one side of the ring his position entitled him to occupy. Here a word should be said about women. Descriptions of the bullring and bullfights from the colonial period to the present make it evident that some women did attend the corridas. Most often these were ladies who sat in one of the boxes on the shady side. Why that was so and why so few of their counterparts came to the arena to sit in the sun will be discussed below.

Much more needs to be said about the bullfight as a metaphor of Mexico's political system, family arrangements, and even certain religious attitudes, but this will be reserved for the discussion of the sports and recreations of those Mexicans who sat in the shade. This elite has been examined largely by evaluating the notions, attitudes, and activities that made up a belief in progress and efficiency regarded as modern; here we will call it the "Porfirian persuasion."

Society had always comprised two major segments, but during the Porfirian regime these divisions came to represent two different, often contradictory cultures. These segments, the elite and the underclass, los de arriba and los de abajo, which Carlos Fuentes has identified as sons of bitches and poor bastards,[2] did not reflect the twentieth-century split between urban and rural residents; rather they existed side by side in the cities and countryside. Although these two cultures appeared together, they lived in two different worlds. By the 1890s, these two aggregations stood in high relief in their occupations, fashions, and pleasures. Pinpointing exactly when those who sat in the shade adopted these modern attributes is impossible because it was a process occurring over a number of years. However, we can point to an event when a number of the fashionable residents of the capital city revealed their self-conscious (perhaps slavish) identification with Positivistic European modernism; the affair was hosted by the Jockey Club.

Before splitting from traditional culture, Mexico City's polite society had a final fling with the old customs in 1884. The bon ton celebrated the birthday of Porfirio Díaz, who was awaiting his December inauguration as president for a second term. In the president-elect's honor, the three-year-old Jockey Club hosted a *charreada,* the traditional display of horsemanship, at the club's Peralvillo racecourse. On September 15, the city's society arrived in charro and poblana costumes for the mid-morning bareback riding, bull-tailing, roping, and other events. The elite joined President-elect Díaz and his wife Carmen in the shade afforded by the awning covering the grandstand; more common spectators thronged a grassy concourse in the sun's glare to watch the displays of equestrian skill.

Although the birthday celebration seemed a great success, never again did the Jockey Club host a charreada. The members, chastened by the sneers of a snobbish Parisian visitor, accepted the views of one C. Bertie-Mariott. This French fop criticized the unseemly morning hours, remarking sarcastically that perhaps the Mexicans knew that it was mid-afternoon in Paris; he scoffed at the traditional costumes worn by both contestants and spectators, finding them shamefully plebian rather than an expression of nationalistic pride. Believing he had attended some kind of horse-race meeting rather than something closer to a rodeo, he questioned the absence of gentlemanly wagering and snickered at the undignified events featuring working horses rather than thoroughbreds. Altogether he found the president-elect's birthday fete distastefully déclassé.[3] His views quickly permeated the Jockey Club; the members dropped the charreada, giving all their attention to the races that they had also initiated in 1882. The fashionable elite, intent on progress, chose amusements after 1884 that seemed more consistent with modernism. Their choices will be discussed in the essay entitled "The Porfirian Persuasion."

This high society first scornfully abandoned traditional culture to the rest of the people; then it vigorously attacked these traditions as backward and decadent customs that did not represent a culture at all, only obstacles blocking the progress and development of the Mexican nation. This assault on tradition and the resiliency of the old ways will be examined in "Rocks and Rawhide: Traditional Culture." And, with information on these two segments of the society in mind, we will consider the conflict between them in the final essay, "Judas at the Jockey Club." All three of these essays first must be placed in the context of Porfirio Díaz's Mexico.

Díaz's thirty-five-year dictatorship from 1876 to 1911 encompassed Mexico's era of modern development. By 1888 Díaz had his administration in place; the efforts of this regime everywhere succeeded in the 1890s, resolving the troubles that had lingered since Padre Miguel Hidalgo first called for independence in September 1810. Four score and a few years had been required to return a rambunctious church to state control, to block the intrusion of foreign invaders, and to halt the centrifugal forces that reduced the viceroyalty of New Spain to little more than the audiencias of Mexico and Guadalajara. Warlord caudillos bowed to the federal army and once-ubiquitous bandits fled before the rurales, the countryside constabulary. Distance yielded to the railroad and isolation to the telegraph. A modern bureaucratic state appeared south of the Rio Grande, where once there had existed a mestizo China.

Díaz had engineered the solutions to these fundamental problems. He fashioned political stability in a land generally regarded as "a poor disintegrated country." One traveler remarked that he "never knew any country in such a desperate condition," in which "civil war pervades the whole country and robbery and pillage and anarchy prevail everywhere." In the space of eight days, he saw two presidents made, and expected to see others grab the office before he could get across the border.[4] Díaz changed all that. The year that he first seized power, 1876, the *New York Herald* printed this astonished notice: "Our advices from Mexico are somewhat startling in their nature, for they indicate that the government had not changed hands for nearly six weeks."[5] By the 1890s the government had changed only when Porfirio stepped aside for his presidential choice to serve from 1880 to 1884; then he returned and the government did not change hands again until the revolutionaries in 1911 chased him into exile. Popular acclaim had accompanied his rule, and when one Arnulfo Arroyo attempted to assassinate Díaz in September 1897, a mob stormed the city jail, forced its way to Arroyo, and hacked the prisoner to death.[6] Here was a violent expression of the intense regard the masses felt for the president—or so it seemed. The people gave many other displays of their esteem, especially enthusiastic public birthday celebrations in the dictator's honor.

8

Díaz resolved Mexico's longstanding disputes with foreign powers. The army, in concert with the United States Cavalry, eliminated the century-old Apache threat. The country almost daily seemed to take on a more western appearance. The programs of Mexico's Liberal stalwarts appeared to be accomplished by 1895. Nowhere was the sense of success greater than in the government's handling of the hierarchy of the Roman Catholic Church. The bitter church-state struggle had ended with the government unmistakably the master. This achievement called forth much overblown rhetoric, such as the statement that resolving the church question "was, in every respect analogous to and was as momentous to Mexico as the abolition of slavery to the United States."[7] Demonstrating that the hostility of this conflict had at last been resolved was the coronation of the Virgin of Guadalupe. This devotion to Mexico's patroness required the permission of the pope and the acquiescence of Porfirio. This religious celebration, which occurred October 12, 1895, symbolized a new working relationship between church and state.[8]

Many Mexicans believed the nation had arrived at modernity by 1890. Self-satisfied soldiers of progress marched in the gleam of the nation's silver production and the export of raw materials. Other Mexicans found clues that modernization had not been nearly as complete or successful as Porfirian prosperity seemed to suggest.

Mud and stagnant water mired the dictatorship's "silver dollar wheels,"[9] just as they had made a swamp of Mexico City since the arrival of the Spaniards. Progressive Porfirian administrators contracted engineers to drain the lakes in the valley of Mexico and to control run-off during the rainy season that turned cobblestone streets into shallow canals. Philadelphia consultants persuaded the capital's city council to cover the cobblestones with a pavement of wooden blocks, beginning with Cinco de Mayo Avenue and then other major thoroughfares. Wooden pavement was chosen because of its low cost and because the surface retained enough friction, even when wet, that horses and mules could maintain footing. Pride in this wooden sign of progress faded in the first seasonal rainstorm. The wooden blocks on Cinco de Mayo Avenue swelled in the rains, causing the sidewalks along both sides of the street to buckle, while the swollen blocks on Monterilla and other streets heaved out and floated about, endangering horses and pedestrians.[10]

Although the councilmen clung to wooden pavements for several years, in the early 1890s they finally abandoned wood and turned to macadam as the surface for the city's streets.

The perils of progress could not deter those who demanded the appearance of modernity, whether or not stone sidewalks sprung into the air or blocks of Philadelphia wooden pavement swirled in the water and mud of traditional Mexico. Progressive American and European city governments expanded their police and fire protection services in the late nineteenth century and Mexico City's councilmen followed.

In an effort to keep pace with progress as expressed in western Europe and the United States and to modernize the agency of order and protection, the government reorganized the capital city gendarmerie in 1878 and 1879 to create a uniformed police force of salaried civilians. Official support eventually effected a larger, better equipped, more professional constabulary; the city's police outnumbered the nation's rural police force by the end of the dictatorship. As in the case of fashion and literature, officials adopted French examples to Mexican circumstances, creating a system similar to the police of Paris, with the precinct station (eight of them in Mexico City) as the center of law enforcement, a secret police engaged in political activities, and an absence of any popular supervision over the inspector generals, who received appointments based completely on their proven, personal loyalty to Porfirio. For all its modern trappings, the police revealed old-styled flaws. Returning to the 1897 lynching of would-be assassin Arnulfo Arroyo reveals a striking example.

After his assault on the president, Arroyo had been taken first to military headquarters, but police inspector general Eduardo Velázquez quickly arrived, claiming jurisdiction in the case. Once he won his point, he had Arroyo gagged, placed in a straitjacket, and escorted to police headquarters in the municipal palace. About two in the morning, after Arroyo had endured twelve hours of interrogation, a mob broke into the police office, overpowered the two guards, and with shouts of "Viva Porfirio Díaz" slashed Arroyo to death. Secret police pursued the lynch mob, firing several shots in the air. When several spectators wandered into the office, they were quickly arrested and charged with the murder of Arroyo. Despite official reports that workingmen had killed the prisoner, within three days those arrested were released and the presidential cabinet learned that Velázquez had staged the murder. Díaz ordered him removed from office to a prison cell. An official investigation into the affair discovered that Velázquez had learned from a judge that the would-be presidential assassin would be sentenced to only a two- to four-year prison term for assault. Velázquez fervently admired Díaz and believed his assailant deserved harsher punishment. The policeman took matters into his own hands, sending his valet to buy twelve daggers while he recruited policemen from another precinct to pose as a working-class mob. He also directed officers at the station house to let the hired lynchers enter, but to break a glass door to make it appear they had crashed into the room.

Within a week of his incarceration, the inspector general's corpse and a pistol were discovered in his cell at Belem prison. A suicide note proclaimed his allegiance to Díaz. Nine of his accomplices were sentenced to death in November, but the following spring an appeal won reduced sentences in prison and three years later a second trial granted freedom to the defendants, some of whom returned to police work. Public opinion remained convinced of the existence of a sinister will behind the death of the assassin, the death of the inspector, and the release of the murderers. Velázquez's complicity in murder called forth sullen nods from many who viewed the reform of the police force as only the development of more systematic and more efficient police corruption. Not until the 1906 installation of a network of 154 call boxes did the public recognize major changes to increase the arrest of criminals. One student of Porfirian law and order, Laurence J. Rohlfes, confirms the popular view of this modern police force, with the statement, "The tolerance of corruption in high places was the greatest failure of Porfirian law enforcement authorities."[11]

Along with uniformed policemen, the city council wanted a modern fire department. The adobe and stone city, which averaged around fifty small fires a year, installed hydrants on the corners of the newly paved streets in 1886. The fire fighters, first organized in 1874, had to attend a gymnastic school so they could be spry in their response to alarms; a little over a decade later the men received new nickel-plated helmets from Germany in 1887, which they proudly exhibited for the first time in the Independence Day parade.[12] A succession of new ordinances during the rest of the century attempted to spruce up the appearance of the city, so it would look modern.

Traditional society ignored these efforts. Villagers still drove turkey flocks through Mexico City. Usually they used the side streets, but as late as 1911 two imperturbable campesinos in unbleached cotton clothes drove about one hundred turkeys the length of San Francisco Street, one of the capital's most bustling avenues, on their way to the central market. Ten years later (1921), turkey flocks still roamed the city.[13] Mexico's heralds of progress notwithstanding, visitors found the capital, with nearly 330,000 residents in 1890, was not yet a city, but one of the world's largest villages.[14] Those who ignored or shunned progress lived much as they had before the Díaz regime. Their lives responded to the rhythms of the liturgical and seasonal calendars; their pleasures came largely in the secular celebrations that complemented both religious and civic rituals. Day of the Dead, Carnival, and Judas burnings joined church holidays, and the people enjoyed the festivals that came with the official celebration of Cinco de Mayo and Independence. Both the government and the elite society during the Porfirian years wanted to end or at least regulate these popular festivals in the interests of order and progress. Occasionally the old society and the new rubbed shoulders despite their mutual dislike; when flinty tradition met steely progress, sparks flew, even at happy celebrations. One such occasion, which reveals much about both cultures, came at the Judas burnings at the Jockey Club.

The
Porfirian
Persuasion:
Sport
and
Recreation
in
Modern
Mexico

With a new self-confidence, Mexicans in 1890 preened before an international audience. With a sense of well-being built on political tranquility and economic success, elite Mexicans adopted a new set of attitudes. Their notions did not represent a political ideology or an economic philosophy; they subscribed to a loose sense of progress, based on Comtean positivism with individual touches of Catholicism or anticlericalism, of Indianism or anti-Indianism, and of greater or lesser doses of the Liberal belief in the efficacy of property. These predilections constituted a somewhat ill-defined but pervasive popular sense of what a number of Mexicans thought about their country and its future. These attitudes and notions might best be called a persuasion.[1] In some sense this popular attitude was little more than a fad that swept across the country as early as 1888, held sway for two decades, and then vanished in the depression of 1905. Certainly it was gone by the time the revolution broke out in 1910.

This persuasion can be seen clearly in the rise of sports and recreation. These leisure activities expressed it better than the government or the economy, where this temper also existed, because Mexicans had clear, unambiguous choices in their diversions. An act of volition was needed to ride a bike, go to the horse races, or join an athletic club; there was no compulsion from the need to survive that exists at least implicitly in political and economic undertakings.

The rise of many organized sporting activities represented the growing influence of the foreign community in Mexico, but simple imitation of U.S. and European sport does not explain this development. Mexicans selected the recreations that appealed to them and rejected those that seemed contradictory to their culture. Football, American style, seemed especially repugnant to Mexico's values, and after its exhibition in 1895, as we will see, it was rejected until after the revolution.

The Porfirian persuasion, this sense of sharing the same activities and attitudes of the international gentry, reveals as well the imitative quality in Mexico so brilliantly examined by Samuel Ramos in *The Profile of Man and Culture in Mexico*.[2] Mexicans saw their country zooming into modernization; hence they rushed to adopt the styles, attitudes, and amusements of other modernized Western nations. Turning to these attitudes, we can find them instrumental in the changing attitudes toward bullfighting, the rise of baseball and horse racing, interest in boxing, and the fascination with bicycling.

Bullfights and Culture

Bullfighting represented a part of Mexico's Spanish heritage. Introduced early in the 1500s, during the three hundred years of the colonial era, the bullfight evolved into the spectator event much like today's corrida de toros. Several secondary features—spearing rings, tailing the bull, climbing the greased pole for a pig, and allowing amateurs from the stands—had disappeared from the bullfight by the time of independence.[3] The rules and etiquette of the corrida emerged and the bullfight became the ritual expressing Mexican cultural values.

During the nineteenth century the essential actors of the corrida included the bull, the president, the matador, picadores, and banderilleros. The drama was worked out in a series of dynamic scenes, essentially three for each bull: the placing of the banderillas on the bull to enrage it, the spearing of the bull in the large shoulder muscles to weaken it, and the entrance of the matador for the killing of the bull, if possible with a single thrust of the sword. Not until after 1930 did the toreador incorporate the daring capework, drawing the bull within inches of his body, that has become the ballet of bullfighting. In fact, during the Porfiriato, an assistant, called the cholo or capa, often preceded the matador into the ring. His role was to wave a "gayly colored" cloth, usually attached to a long pole, before the bull, to tease it to the point of exhaustion. Then, the matador strutted across the sand to deliver the fatal sword thrust. This ultimate scene usually was called the espada (the sword).[4] The graceful killing of the bull, not the ballet of cape and animal, was the essence of the corrida.

The tourist and casual spectator saw only blood and sand. Most English-speaking visitors watched in horror. The fans, the aficionados, knew that the entire event was controlled, in fact orchestrated by one person, the president of the corrida, usually a civil official (Díaz on occasion served). Only the president permitted a bull to enter the ring, only he allowed the progression from scene to scene, and only he signaled for the killing of the bull. This president rewarded the matador with an ear, or two, perhaps even the tail. No honor went to the man who failed to kill the bull or who made a poor job of it. On one or two occasions, the president permitted the bull to live because the animal displayed such gameness and bravery that it overshadowed the men participants. No honors or rewards went to the others, the banderilleros or picadores.[5]

During the nineteenth century the corrida served as a metaphor of Mexican society. The president represented the caudillo, cacique, or patron who governed everyone's endeavors and determined the rhythm of daily activities. Only in a paternalistic society could such a ritual have meaning. The "players" displayed the hierarchy of society in which each man played only his part and left to society as a whole the accomplishment of the task. Although they cooperated, the banderilleros, picadores, and matador did not comprise a team. The matador depended on the others but was clearly of a different and higher level in the hierarchy, and he garnered all the honors.

The matador was the epitome of the event. He had to demonstrate the attributes most valued in this masculine order. The matador faced savage, ruthless nature in its most ferocious form—the raging bull. The matador had to be more than courageous. He had to be reckless, he had to ignore all odds, he had to stand fast in the face of the bull, he had to disregard all his own injuries and fears, and he had to succeed for honors, even his life. Above all, he had to act in a manner of exaggerated courtesy and ultimate decorum.[6] Campesinos, peónes, léperos (street people), workers—the society itself (commentators regularly remarked that the audience represented a cross-section of society), recognized Mexican courtesy, placidity in the face of danger, and the resignation needed to stand up to impossible odds. The bullfight included cruelty, blood, and death, but life itself included these.[7]

During Porfirio Díaz's first administration bullfights were prohibited in the Federal District and several prominent states, including Zacatecas and Veracruz. Two explanations may be given for this prohibition. One exegesis comes from the political and nationalistic ambitions of Díaz. He wanted diplomatic and economic recognition from the United States and Great Britain. Both these countries had been outspoken critics of the backwardness of Mexican society. These commentators not only described Mexico as the land of bandits, kaleidoscopic governments, and unpaid debts, but also they remonstrated against a land that gloried in cruelty to animals. Many referred to the corrida de toros as simple bull-baiting, in which the animal was tormented to distraction and only when the crowd grew bored was it slaughtered. Prohibiting bullfighting in the capital, the major port of Veracruz, and a principal mining zone in Zacatecas meant that few outsiders saw them, and the dictator strengthened his image as the reformer leading Mexico from barbarism into the Western community of nations.

By 1888 Díaz's and Mexico's stock had risen tremendously. Foreign investors rushed into Mexico, railroads tied together the country, peace and stability ruled. Díaz no longer needed to worry about his country's reputation for cruelty and he ignored the petitions from the Society for the Prevention of Cruelty to Animals (whose honorary chairman was his wife) and the Anti-bullfighting Club.[8] Instead, the government gave its attention to such things as requiring pants and felt hats of Indians who came to town, to achieve at least a European appearance,[9] and by 1890 Díaz's success promoted a growing sense of pride in Mexico.

This emergent nationalism revived what it regarded as genuine traditions, though this involved a romantic notion of both the Aztec culture and the colonial epoch. Mexico City's society celebrated "the flowery war," a mock re-creation of the Aztec ritual as a parade of coaches decorated with flowers from which passengers hurled blossoms at each other. Díaz also unveiled the monument to Cuauhtémoc and Aztec bravery in one of the major traffic circles in the city. And, he permitted the return of bullfighting to the capital as one of Mexico's traditions.[10]

Another explanation of the prohibition of bullfighting comes from the anthropological study of "deep play" by Clifford Geertz and of "ritual display" by Susan Birrell.[11] The corrida demonstrated submission to the caudillo in a hierarchical society and called on the individual to ignore all odds in fulfilling the traditional role assigned him. The bullfight was antithetical to the platform that Díaz was mouthing, one that called for rotation in political office, genuine elections, and an end to caudillismo. From 1876 to roughly 1888, Díaz (and Manuel González) consolidated national power by breaking regional and local caudillos, wrecking personal loyalties in the army, and dismantling personal business ties. Díaz promoted central government and capitalistic economics as impersonal and institutional ideals; his consolidation of power would not admit exaggerated individualism or reckless resistance.

By 1888 Díaz had his system in place. He had realigned political power, garnered a national and international reputation, and stood ready for recognition as the father of his country—who would mediate, orchestrate, reward, and punish. This new patriarch was ready for a return to ritual displays of paternalism. Basking in the patriarch's presence, if only metaphorically at the bullfight, was a quality of the Porfirian persuasion.

Abner Doubleday in the Halls of
Montezuma: Baseball Comes to Mexico

Baseball has a shadowy history in Mexico, with its origins as hazy and confused in the popular mind as the origin of the sport in the United States. Without question, baseball represented the growing influence of the United States on the Mexican elite. No one should be surprised to learn that Abner Doubleday's ghost lurks in every Mexican outfield; common knowledge explained that not only had he invented the game in the United States but he also had personally introduced it south of the border.

This apocryphal tale goes: Doubleday was a West Point graduate who served in the United States Army in both the Mexican and Civil wars. In the former conflict, U.S. troops, including young officer Doubleday, occupied Mexico City for ten months in 1847 and 1848. The troops, with little to do, soon organized various entertainments, including sports and dances. According to legend, Doubleday promoted his new game of baseball among the various companies and militia units stationed in the Halls of Montezuma. This story has been exaggerated to the point that the Illinois volunteer who had captured General Antonio López de Santa Anna's wooden leg as a war trophy is said to have used it as a bat in one of these contests.[12] Even if this story were true, there is no record of Mexicans learning and playing anything resembling baseball until the 1880s.

The Doubleday anecdote aside, the first bat-and-ball game, and probably the earliest organized sport in Mexico, appeared when British businessmen and mine owners established the Mexico Cricket Club in 1827.[13] This club survived until 1904, when it merged with the San Pedro Golf Club, which soon became the Mexico City Country Club.[14] Members played cricket sporadically during the nineteenth century. In the late 1860s and early 1870s, the club members divided into Reds and Blues for Sunday morning matches in a season that stretched over four months from November until March. The Cricket Club arranged special trolley service to its pitch at Napolés, and held a formal breakfast at 1 P.M. between innings.[15] The premier test match in 1868 featured the Companies (Barron, Forbes, and Company, the Railway Company, and the Gas Company) versus the Club, in which the only player with a Hispanic name, M. J. Trigueros, of the prominent Mexican sporting family, led the Companies to victory with an inning of sixty-four.[16] The club faced yearly challenges from the Victoria Cricket Club, which Trigueros formed from students at the Escuela de Artes y Oficios. Victoria won a pair of games in 1868, and again the following year, then lost the final rematch in 1870.[17] The game seems to have become dormant for several years after 1870, and George W. Clarke, the editor of *The Two Republics*, feared that this "healthy and manly game" might disappear altogether.[18]

After a period of only occasional activity, the British reorganized cricket in Mexico City in the 1880s coincidentally with Mexico's first games of soccer in Pachuca, a town dominated by the British-owned Real del Monte silver mines. The British colony obtained a field for cricket across the Paseo de la Reforma from Chapultepec Park, and arranged impromptu games. Young Mexican gentlemen took to the game, and the cricket fad swept through the native gentry for a couple of years.[19] A reorganized Pachuca team came to Mexico City for a test match in 1889, the first time in twenty-five years, only to lose before an aristocratic audience.[20] The sport entered a new period of decline in Mexico City in the 1890s, although it remained popular with Englishmen in Puebla, Pachuca, and Monterrey until the end of the century.[21]

The decline of this English game was followed by the rise of baseball within the same Mexico City circles. This change in recreational preference followed the declining influence of the British business community in comparison with that of the United States. Yankee investors surpassed their British competitors by 1890, dominating both exports and imports. With booming economic activity in Mexico, large numbers of Americans of all classes and professions headed across the Rio Grande; to serve this population and bolster United States interests, the number of consular representatives increased as well.[22] These new arrivals, representatives of the hustle and bustle of the industrializing, urbanizing United States, brought their games with them; the economic success of the United States made Mexicans susceptible to U.S. sports. Baseball appeared first in Mexico City in the early 1880s and then at roughly the same time in several places in the early 1890s.

Doubleday's heirs and the carriers of his legend were the Yankee employees of the Mexican National and the Mexican Central railroads, who organized company teams in the summer of 1882 to play scrimmage games. A challenge match pitted the National Baseball Club against the Telephone Company, Sunday morning, July 28. The railroad men, perhaps because of their greater experience, prevailed 31 to 11 before a crowd of foreigners, Mexicans, and some ladies. These teams played on the field at Santiago, but after a few contests, they disbanded.[23]

Another pick-up game was played February 11, 1883, with the Central's road department defeating the mechanical department, 25 to 19. This contest inspired more permanent organization in the summer of 1883. Mexican Central employees in the mechanical department formed a nine to play against coworkers in the supply, road, and transportation departments. The teams played their first scrimmage match, without keeping score, August 4, on the open field just west of Buena Vista station. The combined team soon split into squads representing each department, so that the workers could play a tournament over the summer. New editors J. Mastella Clarke and Walter M. O'Dwyer of *The Two Republics* called on the United States colony in Mexico City to aid the teams in every way possible so that this step to introduce the American national game would not only succeed but become the forerunner of several other "healthful and recreative outdoor pastimes not yet known" in Mexico.[24]

Efforts to promote baseball soon languished, and the teams disbanded. During the next four years only occasional pick-up games were played as a novelty to raise money for charities. One such exhibition matched two Mexican sides at the Corazón de Jesus field, February 21, 1886, to collect funds for the city's poor house, and another February benefit matched Frenchmen against Spaniards in a bungling display of the game before fashionable spectators who had paid fifty cents each to support the French-Belgium-Swiss Benevolent Society.[25] Events outside the capital brought new efforts to establish baseball.

Renewed enthusiasm for the sport came in the wake of reports from both Havanna and Chihuahua City of large crowds attending baseball games in those cities. Baseball had been introduced in Cuba in the 1860s and it soon became the island's most popular sport. In 1887 the Philadelphia Athletics toured the island, inspiring great interest among spectators. Local Cuban clubs drew crowds of fifteen to twenty thousand fans after the Athletics returned to the United States. Other reports indicated nearly one thousand fans crowding the playing field in Chihuahua City to watch baseballers there.[26] These stories inspired the railroad men in Mexico City to make another effort to introduce baseball. Employees at both the National and Central railroads again took the lead in forming teams. Two squads, Railroad and City, appeared and brought the game back to the capital July 26, 1887. This contest brought out a large crowd of Americans and Mexicans, with a fair number of ladies. Only five innings were played because the City team had produced a 27 to 4 score. The City squad was assisted by the three "fly catches of young O'Brien" in the field, so that Railroad yielded.[27]

Railroad's victory instigated a flurry of baseball activity. The railroad men met at the Central line's gym and created a permanent organization. Then all the baseball men in the city met at the Iturbide Hotel, where they established an association with three teams: Railroad, renamed Toluca; City, to be called Tenochtitlán; and a Mexican squad. R. M. Arozarena headed a group to draft the association's rules. These enthusiasts soon inquired of both the Chihuahua City and the El Paso teams asking if the winner of their series would accept an invitation to play in Mexico

City.[28] This outbreak of baseball fever resulted in a series of games played on Sunday mornings over the next several months at the Central playing fields in Buena Vista. On five Sundays, City and Railroad (masquerading as Toluca and Tenochtitlán) played, and on several other mornings scrimmages matched pick-up squads. By the end of 1887 the baseball mania had again declined, for several reasons. The series against the El Paso Browns (who had defeated Chihuahua) failed to develop; fans lost interest in low-scoring contests, which the newspapers blamed on the Mexicans who had never played before and the extremely wet weather that persisted until the Christmas holiday. Nevertheless, scrimmage games continued, preserving some interest in the sport, which resulted in the Mexican workers on the National Railroad forming the first all-Mexican team to play in the scrimmages in 1888. The Mexicans lost their first game, 9 to 8, to their Yankee coworkers.[29] Nevertheless, these Mexicans adopted the game.

The rise of baseball's popularity was facilitated the same year when D. S. Spaulding imported merchandise and Mexican curio shops began selling sporting goods in Mexico City. Spaulding's store offered baseballs, tennis balls, Columbia bicycles, and hunting gear as early as October 1888. Prospective ball players could obtain the proper equipment from this time on without difficulty.[30]

American railroad men reorganized the baseball teams in the fall of 1889. Sportsman H. Remsen Whitehouse, secretary of the American legation, chaired a meeting of thirty prospective players, who first formed the Base Ball Association, then divided into the Hidalgos, led by Walter Gartside, and the Washingtons, captained by Bernard Frisbie. The new association played several Sunday games at Buena Vista field, then in November began a five-game championship series that was swept by the Hidalgos. A second series was initiated but never completed, as it was necessary for the Washingtons to reorganize and the association tried to recruit the team of Mexican players to join them. The second series faltered, but baseball was firmly established.[31]

Outside Mexico City, baseball was introduced in different ways. Yankee sailors from a merchant ship docked at Guaymas, Sonora, in 1877 went ashore, chose up sides, and played baseball before a curious crowd of youngsters. After the ship left, the boys tried the game, using homemade balls and gloves with stick bats. Interest in the sport grew until in

1890 Guaymas challenged Hermosillo to a game of baseball for town pride. Two years later, Guaymas won the first Sonora state championship by defeating teams representing the towns of Hermosillo, La Colorada, Nogales, and Cananea. Baseball became the most popular sport in the state, causing a decline in attendance at the cockfights and reducing the number of spectators at the bullring until it eventually had to close.[32] One mining engineer from the United States, working near Monterrey, taught his workers the game so that they could help him celebrate July 4 appropriately with a baseball contest. By 1900 miners in the state Oaxaca had learned the game from American engineers. Railroad foreman John Glenn taught the game to workers in Durango. Glenn, who later became the U.S. consul in Guanajuato, pitched for the Durango team and arranged contests with neighboring communities. Perhaps the most important boost to the game came from the visit made by the Chicago White Sox to Mexico City in 1907.[33]

Baseball in the capital city was centered in the athletic clubs. The teams playing in 1895 provide an illustration. The city's champion was the Mexican Base-ball Club, comprised exclusively of Mexicans. The Mexicans defeated the American Base-ball Club, the capital city's Cricket Club, Englishmen who adjusted more or less successfully to American rules, the Anahuac Club, named for the valley in which Mexico City is located, and L. P. Frisbie's Mexican National Base-ball Club, a squad of employees of the Mexican National Railroad. The Mexicos played several other Mexican teams organized in 1895, including Demócrata and student squads from the Escuela de Artes y Oficios (the Victoria Club), the Colegio Militar, and the Escuela Preparatoria.[34] After claiming the 1895 championship, the Mexicos played several exhibitions, losing to the Americans in the rematch, 36 to 19, and trouncing the Nationals, 25 to 15. By the end of 1895 another Mexican entry appeared when the Cyclist Union Club, with a chiefly Mexican membership, decided to organize a baseball team and proposed that all the clubs compete for a pennant or trophy in 1896.[35]

These contests were played at the Reforma Athletic Club's grounds, located across the Paseo from Chapultepec Park (the current location of the Tamayo Art Museum). Spectators flocked to the games, lounged under colorful awnings during the contests, and relaxed to discuss the results over elaborate picnic lunches. These games, deviating from the powerful American custom of the time, were usually played in the late hours of Sunday morning; no blue laws prevailed in Mexico.[36]

Baseball teams in other parts of the country traveled for games. International matches took place between Texans and Mexicans, with games between Uvalde and Monterrey and El Paso and Juárez in the mid-1890s, and with exchanges soon established between Monterrey and San Antonio, and other Texas cities. The fans and families of the players usually joined the expedition to play baseball, so that contests always had a festive spirit.[37]

Public interest in baseball continued growing among spectators into the first decade of the twentieth century. Individual players became popular favorites. The first of these stars was the pitcher Valenzuela (first names or initials were not reported), who led his Mexico team to repeated victories over the local Grays, Blues, and Blacks. Valenzuela became a popular hero in November 1903 in a contest against the rival Blacks. He started at shortstop, where he committed three errors that helped put his team behind. In the seventh inning, with no outs, he was called on to pitch. He threw three perfect innings and hit a single and a home run to rally his Mexico squad to a 12 to 11 victory. His teammates carried him from the field on their shoulders.[38]

Valenzuela and Mexico finally lost in 1904 to El Aguila, the club formed the year before in Veracruz. El Aguila regularly challenged the teams from the capital into the second decade of the twentieth century, behind its outstanding fielder Ramón O'Reiling.[39] But after a one-year absence, Mexico reemerged as the strongest team in the republic.

Beginning in 1904, Mexican teams established two leagues, the Liga de Verano (the summer league) for amateurs and the Mexican Association of Baseball for semiprofessionals. Mexico captured the championship of the 1904–1905 inaugural season. Captain Gaspar López emerged as the outstanding player for Mexico, and until his untimely death in 1907, the club held the league's silver championship cup. Four other strong teams, Junior (a student squad), Popo, Olliver, and Country Club, competed in the league, but it was El Record that won the 1906–1907 season and played against the visiting world champion Chicago White Sox.[40]

The White Sox, Charlie Comiskey's "Hitless Wonders," had captured the 1906 world championship by first winning the American League pennant with their nineteenth consecutive victory on the last day of the season and then sweeping through the first intracity World Series over the powerful Cubs, who had won the National League title by twenty games.[41] Comiskey brought the team to Mexico in search of good weather for spring training and the opportunity to pay expenses with exhibition games. He had been the first owner to take a team south for preseason practice, going to Marlin, Texas, in 1904; but for two years the weather had been rainy and cold so he decided the team should go farther south. A party of fifty-six traveled from March 5 to March 10, with several delays including a twenty-four-hour wait in San Antonio, Texas, to reach the Mexican capital. When they finally arrived, they immediately played an intrasquad game between the Blues (regulars) and the Whites (substitutes) before a small crowd of one thousand that included Vice-President Ramón Corral. The following day was spent in two practices preparing for the Mexican champions.

El Record and the White Sox played at the Reforma Athletic field on March 12. The Mexicans lacked a catcher, so the Sox lent them "Babe" Towne and Ed McFarland to team with the crack Mexican pitcher Juárez. Juárez threw well, especially in the early innings, but poor fielding resulted in a 12 to 2 Chicago victory. The Record team included two non-Mexicans, Bell from the University of Nebraska and Tobin of Cornell University. Comiskey was pleased with the contests and immediately made plans to visit Yucatán and Central America in 1908. The Records were not as delighted and refused the opportunity of a rematch. Instead the Sox played four intrasquad matches, which involved several American residents of Mexico City in one contest and featured the Mexican pitchers Juárez and Casas in another. The crowds at these games remained small, probably because of the extremely high ticket prices of $3.50 a seat. The equivalent of seven pesos was nearly three times the cost of a seat in the sun at the bullring. The high price made the trip profitable for the Chicago team but nearly resulted in a riot by the fans at one scrimmage when the Blues, as the home team and leading 9 to 8, did not plan to bat in the bottom of the ninth inning. The regulars decided they had better avoid provoking the audience that had already left its seats in protest, so they took a superfluous turn at bat. After a week in the land of the Aztecs, the White Sox returned to the United States.[42]

Although Chicago newspapermen believed that baseball was still in its infancy in Mexico, the league survived despite Record's loss to the White Sox. Crowds remained largely upper-class Mexicans and foreigners, and seldom numbered more than one thousand before the revolution. Nevertheless, the game was firmly established.[43]

Following the destruction and upheaval of the revolutionary years (1910–1916), baseball was reborn in Mexico. The revolution released new attitudes toward politics, society, education, and even sport. During the first revolutionary regime of Francisco I. Madero (1911–1913), educational reformers created the nation's first university extension program in the capital city. They envisioned diverting workers from the bars and the streets by offering lectures, choir singing, and sports. Renewed violence overwhelmed this plan and with it organized sport until later in the decade, when baseball was reborn. Despite such threatening omens as the assassination of Emiliano Zapata and the imposition of an unpopular presidential candidate that portended another revolt, a press release in December 1919 announced a six-week championship series hosted by the Reforma team. Besides the capital city squad, the international tournament included three Cuban teams, the Havanas, the Alemendares, and the Cuban Stars, and two United States teams, the All-Americans, a club of major leaguers who had been touring Cuba, and the American Giants, a black team. The games were scheduled at the Reforma athletic field and the new Parque Union, with large crowds expected for the excellent play and because of the recent prohibition against bullfighting.[44]

The sport attracted its greatest following in the capital city, where more than fifty-six teams had been organized by 1924 to play weekly Sunday afternoon contests. Once again the United States helped promote the game. President Warren G. Harding encouraged the growth of baseball in Mexico, but Ban Johnson, former president of the American League, became the most active promoter of the game south of the Rio Grande. Johnson attended a game in Mexico City in 1921 and became so enthusiastic that he decided to donate a trophy to encourage the sport. The following year, he presented the Mexican government with a bronze statue of a player sliding into home plate valued at several thousand dollars. He left it to Mexican President Álvaro Obregón to decide how to present the trophy; Obregón overstepped this provision when he took it with him when he left office in 1924. Johnson replaced this trophy and presented the Mexican government with a second statue, a two-foot-high solid silver molding of a left-handed batter with a catcher looking on, to be awarded to the outstanding Mexican team. Mexico honored Johnson for his efforts in behalf of baseball in 1928 by inviting him to attend the final series of the amateur championship in Mexico City. The final contest was played on "Johnson Day." For his part, Johnson donated a set of new uniforms to the winning team. He later explained that he had special interest in promoting baseball in Mexico because he wanted to educate Mexicans away from the savage and cruel practice of bullfighting.[45]

After its rebirth in 1920, baseball flourished in Mexico. During this decade softball appeared as well, resulting in tournaments and the formation of an industrial league in 1929.[46] In 1925 the Mexican Baseball League was reestablished and continues to the present, recognized as an AAA minor league. From that time, Mexicans have made baseball one of their national pastimes, and players such as the second Valenzuela (Fernando of the Dodgers) have made the game an international sport.

The Sport of Kings in the Land of Cortés

Horse racing has a long history in Mexico. Traditionally its beginning is usually traced to the day Hernán Cortés landed in Veracruz in 1519. Cortés, in order to impress the messengers from Montezuma, ordered several riders to race in pairs across the sands. Racing continued throughout the colonial years, but always in this informal manner between owners who rode their own horses for variable stakes. Not until British and American diplomatic representatives arrived after independence did the sport become somewhat more formal. The British insisted on the style they knew, including circular tracks, jockey clubs, and studbooks. By the 1840s, Mexicans organized clubs to hold occasional meetings. Tracks remained short (1,000 to 1,500 feet) because of the widespread belief that horses could not tolerate longer distances at Mexico's eight-thousand-foot altitude.[47]

These informal races notwithstanding, the editor of *The Two Republics* in 1869 called for both the Mexican and foreign leaders in Mexico City to join with hacienda owners to form a club dedicated to improving Mexican horseflesh. The editor explained that nearly all improvements in European and American stock had resulted from breeding the best imported stallions to the best native mares. Club members, he asserted, should establish a course near the capital for trotting, running, and other races that would result in improved breeding for Mexico.[48] But this editorial had little effect, and informal races remained the order of the day. Occasionally the newspapers would report on these contests, such as the trotting match on Chapultepec Road (the Paseo de la Reforma today) in which one Señor Portilla drove to victory and collected a $1,000 bet from his unnamed opponent.[49]

The leaders of the Mexico City elite finally answered the call to organize the country's horsemen and founded the Jockey Club in late 1881.[50] At its January 1882 meeting, the members determined to purchase a large tract of land near the Peralvillo Gate, between the city and Guadalupe, for the construction of a track. Club members placed the construction and supervision of the course in the hands of Richard de Bergue, who had some familiarity with racing because he had attended races in France, England, and the United States. De Bergue designed a course with a mile-long outer track and an half-mile inner oval. The grandstand seated 720 persons, with a concourse admitting 4,000 more fans. Members selected Easter Sunday, April 9, as the first race day, with the meeting to extend for the three following Sundays, featuring four races for various classes at different distances, and with prize money ranging from $150 to $1,500.[51] Disappointing the elite, who had returned from Santa Anita on Easter Day for the races, construction delays prevented the opening of the season.

Peralvillo track opened Sunday, April 23, 1882, to all Mexico City's "wealth and fashion," including President Manuel González, his cabinet, and the diplomatic corps. The first day's card featured four races for the horses of gentlemen owners. General Epifanio Reyes, who soon afterward became the zone commander in Morelia, and José Zoliélliga watched their horses win the first two races. Pedro Rincón Gallardo, another military officer and governor of the Federal District, owned the winners of the next two events. The last race, without a purse, matched military officers on their own mounts.[52] A large crowd returned for the second day of racing and the spectators increased again on the third day. The horses on this third afternoon won purses of $200 to $1,000 for a new set of owners, including Mauro Elías, Guadalupe Ortega, and President

Manuel González. González had purchased his horse Carey, which had won the first-ever Jockey Club race, from General Reyes. J. G. Tucker drove Halcón Negro to victory in the track's first trotting contest.[53]

Trotting proved popular and was featured again at the last day of the meet. Even more popular on the final day was the steeplechase, 1,500 meters long over a course interrupted by a wall, a ditch, a second fence, a double ditch, and ending with two more fences. The season's largest crowd cheered W. H. Keller, F. Koelig, C. Clinch, and Mr. Struck, all of whom suffered minor accidents, galloping to the work of art offered to the winner at the finish line.

The initial race meeting proved a financial success as the Jockey Club collected $6,000 in receipts during the four days of racing. The only serious problem confronting the club came from the severe dust clouds created by the galloping horses, but the members voted to sod the course to eliminate this difficulty. On the basis of their intention to improve Mexican horseflesh, at the end of the first session members sought an exception from the city council so they would not have to pay the municipal tax levied on public amusements.[54]

The Jockey Club's fall meeting of four Sundays began October 25 with President González again in attendance. Streetcars carried large crowds from the Zócalo to the track. Most of these spectators placed at least the minimum bet of one dollar on each of the events. The first day featured one race for rural guards in uniform and another for mounts owned by officers of the rurales. The third and fourth races matched foreign and Mexican horses; gentlemen owners entered, among others, Halcón from Mexico, Taxation from the United States, Constitution from England, Jupiter from Jamaica, and Caracol from France. Only nonprofessional riders could compete for the work of art offered to the victor of the last race of the day. Succeeding Sundays offered races for Mexican horses only, half-bred Mexican horses, horses owned and ridden by army officers, handicapped events, and steeplechase for horses owned by officers and ridden by sergeants or lower ranks. The last race day included events for horses that had not won during the fall meeting, another steeplechase, and a race for trotters and buggies.[55]

Success encouraged the Jockey Club to announce improvements for the 1883 season. Plans called for increasing the number of seats in the grandstand, sinking two artesian wells, and grading a roadway from the entrance of the property to the grandstand.[56] The social importance and political potential of the club was revealed clearly in the election of officers for 1883. The executive committee members represented the social, political, and economic leaders of the restored republic and the men who became the Porfirian elite of the 1890s. The officers were Manuel Romero Rubio, president; Pedro Rincón Gallardo, first vice-president; Samuel Knight, second vice-president; José Gargollo, treasurer; Román G. Guzmán, sub-treasurer; José Limantour, secretary; Manuel Nicolín, sub-secretary; Pablo Escandón y Barrón, Luis de Errazu, José Izita, and Francisco Suínaga, directors; Miguel Cortama, Guillermo de Landa, Antonio Riva, and Francisco Algara, alternates.[57]

Beyond the immediately recognizable names of Romero Rubio, Mexico's social leader, Positivist spokesman, and Díaz's father-in-law; Limantour, the father of Díaz's acclaimed minister of finance; and Rincón Gallardo, longtime governor of the Federal District, this executive committee included Guzmán, the financier who organized the street railway company for Mexico City and the Mexico–León Railroad; Escandón y Barrón, who later served as Díaz's chief of staff and governor of Morelos in 1909; Landa y Escandón, wealthy senator for Morelia, later for Chihuahua, and governor of the Federal District, 1903–1911; and Algara, the brother of the leading member of the Mexico City Cabildo.[58] Porfirio Díaz and Manuel González headed the list of fifty-nine Mexicans and five foreigners who composed the membership.[59]

The prominence and the popularity of the club stirred enthusiasm in the capital and imitation across the country. Newspapers soon carried results of races in Veracruz, Amatlán, and León. The German colony in Mexico City sponsored a one-day event in 1883 with races for quarter horses, steeplechasers, and trotters ending with a champagne dance that became an annual fall celebration. Matamoros announced the formation of a jockey club in 1883 and the following year Guadalajara held its inaugural race meeting. In Chihuahua, Colonel Juan Manuel Gómez undertook construction of a new hippodrome that was scheduled to open May 5, 1892 (the structure was situated on land furnished by Pedro Rey across from the Fifth Regimental barracks).[60]

Not all sporting gentlemen in Mexico City approved of the Jockey Club and its track at Peralvillo. Some horsemen preferred Mexico's traditional equestrian event, the Charreada, held at Coyoacán. Here charros appeared in their traditional wardrobe. Even more important to these critics, women wore the china poblana clothing rather than displaying the latest in foreign fashions. Moreover, these traditionalists believed the charreada demonstrated horsemanship while the Peralvillo races substituted gambling for equitation.[61]

Despite its critics, horse racing emerged by the 1890s as a major Mexican recreation. The Jockey Club served as the center of Mexican gentlemanly activity at its home, the Casa de Azulejos, purchased in 1896.[62] Other Mexicans and foreigners frequented the Piñón Turf Exchange, where horsemen shared information on horses, placed bets, arranged races, and discussed race meetings; it also served as a club with reading rooms, selling drinks and tobacco to patrons. These horsemen sponsored regular meets at Peralvillo track during the 1890s.[63]

Another race meeting began in 1894, when Colonel Robert C. Pate built the Piñón Race Track and promptly lost $100,000. Some explained the fiasco by the track's unattractive location; others suggested the failure resulted from the poor grandstand seating and Mexicans' inexperience with the North-American system of betting. This St. Louis horseman refused to give up, and the following year organized the Robert C. Pate Company Racing Association, purchased property, and constructed the Indianilla track in the suburbs on La Piedad road. The track was a one-half-mile oval with the regulation sixty-feet width, spacious grandstand, and grassy concourse. A popular feature of the Indianilla track was the importation of necessary equipment so that patrons could bet in the latest Paris Mutual manner that automatically determined odds by the bets that had been placed. More than seventy-five horses from the United States joined about a third that number of Mexican mounts for the meeting that lasted two months. Pate's track excited great public interest by matching the best Mexican ponies against thoroughbreds from Texas and Kentucky. A favorite on race days was the regular race featuring gentlemen owners in the saddle.[64]

Horse races were society events. Opening day at Indianilla drew four thousand patrons that included the city's Mexican aristocracy and the English-speaking colony, who were entertained between races by the president's personal band, the famous 8th Regimental group. Pedro Rincón Gallardo, governor of the Federal District, General José Mena, minister of public works, General Mariano Escobedo, prominent member of

Congress, and José Limontour, minister of hacienda, as well as various other members of the national congress were regular patrons of the races. All the city's fashionable ladies also attended. President Díaz and his wife remained officially in mourning for the death of Manuel González the last two months of 1895, but the presence of his personal band indicated the president's interest. The Jockey Club in October 1910 opened its new and elegant hippodrome at the Hacienda de la Condesa in Chapultepec Forest. Mexican horsemen flocked to the track to celebrate the great Mexican horse Tecoác and attend the Mexican Derby, first run in 1896.[65]

The crowds demonstrated what horse racing represented to the society. This was the occasion for ostentation by the ladies, who came in their most fashionable frocks. The desire of these women to promenade persuaded Pate to expand the grassy concourse in front of the grandstand. Of greater importance, the races provided the opportunity for men, both Mexican and foreign, to demonstrate their willingness to take risks. For a few, the risk came by riding in the gentlemen owners races. Mexico's favorite sportsman, Joaquín Amor, was so seriously injured in one of these feature races at Indianilla that spectators initially believed he had been killed when his horse tossed him several yards and he landed head first. But most spectators could only race vicariously, so they demonstrated their courage, their stoicism in the face of odds, by betting excessively. Gambling on any kind of event, but especially these races, gentlemen regarded as the trait of a true Mexican. This behavior coincided in most ways with the values and attitudes of gentlemen from England and the United States, in which normally hard-headed financiers regularly bet more than a sensible amount, and won or lost with no apparent concern for the result.[66] Through gambling spectators had the opportunity for conspicuous consumption and ostentatious display, so crucial in an emergent capitalistic society, and for the demonstration of the willingness to take chances.

Mexican Gentlemen Learn the Sweet Science

Boxing has no pre-Columbian or Hispanic precedents; it represents clearly the impulse of mimicry by Mexican gentlemen of the 1890s. Indigenous cultures had a variety of ritual sporting contests, which included a form of wrestling and mock combat with various weapons, but not fisticuffs.[67] The medieval Spanish tradition included tournaments matching individuals or an individual against a bull, but pugilism was never an event.[68] Impromptu fights to settle differences in New Spain and nineteenth-century Mexico led to the use of weapons, either knives or later guns, not fists. In fact, when Governor Rafael Cravioto agreed to allow a prize fight in Pachuca, Hidalgo, in 1895, he did so with the comment that he hoped Mexicans would take a lesson from the exhibition and learn to settle differences "without guns."[69]

Duels often provided the recourse for high-society gentlemen with grievances. The government of the Federal District tried to prevent such affairs of honor in the 1860s and 1870s by repeatedly passing laws prohibiting duels, but these laws were broken as regularly as they were issued. As an alternative to pistols at ten paces, Monsieur Nicolas Poupard opened a fencing academy in 1867. Colonel Thomas Hoyer Monstery, newly arrived from the United States, opened a second school of the combative arts in February 1868. Monstery claimed the title of Mexico City's master-at-arms, based on his training at Denmark's Royal Military Institute of Gymnastics and Arms and his experience as an instructor at the United States Military Academy. He offered classes in foil, broadsword, sabre, bayonet fencing, knife, and boxing. As an advertisement of his skills, he challenged Poupard to an assault-at-arms and boxing demonstration, with the public invited. A large crowd, including many Mexican army officers, packed the Fencing Academy on the second floor above the Café Concordia, Sunday morning, February 15, 1868, to watch the combat. Monstery so dominated Poupard with the foil that the Frenchman conceded all events to his rival. Monstery then sought volunteers from the audience to exhibit the other weapons, and after much badgering persuaded Captain Baker, late of the United States Army, to compete with sabre and bayonet. The morning's finale was a sparring match between Monstery and one of his pupils, Sr. Valdez, a subcabinet minister. Valdez's efforts won acclaim in the newspapers. "As boxing is not the peculiar amusement of Mexicans," wrote one reporter, "his acceptance of the challenge produced as much surprise as his performance elicited admiration." Spectators reported that Valdez "took good positions, eyed his adversary and threw out, and altogether handled his gloves to the great satisfaction of his friends." Despite the admiration they had for Valdez's ability to eye his adversary and handle the gloves, few young Mexicans, whether army officers or not, took the opportunity to enroll in the academy.[70]

Before Mexican gentlemen would evince any interest in prize fights, a social situation had to exist that would enable them to choose to attend this kind of sporting event. The circumstances that precluded boxing until the 1890s demonstrate the theoretical argument of sociologists Norbert Elias and Eric Dunning, who have examined the rise of sport in the United States and western Europe. They identify the impetus to organized sport as "the quest for excitement in unexciting societies."[71] They argue that this craving does not surface in frontier communities, boom towns, or lawless societies. The "excitement" of constant golpes del estado (fifty-five presidents from 1821 to 1884),[72] foreign intervention (Spain, 1829; France, 1838; United States, 1846–1848; Spain, England, and France, 1862; French occupation, 1862–1867), and religious controversy (most viciously, the War of the Reform, 1858–1861)[73] made Mexico an unlikely location for the rise or the enjoyment of sport until the Porfirian system was well established. Then the dictator's peace reduced the struggle for survival and success to the point that upper-class Mexicans sought the thrill of excitement in the risks of sport.

By the mid-1880s boxing exhibitions appeared in the capital city. Foreigners promoted the demonstrations but clearly hoped to attract Mexican spectators. The government of the Federal District granted a permit to H. C. Laflin in April 1887 for a boxing demonstration that he planned to hold in one of the city's bullrings. By the next decade these exhibitions had become more common as a feature in the theaters that had also begun to attract crowds by presenting the cancan and other sensational performances. The Davis Brothers sparred before appreciative crowds at the Principal theater in 1891, creating a small following for the sport.[74]

The high point of boxing interest during the Porfirian years was the contest between Englishman Billy Smith, the middle-weight champion of Texas, and an American black, Billy Clarke, champion of Central America, in Pachuca, November 24, 1895. This spectacle was the promotion of Professor James "Jimmy" Carroll, who owned the Mexican National Athletic Club and operated the saloon in the popular Hotel Iturbide. Carroll arranged ten special coaches, including a buffet car, for the five hundred fans who took the train from Mexico City to Pachuca. The "respectable and orderly" crowd of about eight hundred, mostly Englishmen and Americans, but with a sizable number of prominent Mexicans, flocked to the bullring to watch a series of exhibitions before the main event. Carroll's oldest son Charles gave a display of bag punching, followed by a sparring demonstration by Charles Carroll and Fred Steinbuch. Two youngsters, Arthur Carroll and George Williams, delighted the crowd with their bout. The fans wildly applauded the superb "scientific exhibition" between Jimmy Carroll, the former light heavyweight champion of the world, and Ed Price, the former champion of California. An intermission was required for the erection of the twenty-four-foot ring.

The main event lasted only four rounds. Trinidad Vázquez, mayor of Pachuca, presided over the gloved match with three-minute rounds; G. H. Hewett acted as the referee. Clarke won the first round, with several vicious blows; Smith staggered his opponent with a terrific left to the nose in the second; becoming confident, he landed a flurry of punches in the third; he turned Clarke into a punching bag, finally knocking him down in the fourth. Clarke recovered before the ten count, staggered to his corner, and fainted. He remained unconscious and could not answer the bell for the fifth round. Smith was awarded the knock-out victory.

Before the fight little Arthur Carroll had presented Smith with a mascot, a small yellow shoat decorated with green ribbons. The pig was taken to his second-floor room following Smith's knock-out victory and the pig leaped from the balcony to its death. It was widely commented that the piglet committed suicide after seeing Smith's pugilistic ability.

The reporter covering the fight for *El Universal* and the *Mexican Herald* said that he had been a spectator at the Olympic Club in New Orleans when James J. Corbett defeated John L. Sullivan, and that the Clarke-Smith fight was every bit as good. The writer praised Carroll's promotion and expressed the hope that Mexico would soon witness other prizefights. Even Mexico's graphic caricaturist José Guadalupe Posada evinced an interest with a sketch of don Chapito, one of his stock characters, watching the bout.[75]

Mexican and foreign residents did demonstrate a greater interest in boxing following the fight. Carroll had to hire an additional boxing master for his gym and Clarke opened his Olympic Club expressly for Mexican sportsmen who wanted to learn the manly art of self-defense. After the first of the year, when Carroll returned to the United States in an effort to claim his share of the Fitzsimmons-Maher fight winnings (he had been in Fitzsimmons's corner as a tactician), he sold his athletic club to Pedro Quintero and the establishment passed permanently to Mexican management.[76] Billy Smith took his winnings and went north to El Paso, where he opened a sporting club in March 1896, only to return to Mexico in 1898.[77]

Newspapers carried boxing information from the United States, giving widespread coverage to the on-again, off-again Corbett-Fitzsimmons championship bout, even suggesting they fight in Mexico. Enough Mexicans took up the sport that they occasionally fought in both Mexico and the southwestern United States. Jack London, after inspecting the Mexican Revolution in 1910–1911, wrote a short story about one rebel who fought in Los Angeles, California, to raise money for the cause.[78] But it was not until the 1920s and 1930s that boxing took on a distinctive Mexican character, and today it has become one of the most popular sports in the country. During the Porfirian years it demonstrated only the influence of foreigners, the imitative quality of the Mexican elite, and the desire for excitement in a comfortable, secure society.

Climbing Popo, Mexico's Smoking Mountain

Mountaineering developed rapidly during the Porfirian years, but not among Mexicans. Popocatépetl, the volcanic cone reaching 17,520 feet above sea level, dominates the city of Mexico, the surrounding valley, its neighboring peak, Ixtacihuatl (17,330 feet), and the imagination of visitors to Mexico. The Aztecs, or some earlier Toltecan people, named it "Smoking Mountain," because it belched fire and sulfuric steam with notable eruptions in 1347, 1354, 1519–1530, 1554, and most recently 1920 to 1926. This peak, rising nearly two miles above the valley floor, had lured the adventuresome even before the Europeans arrived.

Pre-Columbian records reveal that the people of Tenochtitlán climbed Popo (as it is usually known) but offer no details of the purpose or the reaction of these anonymous adventurers. Once Cortés arrived, we have more information. The conquistador captain ordered Diego de Ordaz to take captured Aztecs as guides and porters and climb the volcano in search of sulfur to use in making gunpowder for his cannons. Ordaz was doubtlessly successful, reaching the rim of the crater and securing the necessary mineral. Again needing sulfur, Cortés sent a second expedition up the slopes of Popo the next year.

The first recorded ascent made simply from curiosity occurred when Fray Bernardino de Sahagún climbed to the edge of the crater in 1545. Others followed Sahagún, but no records of these expeditions exist for the next two centuries. Mineralogist Federico Sonneschmidt climbed to the timberline in 1772, then turned back because of the snow fields. Alexander von Humboldt, during his memorable tour of the Western Hemisphere, also turned back when he reached the snow line. William and Frederic Glennie led the first scientific expedition to climb the mountain in 1827. Heavy storms forced down the first effort of Baron de Gross and Federico von Geroldt in 1833, but on their second effort they reached the summit and collected a great deal of information on the flora and geology of the volcano. The most successful and intrepid of these early-nineteenth-century explorations was the Laverriere and Sontag expedition which reached the rim in 1857, and descended into the crater. These explorers recorded simultaneous temperatures of seventy-one degrees centigrade on the crater floor and twelve below zero on the rim at midnight. Humboldt excited great interest in the peak among his late-nineteenth-century readers because of his erroneous assertion that Popo was the highest peak in North America. In fact, it stands third to Mount McKinley in Alaska (22,000 feet) and Mexico's Orizaba (18,320).[79] Nevertheless, during the era of Porfirio Díaz many foreign adventurers made the climb.

Mexicans had an almost exclusively economic interest in the mountain. While explorers and scientists made periodic attempts to reach the summit, workmen continued to collect sulfur from the fissures and even the crater itself. Philip Terry estimated that one hundred million tons of sulfur had been brought down the mountain in leather bags, containing one arroba (about twenty-five pounds) each, between the conquest and 1900.[80] This individual enterprise became a monopoly when the national government issued a concession to General Gaspar Sánchez Ochoa. Sánchez Ochoa had had a successful military career, joining the Ayutla rebels against Santa Anna, fighting with the Liberals against the Conservatives in the War of the Reform, taking part in the brilliant victory over the

French in the first battle of Puebla, being captured by the French and then escaping and undertaking a secret diplomatic mission to the United States for President Benito Juárez. Juárez rewarded him for his years of devoted service with a concession for the sulfur on the volcano. The general retained his rights even when he opposed Porfirio Díaz's rise to power.[81] Soon reconciled to the Díaz regime, Sánchez Ochoa received the position of chief of engineers in the Ministry of War and Marine and served as a judge on the Supreme Court. This man who owned a volcano died in 1909, having lived well on this income from the mountain's sulfur.[82]

During these Porfirian years, the Díaz government did send one scientific expedition up Popo's slopes to survey the volcano and collect geological information. This expedition remained several weeks near the timberline and its efforts received aid and support from Sánchez Ochoa.[83]

Foreigners who wanted to climb the peak during the Porfirian years needed to secure the general's permission. These outdoorsmen obtained his aid if they had proper introductions. When he was disposed to help, he would send orders for his workers to assist the expedition in every way possible, including reaching the floor of the crater.

Howard Conkling, grandson of former U.S. minister Alfred Conkling, presented letters of introduction to Sánchez Ochoa, who arranged for Conkling's 1883 climb. Conkling followed the custom of first traveling by rail to Amecameca, a village about forty miles from the Zócalo, where he presented the general's letter of instructions to the superintendent. The mayordomo arranged for guides and equipment and the key to the Rancho de Tlamacas, a short distance from the permanent snow line. From Amecameca, Conkling and his party, which included his brother, another North American, and the guides, made the day-long horseback journey to the rancho. Tlamacas offered little in the way of hospitality; the scattered huts without windowpanes, bedsteads, or fireplaces scarcely provided shelter. The round-trip from Tlamacas to the peak required an early start. The party rose at 3:30 A.M. and prepared for the ascent. "I wore an ordinary heavy business-suit," wrote Conkling, "with canvas leggings and shoes purchased for the occasion. A large straw hat, a havelock [a covering attached to the head to protect the neck from the sun and the weather], and a pair of green goggles." He completed his outfit with mittens and an alpenstock. The party rode their horses to the snow line, then hiked through the snow to the rim of the crater. About two thousand feet from the summit, Conkling began to suffer from altitude sickness, feeling drowsiness, a peculiar clicking and singing sensation in the ears, accelerated breathing, palpitations of the heart, and a violent headache. His brother, who had climbed many of the peaks in the Alps, had none of these symptoms. The party reached the rim at about noon, where they enjoyed the panorama of Mexico City, Puebla, Cholula, Ixtaci-huatl, and in the distance, Orizaba.

After the party had passed several dangerous stretches on the way down, the guides suggested that they slide the rest of the way to the horses. Each guide had his petate, a straw sleeping mat that served as a makeshift sled. The adventurers sat behind the guides, who pulled up the front of the petate, and they whizzed to the lower end of the snow. After spending another night at Tlamacas, the Conklings returned to Ame-cameca for lunch before taking the afternoon train back for dinner in the capital. Conkling summarized the adventure: "Several days are required to make the ascent, and the severest physical exertion, personal risk, exposure and hardship, must inevitably be encountered."[84]

"I do not know whether I advise everybody to climb Popocatépetl," wrote William Henry Bishop, who had done it in 1881; then he commented on its allure: "There it is always on the horizon, the highest mountain in North America, and one of the few highest in the world—a standing inducement to the adventurous."[85] Butler cautioned prospective climbers that they needed to obtain their kits in Mexico City, as they would be unable to acquire anything useful in Amecameca. An experienced outdoorsman, he warned especially about keeping the feet dry during the climb through the wet snow. He had used wool socks, but reported that the guides recommended strips of coarse cotton cloth, bound around in the Italian contadino fashion. Bishop believed this was deliberate bad advice, because the feet would soon be soaked. Since the climber would retreat down the slope, the guides would receive their pay without climbing to the summit.

The truly intrepid could descend into the crater by means of the windlass used to lower and raise the workers and the bags of sulfur. When Bishop reached the top he learned that the workers had gone on strike, so he did not have to stiffen his back and take the trip to the floor of the crater. He did report on the working conditions. The men lived for a month at a time in a cave near the summit, going down into the crater to fill the bags with sulfur. Once the bags had been hoisted to the rim, they would be sent sliding through the snow fields, where other workers collected them and took them to the rancho.[86]

Thomas A. Janvier wrote a guidebook for the traveler to Mexico, and he described the ascent of Popo. He advised climbers to obtain light but warm woolen clothing, including mittens, cotton-cloth swathings for the feet, smoked glasses, plenty of nourishing food such as canned meats, wines, and liquors, and blankets, all of which should be purchased in the capital. The Hotel Ferrocarril in Amecameca, he reported, had everything except provisions but charged exorbitant prices. Guides could be arranged through Juan Oriega Mijares, owner of the shop La Flor de Amecameca. Janvier, on his 1885 climb, did get into the bucket and the workers lowered him to the floor of the crater. The mid-1880s cost of his railway ticket, guide, and provisions totaled about twenty-five dollars.[87]

By 1890 enough expeditions had climbed the mountain that much of the mystery and romance had disappeared. Rather than an arduous, dangerous undertaking, it quickly became regarded as a pleasant weekend adventure. "A jolly party" from the American colony in Mexico City decided to combine a bicycle excursion and climb to the summit of Popo in November 1895. The party included the well-known cyclists Mr. and Mrs. Johnstone, S. W. Reynolds from Boston, on a big-wheel bicycle, and Lieutenant Dwyre, the U.S. military attaché, and several other couples. The expedition pedaled to Miraflores, then took the train to Amecameca, and under moonlight rode horses to the timberline. The next morning they started again at 2:30 A.M. and climbed until they were within a thousand feet of the summit. Then the adventurers slid back to their horses on petates and were back in Mexico City for dinner. This expedition was remarkable when compared to those of the 1880s, because it consisted of men and women, without guides, nor extraordinary preparations, who simply made a weekend holiday out of what a decade earlier had been the adventure of outdoorsmen.[88]

During the last decade of Porfirio's regime (1900–1910), climbing Popo was regarded as one of the attractions of Mexico that should not be missed. Even those with serious heart conditions were encouraged to make the horseback trip to the timberline. E. H. Blichfelt expounded this view, saying that Popo was "doubtless one of the easiest mountains on the globe upon which to reach so great a height. There are no glaciers, no treacherous ravines, none of the special terrors that attend mountain climbing elsewhere." Nonetheless, he conceded that only the most hardened climber would consider the climb commonplace.[89] Philip Terry found the excitement of the climb to be in the view one obtained from the rim and in the descent, sliding "*a la tobaggan*" to the timberline. He described the adventure: "When the snow is smooth and does not cake, the journey is made seated on a straw mat (petate) guided by the Indian guide carrying a long alpensock — a man who knows every foot of the road and who skillfully avoids rocks and crevasses. He seats himself on the mat, pulls up the front edge, grasps his stick, which he uses as a brake, is in turn grasped around the waist by the passenger seated behind him, and in a vertiginous and extraordinary exhilarating swoop, the traveller finds himself at snow-line almost before he has realized that he was underway."[90]

A semi-scientific expedition climbed the peak in 1908 in order to take photographs for the American Museum of Natural History. The explorers, led by Edmund Otis Harvey, reached the summit of Nevado de Toluca, the volcano of Colima, and Popocatépetl. The most enjoyable according to the party was Popo, and they shared the excitement of earlier climbers by sliding down two thousand feet on the snow fields.[91]

Tourist possibilities of the volcano attracted Donald Stewart, who spent several days on Popo examining the possibility of constructing a wire tramway from the base to the rim, and down into the crater of the mountain. The proposed cable car would travel a distance of ten miles, the longest tram in the world. This 1894 proposal never came to fruition.[92]

This mountaineering episode points up the difference between the Anglo-American and the Mexican sporting ethic. The Anglo-American tradition in the nineteenth century centered upon the Protestant Muscular Christian ideal in which the individual could testify for God by developing his body and display divine inspiration by accepting the challenges of the environment by mountaineering and hiking. The outdoors ethic merged with Muscular Christianity in the Anglo-American culture. No such thing existed in Mexico. Mexican sportsmen took up many of the sports of Victorian society, or perfected work-related sports such as the charriada. They challenged nature, but in animal form, through horse-manship and the bullfight. The idea of physical fitness for itself had no appeal. Outdoors activities that could not be accomplished on horseback or bicycle attracted little attention. The possibility of a Mexican Teddy Roosevelt flaunting the ideas of the rugged life based on living in the great out-of-doors did not exist. The Mexican guides never seem to have viewed the climb as anything more than a job; nor did the sulfur workers find the experience uplifting or inspiring. Moreover Mexicans were jaded with the sight of Popo in the same way New Yorkers take the Statue of Liberty for granted. Not until the 1922 founding of the Exploration Club of Mexico did Mexicans display interest in climbing the peak. Today the Exploration Club provides guides and a rescue group on Popo. Climbers no longer need permission to stay at Las Tlamacas, but can rest at the recently built Vicente Guerrero Lodge at the 13,000 saddle between Popo and Ixtacihuatl and enjoy climbing in the newly created Ixta-Popo National Park.[93] During the Porfirian years, the climb of Popo was part of the Victorian quest for intense experiences that led Englishmen and North Americans up peaks and into the wilderness around the world. Climbing and trekking became a kind of mania among them. Hardly would a party return with stories of its climb up Popo, before another individual reported the exploits of his party's climb.[94] Mexicans found other outlets in their search for adventure.

Bicycles and Technology

Bicyles were first shipped from Paris and Boston to Mexico City in 1869. The cycling rage, called the "Parisian mania," reached the capital when a French three-wheeled velocipede appeared on the streets. Soon a vehicle of Mexican invention, with four wheels, a seat at the back, and an umbrel-la that overspread rider and machine, took to the Paseo. By mid-summer, another Mexico velocipede appeared, this one a tricycle built for two. The unidentified Mexican inventor announced plans to build a machine for a family of five or six to ride together. This fad faded quickly as attention focused on the unsettled political situation that remained several years after the execution of the Emperor Maximilian, and because the common type of wheel, called the boneshaker, proved both difficult and uncom-fortable to ride. The only bicycle that the Mexicans knew much about before 1880 was the one ridden as part of a clown act at the Chiarini circus.[95]

Another shipment of bicycles from the United States arrived in Mexico in 1880. These were the so-called "ordinaries," high-wheeled bicycles famed for the headers taken by riders when they were hurled over the handlebars. Cycling received encouragement from 1880 to 1884 when a Michaux bicycle outlet was opened on the north side of the Alameda to rent machines and to offer instructions to prospective riders. Converts to the wheel soon organized the Club de Velocipedistas in the capital to sponsor excursions led by President Wiener to the countryside. Dressed in a uniform of hunter's green, the riders traveled to El Desierto and neighboring suburbs.[96]

More competitive club members organized velocipede races, at first down two streets bordering the Alameda, turning at the glorieta, and returning. Mario Garfías became the first champion racer. Despite his popularity after winning several races in the spring of 1884, interest in cycling soon waned. The ayuntamiento contributed to the decline of cycling. The council ruled that no wheels could be ridden in the Alameda because of the number of accidents and upsets that had occurred there. The dormant bicycle club roused itself to arrange races down Cinco de Mayo Boulevard as part of the 1887 Independence Day celebration (although heavy rains forced the races to be held at the French hippodrome at the La Piedad, October 2). Nevertheless, the fad attracted only a few partisans in the early 1880s because of the high risk of accident on these vehicles. At the end of the decade, a prospective cyclist still had to order his machine from Boston. The public did not rush to purchase boneshakers, or even the more stable Brown quadricycle, with two small front wheels, the usual large wheels at the back, and steered by a joy stick. Few ordered them from the Massachusetts dealer.[97] Mexicans waited for a better machine.

The machine that created a craze was the "safety" bicycle that arrived in 1891 with the opening of the Columbia Bicycle Agency on Cinco de Mayo Avenue. The safety was a machine with equal-sized wheels and soon came equipped with pneumatic tires. It was called the safety because it greatly reduced the number of headers suffered by riders. Moreover, the air-filled tires made it possible to ride on Mexico's nearly impossible cobblestone streets and rutted roads. When the Germans Hilario Meenen and Carlos Deeg imported safety bicycles in 1891, enthusiasm leaped forward, and by the following year safeties appeared throughout the capital, especially on San Francisco and Corpus Christi streets and the Paseo de la Reforma. Newspaper reporters predicted the cycle would soon become the major means of transportation in the nation.

Cycling clubs sprang up across Mexico. For example, Meenen, Deeg, M. Biguard, and others founded the Veloce Club in July 1891, with riders usually adopting North-American models, such as the Victor. Prospective riders could buy American bicycles at Mexico City's Spaulding outlet (a Columbia agency), or the W. G. Walz Music Store, or from company agents such as Eugene Roller, who represented the Pope Manufacturing Company, Columbia Bicycles, Meridian Britannia Company, D. M. Osborne Company, and Mason Hanlon Company, or Holmes and Trachsel, sole agents for Victor bicycles.[98] One customer learned he could make the best purchase of a wheel from a protestant missionary who sold bicycles as a sideline to saving souls.[99]

The popularity of bicycling received a boost from touring racing teams. The Sterling bicycle team visited Mexico City and Puebla in 1894. A more elaborate tour occurred the following year, when an all-star racing team from the United States visited Mexico from January to March, 1895. H. T. Roberts, of Roberts & Pomeroy Cycle importing company and owner of the Bicycle Riding School, had arranged the trip for Mexico's cycling clubs through promoter F. E. Spooner of Chicago. The five-man team included the nationally known professional riders L. D. Cebanne, the owner of the half-mile unpaved course record of twenty-five seconds; Dr. A. I. Brown, quarter-mile record holder; L. A. Callahan, road and track champion; E. F. Leonart, straight-away champion; and, A. J. Nicolet, trick rider, who also served as photographer. The party comprised ten persons, including coaches and trainers.

The schedule called for races in Mexico City (opening January 23), with appearances in Guadalajara, Puebla, Monterrey, Durango, and San Luis Potosí. All these cities reportedly had active cycling clubs and racing tracks. The tour was to teach Mexicans how to attain higher speeds, especially with the use of pace-makers. The riders, in exchange, would receive fees, expenses, and become acquainted with Mexican society through balls and dances, and the nation's sights through special excursions.[100]

The all-America team left Chicago for Mexico City on January 13, but did not have a chance to race until February 17 because the new La Piedad track experienced a three-week construction delay. This velodrome, located at Rancho Anzures, had a track that was a hard, smooth adobe oval three miles long, with a spacious grandstand a quarter mile long, ten rows deep, and topped with boxes, and a concourse accommodating more than two thousand spectators.

On opening day L. A. Callahan won the open mile and delighted the capacity crowd, who also enjoyed the one-mile novice race won by local favorite Felipe Flores, followed by Eduardo Trigueros. Another Mexican, G. Licea, captured the handicap contest, and the following week won both races open to amateurs. The second day again drew more than two thousand fans, despite the fact that it was Carnival weekend. The audience gave its hardiest approval to the cycling tricks performed by Nicolet, who was persuaded to give a special benefit performance at Orrin's Circus before the tour left the capital.[101]

The delay in Mexico City severely abbreviated the tour. The team immediately headed for Guadalajara for its last stop in Mexico. The Biciclista de Occidente (the Western Bicyclist Club) sponsored the riders, and had prepared for their visit by financing a new $2,000 track made of volcanic ash. Before leaving for El Paso, Texas, the Americans gave two exhibitions that were both well attended by the Tapatíos, the residents of Guadalajara, even though they occurred during the Lenten season.[102]

The exhibitions boosted cycling. The sport increased in popularity, but not with everyone. Members of what Silvestre Terrazas identified as "the lower part of the population" sneered at the vehicles and jeered at their riders. Their least offensive insults, reported Terrazas, included "locos" and "white devils." Many tossed rocks along with their catcalls. The capital's city council cast a jaundiced eye at the wheel as well, and in 1891 banned both boneshakers and safety bicycles and any similar machines from the center of town, defined by a circle running through the city tollhouses (the garitas) and passing through the statue of Carlos IV. The wheel was thus excluded from the Zócalo, the Alameda, and neighboring shopping districts. The statute allowed bicycles in only one fashionable district, the suburban residential area developing at the Hacienda de la Condesa in Chapultepec Forest. Members of the Veloce Club immediately petitioned to have the law modified or reversed, but the ayuntamiento stood firm against them. The riders then sent a delegation to President Díaz. Cycling enthusiast José O. Pastor headed the committee and presented a request that the president intervene in behalf of the sportsmen. Díaz assented to the committee's proposal and ordered the city ordinance revoked. The law remained in force for only a few months, but it indicated clearly that not everyone accepted the bicycle or the changes it represented in the Mexican traditional mentality.[103]

Opposition to the wheel and opportunity to share excursions both encouraged riders to join clubs. Organizations similar to the Club Veloce quickly appeared around the country. Enthusiasts in Puebla organized the Colón Club, October 12, 1892, and other communities followed. A second bicycle group appeared in the capital city when Mexican riders formed the Cyclist Union Club, New Year's Day, 1883. José Hilario Elguero, Federico Trigueros, Alejandro Riva Fontecha, and Francisco Rivas were the club's founders and they held the executive position for the next several years. In 1895, for example, members elected the following officers: José H. Elguero, president; Alejandro Riva, treasurer; and Federico Trigueros, secretary and trainer. The club's excursions to neighboring villages and tourist sites, such as El Desierto, attracted many ardent cyclists, beginning with 70 riders on the first trip, 104 on the second, then 120 on the third, all in the first year of its existence.[104]

Club members and other wheelmen displayed the attitudes, including the acceptance of technology, of modern society. These included secular expectations, equality of competition, specialization, rational rules, bureaucratic organization, record keeping, and production (in sport, the drive to set records, especially for speed).[105] The Cyclist Union Club financed the $25,000 La Piedad bicycle track, built by developer Salvador Malo. Club members clocked laps and races, recorded elapsed time to suburban towns and farther to Amecameca and Cuernavaca, had its own bureaucracy, and maintained records of the first woman to ride from one place to another, the fastest Mexican in the mile, and other distances. These events sprang from exhibitions during Lent, demonstrating a new secular attitude.[106]

Speed lured many from biped to bicycle. Mexican cyclists developed an interest in the capabilities, especially the speed, of their metal steeds. This concern resulted in an awareness of mechanics, new models, different brands, demonstrations, and above all racing. Tlalpan hosted the grand races of May 1893, dominated by René Sarre, who earned accolades as the first champion of Mexico. Shortly afterward, Puebla's cyclists inaugurated their new track with a series of races. The capital city riders sponsored races on Plateros and San Francisco streets (in the area the city council had once closed to riders) in September. Once again Sarré dominated by winning four of the events. The following year a new champion emerged when Luis Brauer won the championship of Mexico at both long and short distances. These Mexican cyclists, along with Lecca, Flóres, Trigueros, and Jiménez, became popular figures. Society was stunned when one celebrated rider, Carlos Buenabad, died of typhus, November 7, 1895. His funeral cortege was escorted through town by all the city's bicycle clubs.[107]

The drive for speed, equality of the conditions for competition, and specialization served as motives for the construction of new cycling tracks. The official inauguration of the La Piedad track with a full season of racing in December 1895 saw the new '96 Rambler bicycles win three of five races. Customers quickly bought the entire shipment of new Ramblers.[108] These purchasers had adjusted to the planned obsolescence that apparently originated with bicycle manufacturers and became a part of their marketing strategy in the United States and elsewhere in 1895. Demonstrations of different brands occurred with the arrival of company agents and riders in Mexico. Colonel Albert Pope,[109] whose company manufactured the Columbia, traveled to Mexico in the winter of 1894–95, and there was great disappointment when he announced that he would have to cancel his 1895 return.[110] The E. C. Stearns Company sent Howard F. Tuttle, who stayed with Federico Trigueros while displaying his machine for admiring wheelmen. California's outstanding rider, M. Stewart, arrived to exhibit his new racer.[111]

Mexico's wheelmen were a cosmopolitan crowd. In the capital, the editor of the *Mexican Herald* commented on the widespread interest in bicycling, saying he had observed "Mexicans, Americans, English, French, Spaniards, and an African or two" riding through town.[112] Young Frenchmen formed the Velo Club Touriste with M. Clement as chairman. Most of the riders chose French bicycles, but a few imported their mounts from the United States.[113] Englishmen belonged to the older and more sedate Bicycle Society, Limited, but the largest and most active club remained the Mexican-dominated Cyclist Union Club.

The cycling clubs corresponded with counterparts in Puebla, Monterrey, and other towns around the country and obtained information on cycling matters in the United States, England, and the continent.[114] Newspapers included a wheelmen's department, with international news, such as the report that Colombia's President Miguel Antonio Caro's son had imported and begun riding the first wheel in Bogotá.[115]

As in other nations, cyclists in Mexico worked for better roads and traffic management and claimed that the bicycle itself would reform society. These efforts were credited with the decision to pave one hundred blocks of streets in Mexico City with asphalt.[116] Another proposal called on the city council to purchase the Hacienda de la Condesa, near Chapultepec Castle, to convert to a park with paths for horsemen and wheelmen. This proposal explained that Mexico City had no genuine park; the Alameda, although beautiful, was too small; the Zócalo, the central garden of the Plaza Mayor, was the breathing spot for the lower classes; Chapultepec Forest offered possibilities, according to the plan, if the commissioners acted wisely in their efforts to preserve the giant cypress trees. the *Mexican Financier* argued that the city council could provide a park, if it would buy the Hacienda de la Condesa from the Escandón family, and it could reclaim the cost by developing a residential district in one section of the property for those who wanted to be near an ideal location for cycling.[117]

Thefts, accidents, collisions with pedestrians and carriages, and conflicts over the right-of-way on streets raised questions of traffic management. Reports of stolen bicycles pointed to the need for a licensing policy; the city council began selling license plates, good for a two-month period for $1.25 pesos. The licenses may have helped the police identify the missing wheels, but thieves continued to sneak off with Ramblers, Stearns, and Columbias. Charles Van der Velde rode his Victor, license 238, to the YMCA reading room one evening. As his bicycle could not read, so he explained, he left it outside, and a daring thief rode off on it. Bicycle clubs soon raised a fund to provide rewards to witnesses that helped bring bike thieves and hit-and-run coachmen to justice.[118]

Collisions and injuries resulting from questions of right-of-way represented more serious problems for the community than the individual loss of bicycles. As early as January 1891, a bicycle rider collided with a goat cart in the Alameda. Both the rider and the goat escaped injury, but the animal displayed its displeasure by chewing up one of the vehicle's rubber tires.[119] A number of accidents occurred in 1895. Pedestrians received a warning that at intersections anyone walking the streets would be held responsible for damages in the event of a collision with a wheelman.[120] More serious than pedestrians for cyclists were the crashes with coaches and hacks. Jean Girard, a young Frenchman, was run down on Juárez Avenue by a Red Hack in December 1895. Girard suffered no permanent injury, but John C. Hill, from the United States, while riding his bicycle, was struck and killed by a hit-and-run coach. Hill's might well be the first traffic death involving a bicycle in Mexico. Officials reacted quickly. United States Consul-General Thomas Crittenden demanded that all efforts be made to arrest the unknown coach driver and that new laws be drafted for the protection of riders.[121] The governor of the Federal District, Pedro Rincón Gallardo, pressured the police to complete the investigation (which proved unsuccessful) and reissued a set of rules that supported this technological innovation.

Rincón Gallardo had first opened all streets of the city, the towns of the Federal District, and adjacent roads to two-, three-, and four-wheeled vehicles during Holy Week of 1892. His restrictions prohibited use of the sidewalks, immoderate speeds, and traveling more than three abreast. he also warned that beginners attempting to master the wheel would not be tolerated on the streets. His safety measures required a bell, a lamp at night, riding on the right-hand side of the road, and passing on the left; the decree prohibited riders from lifting either foot from the pedal since this might result in loss of control. His proclamation concluded with an order for the police to protect wheelmen, arresting anyone who assaulted, whistled at, swore at, or annoyed the riders in any way. With official protection, the bicycle remained popular in Mexico until the advent of the automobile. This decree was reissued in September 1895.[122]

Wheelmen believed their metal mounts offered a way to speed the progress of society. Healthy, wholesome exercise was the most apparent benefit. One Mexican father outfitted his three teenage sons with bicycles costing $750 in the hope that cycling would keep them away from barrooms. A Boston journalist, reporting the popularity of the wheel in Mexico, said, "The sport is in high favor among progressive people, who see in it a means of giving vent to the surplus energy of youth." The same anonymous reporter claimed that the bicycle worked against Mexico's national preoccupation with pills, potions, and patent medicines, which soon "give way to a passion for exercise, and we shall see here a wonderful change." The greatest opposition to the wheel, he asserted, came from the apothecaries, who saw an end to their lucrative business in patent medicines.[123]

Silvestre Terrazas, a Chihuahua journalist, wrote Mexico's first book on bicycling in 1896. In his volume he stressed speed, health, and self-reliance through the mastery of basic mechanics to do maintenance and repairs. The book demonstrates clearly the author's acceptance of modern notions and his effort to promote them among other Mexicans. For prospective racers, Terrazas translated Thomas W. Eck's primer, *Points of Training*, because the methods were the ones known and used by all the top Mexican racers. He recommended that the ideal age to take up Eck's training program for racing was between eighteen and thirty years of age, recalling that Carlos Buenabad, one of the outstanding Mexican racers, had been fifteen at his untimely death that prevented him from becoming one of the world's greatest cyclists. Terrazas's own counsel contains much good sense, for example, reminding corpulent riders that their bodies create too much wind resistance for them to expect much success on the racing circuit. Moreover, he insisted that the successful racer needed what he described as two moral conditions: intelligence and energy—the first to develop sound strategy and to recognize the slightest advantage that could be used to claim victory; energy, he explained, enabled the rider to overcome difficulties during the race and to struggle until the opportunity came that would enable the rider to win. Riders fell into three categories as racers: the formidable, the less formidable, and duffers. The Cyclist Union Club divided racers according to the International Cyclists' Association classification, which recognized amateurs and professional riders.

Eck's advice began with a trumpet call for hygiene and fashion. The unkempt rider he declared was "repulsive"; he counseled that a man should dress in clean clothing for racing just as he would to walk out in the streets, because one never knows "when he will be seen by ladies or gentlemen." In his section called the "Development of Speed" Eck suggested a reasonable twice-daily program of endurance training and sprint intervals, with the caution that the prospective racer should begin "the work" of repeating these exercises as much before the race as possible, preferably in the early spring. Following each workout, the rider should go immediately to the locker room to towel off and rub liniment into the skin to prevent catching cold. For supple muscles and soothing relief, he encouraged the use of a mixture of bay rum and alcohol.[124]

Besides his own and Eck's advice to prospective racers, Terrazas also provided encouragement for those duffers who wanted to ride for their health. He included a chapter of medical advice for riders, waving away critics of the sport with the assertion that eminent doctors of all nationalities had praised cycling for its contributions to physical fitness. Most of his information he drew from two doctors from Chihuahua City, Angel J. Nieto and D. J. Enríquez y Terrazas, both of whom had published articles in local newspapers. They reported that the bicycle contributed to wholesome skin, because the rider was exposed to the sunlight, and his muscles gained from the exercise; but they argued the nervous system received the greatest benefit from the good circulation of blood. Moreover, cycling encouraged the secretion of gastric juices, aiding digestion. Finally, Terrazas concluded that cyclists should learn to breathe correctly to garner the greatest benefits from the exercise; the cyclists' breathing method called for the rider to inhale through the nose and exhale through the mouth. Altogether cycling created a happy, robust individual.[125]

Terrazas offered information for the beginner. His concluding chapter reprinted instructions from several newspapers on learning to ride. This basic information was supplemented with a glossary of cycling terms, including the parts of the vehicle and the racing vocabulary (including many words borrowed from English, such as *handicap, mile,* and *Time-Kipper*), illustrations showing how to change and repair a tire, and a discussion of the parts and accessories to reduce vibration, to alter gear ratios, and to increase the enjoyment of the bicycle.[126]

Knowledge of the machine, its parts and repair, modifications for speed, preparation for racing (understood and described as work), a training regimen comprised of the repetition of the necessary functions (e.g., sprinting) for the production of speed—by promoting all of these, Terrazas offered Mexicans the experience of modern life through bicycling.

The bicycle also represented modernization as it challenged traditional behavior, demeanor, and fashions of Mexican women. Señoritas looked on the sport as an opportunity for a freer life. They could escape the humdrum of a shut-in existence by mounting a wheel, often riding off in the company of a young gentleman, leaving behind the dueña who could not or would not learn to ride a bicycle.[127] These señoritas could not ride in the traditional dress, so had to modify their wardrobe. Some of them adopted the daring "bloomer" costume. "To be or not to be" in bloomers, described as "a pair of trousers very baggy at the knees, abnormally full at the pistol pockets and considerably full where you strike a match," was the question agitating the feminine mind in Mexico City. Opponents argued that women should be held responsible for accidents caused by their provocative garments; others averred women would tarnish their reputations by appearing nearly disrobed in public. Reports soon circulated that shoplifters were renting the cycling costumes because the roominess of the garment made it easy to hide stolen goods. Despite critics, the wheelmen and women believed progress was the result of exercise, mobility, new fashions, and companionship offered by the bicycle.[128]

Progressive society returned to Mexico City from their suburban homes along the Viga Canal on two pneumatic tires during the Lenten season. Traditionally high society had escaped the onerous rules of Lent by retiring to the suburbs, but the wheel brought them back beginning with the tour by North American riders in 1895. The following year, the capital's city council arranged a bicycle parade to celebrate the Carnival season, offering over $500 in awards to winners. The display was regarded as a stunning success. Federico Trigueros, dressed in a red, blue, orange, black, and white costume with his wheel decorated with "rare tropical flowers, shaded by a canopy of gardenias," tied for first honors; but Zozaya claimed the prize with a coin flip. Only the presence of large numbers of the rabble, who could not be controlled by the police, marred the event, according to reporters. After this 1896 parade, riders began to spend the entire Lenten season, with reduced regulations, in the city. These events soon led to pushing the traditional celebration of such Holy Week events as the burning of Judas out of the Zócalo into the plazas and streets of the working-class neighborhoods.[129]

With all the interest in the bicycle, eventually commercial efforts to repair them and manufacture them had to come. R. R. Shepard opened a repair shop in the Calle de Dolores in 1896, offering spare parts and making adjustments. Charles Leo Browne obtained contracts on November

15, 1905, and March 12, 1908, to establish a factory to manufacture both bicycles and automobiles. For reasons that remain unclear, Browne's efforts never went beyond the planning stage, and February 10, 1909, the government rescinded his contracts. Nevertheless, for the modern Mexican mounting his wheel and weaving in and out of the crowds during the afternoon's paseo on the Reforma demonstrated his wealth, position, and above all his progressive character.[130]

The leisure interests of Mexicans in the 1890s revealed attitudes, notions, and proclivities that constituted the Porfirian persuasion. This temper showed a rush to accept European and especially American activities, which included sport. Baseball particularly reflected the growing influence of the Americans, the most important group of foreigners in the country, whether measured in number of residents, importance of occupations, or value of investments. Boxing not only expressed this mimicry but also revealed the new security and routine established by the Díaz regime that resulted in a quest for excitement in what had abruptly become an "unexciting" society. Above all, Mexicans recognized the importance of progress, speed, and modernization through technology as they turned to bicycles. Cycling became the sport of the times. Perhaps these attitudes do not seem surprising to those familiar with the Porfirian economic and political system. But no political pressure or economic necessity compelled the adoption of these diversions. Mexicans freely chose the sport that expressed the Porfirian persuasion.

Game Fit Only for Cowboys

Not all foreign sport made an impact on Mexico. The Porfirian haut monde imitated the western bourgeoisie in many amusements, but had acquired the self-confidence by the 1890s to reject recreation that they found repugnant to Mexican culture. One example can be seen in the events surrounding the first football games played south of the Rio Grande.

The United States colony, so influential in shaping the sporting traditional of Porfirian society, included several men who had played football in college. They wanted their sport to join baseball, horse racing, and bicycling as Mexican pastimes. They found the promoter they needed when they negotiated with George A. Hill of Austin, Texas, an entrepreneur, a land promoter, a railroad investor, and most important of all, a football fan. Hill, who had organized several tours to Mexico, was persuaded to combine a Christmas excursion with a pigskin exhibition in Mexico City.

Hill took advantage of circumstances. The University of Missouri football squad had arrived in Austin for a December 14 game against its old coach Harry Orman Robinson and his University of Texas team. Hill offered the players and Coaches Robinson and Frank Patterson an all-expense-paid trip if they would play a few exhibitions in Mexico. The Texans immediately agreed. Missouri's players voted for this postseason excursion and settled down in Austin to enjoy themselves.

First they played the Texans. After withstanding a Ranger (today called the Longhorns) drive that ended on their two-yard line, the Tigers rushed for two scores and a 10 to 0 victory. The night after the contest, the university German club feted the players. The Missouri yearbook editor reported that "the entertaining powers of the young men, together with the exceptional charms of the young ladies, made it one of the most pleasant affairs of the kind it has ever been the good fortune of the scribe to attend." This holiday spirit dominated the tour of Mexico.

While waiting for the Texans to finish their fall classes so the tour could begin, the Tigers won three exhibitions over the Texas Deaf and Dumb Institute (39 to 0), the San Antonio Athletic Club (29 to 0), and the Austin Athletic Club (21 to 0). Officials in Missouri expected the squad to return shortly.[131]

Preparations for the excursion hit a major snag with the administration of the University of Texas. The university president had no objection to the team's traveling to Mexico, but he would not allow the players to schedule a game for Sunday, December 27, because the long-standing Protestant ethic required keeping the Sabbath free of frivolous activities. His decision created a serious problem since Sunday was the traditional day for recreation in Mexico City and therefore the day on which the teams could be expected to draw the largest crowd of spectators. Hill had no choice but to accede to the president's prohibition of a Sunday contest. The promoter made other plans.

On Christmas eve, a party of 150 excursionists including 31 football players left Austin. Travelers paid fifty dollars for the ten-day tour; local merchant Philip Hatzeld paid the players' expenses. The entourage traveled on a special train on the Mexican National Railway with five sleepers, a day coach, a diner seating forty-eight persons, and a baggage car. First stop was Monterrey on Christmas Day. Several hundred curious Mexicans and Americans joined General Bernardo Reyes, governor of Nuevo León, at the athletic grounds to view *futbol americano*. The teams, with both coaches playing, struggled throughout the hotly contested game that was finally won by Missouri, 12 to 0. This proved the most evenly played contest of the tour.[132]

Meanwhile preparations for the arrival of the football players proceeded in Mexico City. Arrangements included hiring the Indianilla track and grading its infield for the game. The owner, Colonel Robert Pate, decided to charge an extra fee for those who wanted box seats. He justified the price increase on the basis that in the United States the most fashionable people attended football matches and at the recent Yale-Princeton game box seats had cost ten dollars to limit the crowd to the well-educated.

Newspaper publicity included an explanation of how the game was played for first-time spectators. The reports described the parallelogram field called a gridiron and the scoring of touchdowns (four points each) and trys (two points for kicking the ball between the goalposts after a touchdown).

Announcements filled the newspapers about the impending arrival of the teams in Mexico City. Reporters touted the Missourians, holders of the Western Championship, informing readers that the proper cheer was "Rah! Rah! Tigers!" Prospective fans were informed that the Tigers wore yellow-and-black-striped jerseys and the Rangers dressed in yellow and white. The Texans flaunted their yellow-and-white silk banner that only recently had been presented to them by the young women of the senior class. The advance publicity contained a curious notice: traveling with the university teams were the players of the Star Athletic Club and the Crescent Athletic Club. The clubs were scheduled to play an exhibition match at Indianilla on Sunday, December 27.[133]

In Mexico City, a crowd of two to four thousand attended the Sunday afternoon game between the Stars and the Crescents. Pseudonyms may have fooled Mexican spectators, but the other excursionists recognized the teams from the University of Texas and the University of Missouri. Those who knew the players connived with Hill's subterfuge to honor

Protestant blue laws. Attendance disappointed the promoters, who had expected about twice the number of fans and who had been personally assured that President Porfirio Díaz would attend. Although Díaz failed to appear, the city's mayor, the diplomatic corps, and the leaders of Mexico City society and the Anglo-American colony attended. Colonel Pate took advantage of the halftime for a matched horse race that was won by the popular local horse Portuguese.

Two Yale graduates, E. H. Morton and F. M. Patterson, served as the referee and umpire of the contest. In a game that baffled most of the spectators, the Crescents scored two touchdowns and two trys to win 12 to 6 over the Texans masquerading as the Star Athletic Club.[134] The use of pseudonyms was already a habit for several of the Missouri players. Two Tigers, in fact, were not even students of the university. The Rangers did not protest against them because the use of so-called "tramp" athletes was common in the 1890s.

An even smaller crowd turned out for the second contest, this time played in the name of the University of Missouri and the University of Texas. One of the Missouri backs, Crawford White, was betrayed by his memory several decades later when he recalled that the game was preceded by a bullfight. Perhaps he remembered a corrida de toros before one of the entertainments given for the players such as the dance at Mrs. Tennant's home. As part of their excursion, the players probably attended that spectacle on some occasion, but on game day (December 29) the only other events were halftime horse races.

The footballers played poorly in their third contest in five days. Some fans attributed the sluggishness to the effects of the high altitude, but one Texas fan gave a different picture of the poor play of his team. "The boys raised hell after they got down there. We didn't have any sissy boys on the team. They'd go out and get drunk, stay up all night, and come in and play a game the next day." Whatever the cause, in their third rematch in Mexico, the Tigers and Rangers played to a scoreless draw.[135]

Bernard Frisbie, one of the leaders of Mexico's Anglo-American sporting fraternity, joined George and Oscar Braniff and George Patterson in collecting a local team to play some of the college boys. But the collegians could not muster enthusiasm enough for another match in the Aztec capital.[136] The excursion train left Mexico City December 30 for the border.

The players played a final game at the Laredo Bicycle Park on January 2, 1897. The contest had been arranged for New Year's Day, but a wreck on the Mexican railroad line delayed the train and the contest. Only three hundred curious fans turned out a day later, to watch Missouri win once more. The exhausted players climbed into their pullman and headed home. The Missourians had to face the wrath of parents and college administrators because Coach Patterson had returned all telegrams inquiring about his team's activities marked "whereabouts unknown" and "return to sender."[137]

The Tigers chugged into Columbia on January 4, after traveling six thousand miles and being "lost" for three weeks. The university administration reacted swiftly: the president fired Patterson and suspended the players from the university. The suspension of the players was lifted before the 1897 season, but Patterson remained fired. Despite the rather unhappy ending, the yearbook editor concluded, "While their conduct was not at all times strictly decorous, they were always gentlemen and were ever mindful of the duty they owed to the school and the state."[138]

The tour had no permanent impact in Mexico. American workmen announced plans to organize teams representing the Mexican Central and the National railroads. But these plans were never realized, nor did the games create any spectator interest. Before the revolution, the only games played matched Mexico's American School and the British branch of the YMCA.[139] Those who watched the exhibition games in Mexico City could not understand why the players wore such heavy clothes, ankle protectors, and guards for the ears and nose.[140]

Mexican journalists expressed confusion or criticism of the contests they had witnessed. *El Nacional* reported the game became somewhat "rough as well as savage, unpolished, and dangerous," adding it was "unlikely that the game will become naturalized here." *El Tiempo* hoped football would not become established among Mexicans, "for in it, brute force plays a greater part than skill." *El Monitor* provided a fuller account: "The players jumped on the top of one another, charged, bucked, and struggled, forming a human tangle very disagreeable to behold. We must say the spectacle did not please, but on the contrary, produced a sentiment of disapproval." *El Mundo* spoke for many Mexican witnesses, saying, "The funny part of it is that after the rough and tumble struggle, the players came away as happy and as friendly with one another as if they had just had a drink together. We are decidedly of the opinion that this game will not find many votaries here. Our temperament and character would not allow it. Each game would degenerate into a row. On receiving a blow, we would not continue to think of the ball. We are not made that way." *La Patria* snorted, "It was a game fit only for cowboys." The distasteful memory lingered, and a year after the event *El Hijo del Ahuizote* published a satirical cartoon picturing a brutal pile-up of players, with the comment, "En El Foot-ball (Barbaro juego de pelota yankee) [Barbarous Yankee ball game]."[141]

Football might not respond to the interest and cultural convictions of Mexico's frock-coat crowd, as the respectable classes were derisively called, but it showed how foreigners made themselves at home in Mexico, demonstrating the security they felt in the dictator's country. Several foreign groups had established casinos or clubs as the center of their activities by 1890.[142] Capital city Germans, for example, hosted a Swiss musical troupe and Miss Allie Torbett, a violinist from the United States. Other Germans in Puebla quickly began brewing Vogel beer, and sales in Toluca became so successful that owners ordered a team of Clydesdales from St. Louis to pull the wagon-loads of beer to customers. The brewery soon opened a Tivoli garden with regular Sunday afternoon concerts and entertainment for the town's society. The beer garden also offered facilities for bowling and billiards.[143]

Spaniards in Mexico City, accused of being either grocers or priests, wanted to enjoy old-country recreation, so they subscribed to a building fund that financed the construction of a jai-alai frontón for playing what was then called eder-jai. The building had the necessary playing area, lounge, restaurant, grandstand and additional seating for 1,500, a section reserved for the military band provided by Díaz, restrooms, and, of course, a betting room. The Spanish national champions came to Mexico in December 1895 to inaugurate the frontón. They divided into the Reds and the Blues and gave a series of exhibitions before an appreciative audience that included several members of the presidential cabinet. Díaz did not attend, but sent his regrets, saying he was still officially in mourning for the death of General Manuel Gonzáles.[144]

Other foreigners had by 1890 established their favorite sporting recreations in Mexico. In Pachuca, English miners introduced English football or soccer, which became Mexico's most important spectator sport, while their Cousin Jacks organized Cornish wrestling for their pleasure. Englishmen also flocked to cricket matches at the Reforma Athletic Club, and organized a Rugby team to challenge Pachuca's Rugby Union Football Club, which published an offer to travel anywhere in the republic for a match. Other teams sprang up in Monterrey and Ciudad Porfirio Díaz. Mexican gentlemen often attended these events, and formed their own Club Atlético first to play cricket, then baseball against teams of foreigners.[145]

Scotsmen enjoyed broadsword and one-on-one competition with lances and other weapons introduced by Duncan C. Ross. This Boer War hero toured from Monterrey to Mexico City in 1895 and 1896, giving athletic and combative demonstrations. He dueled, wrestled, and offered to roller-skate against all comers in the capital city. Highlanders, as well as many other residents of Mexico, packed his performances.[146]

Yankees in Porfirian Mexico also enjoyed their favorite sports. These foreigners, numbering seven thousand in the capital by 1911, included many sportsmen, who established a country club in Churubusco that offered a golf course, tennis courts, a hall for theatricals, dances, and concerts, and accommodations for travelers. Other Americans organized the Reforma Athletic Club, which provided tennis courts, baseball and cricket fields, and space for track events to both foreign and Mexican gentlemen and ladies. Yankees founded the Monterrey Gymnastic Club, which served as the center for anyone interested in Indian club juggling, physical training, boxing, wrestling, track, or baseball.[147]

Perhaps the most persistent, and ultimately the most successful, promoter of Anglo-American sports was the Young Men's Christian Association. A young men's Christian society had been organized to sponsor a reading room in Mexico City in the 1880s; this small group became the nucleus for a Y. affiliate established in 1891. George N. Taylor, who had served the Y's International Committee, became the first secretary in Mexico. Just before his death in 1893, Taylor secured a building for the group. Edward P. Gaston, an American businessman also with Y experience, became the new secretary and gained support from prominent Mexican government officials and established the best-equipped gymnasium in Mexico City. Gradually the Y opened its facilities to Mexicans, but they could not become members. Regarded as a center of Anglo-Americans and a missionary center for Mexicans, the Y achieved little success and soon lapsed into such inaction that in 1900 it was no longer recognized by the international YMCA. Change came with the arrival in 1902 of George I. Babcock, who first established an association for English-speaking railroad workers (as part of the Y's effort to proselytize among workingmen that began in 1868 and had its greatest success among the railroaders). Two years later he opened a branch for Mexican workingmen, using as a base the surviving organization and facilities of the 1891 group, and in 1907, in an action without precedent, he joined the railroad and Mexican groups into one YMCA.[148]

Merger of the English-speaking and Mexican associations altered the membership test of the international YMCA that had required affiliation with an evangelical church. Babcock listed Baptist, Congregational, Episcopal, Methodist, Presbyterian, and Roman Catholic churches as fulfilling this definition. His action, eventually ratified by the international organization, allowed rapid expansion in Mexico and other Roman Catholic countries. By 1911 the only religious requirement was good standing in any Christian church for membership in the Y.

From his arrival Babcock devoted much attention to what the YMCA called "Boys Work," programs for youths under the age of eighteen to aid in their physical, mental, and religious development. The Y attempted to make the gym an alternative to the cantina and the calle. As in the United States, promoters used sport to attract young men; physical education directors A. C. Stewart and Charles Westropp organized the first basketball and swimming teams in Mexico. By the time of the 1910 centennial celebrations of Mexican independence the Y required a larger gym to accommodate its classes and the two English gym directors had been succeeded by Mexicans Julio Marín, Enrique Aguirre, and Pancho Lara, all three of whom had attended the training classes at the Springfield (Massachusetts) YMCA Training School. With a new building and a larger gym, the number of calisthenics classes increased and were enlivened with piano accompaniment by a Señora Cervantes, who remained at the YMCA's piano for thirty years. Of course, sport and exercise were complemented by hygiene and health lectures. The YMCA continued its efforts into the 1920s, when it organized track teams and established Campo Williams in Tepostlán as a place for boys and workers to get away from urban life.[149]

Private individuals opened clubs in Mexico City for the paying public interested in athletic instruction and training. Professor Jimmy Carroll owned and managed the Mexican National Athletic Club, where he taught the art of pugilism, and had a staff of three other boxing masters and one dumb-bell teacher. The American Olympic Club was a rival business, operated by boxing champion Billy A. Clarke, who taught boxing and gymnastics to enthusiastic foreigners and young Mexican gentlemen. H. T. Roberts rented costumes and wheels at his Bicycle Riding School on the Paseo de la Reforma to those who wanted to master this machine.[150]

The rise of these sporting activities demonstrates the welcome given to foreign activities in Mexico and the comfortable feeling that foreigners enjoyed during these years of the Porfirian regime. Traditional Mexican diversions also were increasingly affected by foreign influences. The theater, long a leisure activity of the Mexican population and the target of foreign critics, began featuring foreign troupes, not just from Spain, but from England, France, and the United States. Beginning in the 1870s, a regular opera season brought non-Mexican artists to Mexico City, and by the 1880s such renowned troupes as the Sieni Opera Company made annual appearances. Theatergoers rejoiced when world famous diva Adelina Patti agreed to a season in Mexico City in December 1886 and January 1887. The visit started on a bad footing when a confidence man who posed as the singer's advance agent sold out her performances and absconded with the funds. Nevertheless, Patti's seven performances played to sell-out crowds who paid $87,000 to listen to the person proclaimed by the newspapers as the "greatest songstress on earth."[151]

Less than a month later Sarah Bernhardt arrived, making Mexico City one stop on her American tour. The world's most celebrated actress appeared on the stage of the national theater ten times in the role of Theodora, and took away pesos valued at some $35,000 from an enthusiastic audience who paid the equivalent of four dollars to see her perform. Although Mexicans welcomed non-Mexican performers, they maintained traditional customs of wearing their sombreros, smoking cigarettes during performances, and selling tickets for each act of the opera or play.[152]

Theater amusements of the lower social groups began to change in the 1870s as owners started to integrate non-Mexican techniques and attractions into their productions not simply in imitation of the foreign stage but in a successful effort to increase profits. Itinerant circuses established permanent locations and introduced the English clown with red hair and nose and baggy trousers; neighborhood theaters encouraged the exchanges between audience and actors that typified traditional puppet performances and drew spectators, and, after 1869, they featured the cancan, a dance sensation that drew sell-out crowds. These local theaters soon developed into music halls called the *teatro frívolo*, which became one of the centers of social life for the lower and working classes during the Porfirian years.[153]

The Mexican elite took up some of the high-society recreations of England and the United States. Boating received a response first in the ports of Mazatlán, where sailors from the *Mexico* won a regatta in 1886, and Veracruz, host of a yacht race as early as 1888. The capital city's English-speaking residents in 1890 held a meeting to form a boating club. These gentlemen elected the British minister, Sir Spenser St. John, as president and chose Edward C. Butler, three years later named first secretary of the United States legation, to head a committee to tour Lake Chalco for a suitable site for the clubhouse. The initial plans called for racing and sailing, and a club equipped with a tennis court, croquet ground, and dance floor.[154] Officially founded in 1891, the Lakeside Sailing Club included numerous Mexican members. The club held regular regattas on Lakes Chalco and Xochimilco and traveled on at least one occasion to Veracruz to sail with that city's yacht club. The National Military Academy organized a crew that often rowed against the lakeside team.[155]

Still other Porfirian gentlemen participated in the annual Christmas polo matches, first played at the Hipódromo Frances in the 1880s. In 1888, Mexican aristocrats organized a polo club, with its home grounds at the Condesa hacienda (today part of Chapultepec Park). In the same year, British employees of the mines in Pachuca organized a team as well. The two clubs met the following spring in Mexico City before an elite audience who attended by engraved invitations only, including President and Mrs. Díaz. The capital team, dressed in regulation polo clothes and riding banged-tailed ponies, easily defeated the Pachuca squad, which appeared in charro uniforms, mounted on Mexican stock. Mexico's team consisted of Manuel and Pedro Escandón, Ignacio de la Torre, Alfredo Zaldivar, A. H. Clinch, Lionel Carden (British consul and later British ambassador to the government of Victoriano Huerta), and H. Ramsen

Whitehouse. Whitehouse, secretary of the United States legation, had such confidence in this team after its victory that during a furlough in New York City he challenged the Meadow Brook Polo Club. A match was arranged for Mexico City in late February or early March, 1890, and called for several days of competition that would include baseball, cricket, and tennis after the polo meeting. This prospect apparently died when Whitehouse left his diplomatic post in Mexico in early 1890. The capital city polo group later merged with the Reforma Athletic Club in 1892. Then, to avoid the distraction of other sports, devotees founded the Polo Club in 1905, with thirty members representing the elite of the capital.[156]

Even more popular with Mexican society was the roller-skating fad. As early as 1871, *The Two Republics,* an English-language newspaper often reprinted by the capital's other editors, called for construction of a rink where Mexico City residents could enjoy the "respectability, morality, and healthiness" of skating on wooden rollers. This rage, which had already swept the United States and western Europe, finally arrived in Mexico in December 1875, when the Tivolí de Ferrocarril opened a roller rink so that patrons could attempt this "exciting and fascinating diversion" to the music of a select orchestra.[157] A second rink opened at the Tivolí de Eliseo in 1877, first for Sunday-only skating, which immediately became popular with persons from the middle class. The Orrin brothers, owners of the capital's circus, inaugurated a third rink which offered three sessions daily and classes for beginners taught by the Fletchers, the well-known skating professionals. Patrons flocked to watch the demonstrations of fancy skating given by the Fletchers each Monday and Thursday evening, to cheer the students who competed at the conclusion of the course for a pair of Plimpton roller skates, and to laugh at the antics and juggling of a clown on rollers.[158]

Interest grew in skating as both an entertainment and a recreation. The managers of the Abreu, a second-class theater, lured audiences by offering a variety program that included illusionists, the Berlands, and roller-skating star Frank Fuller, in 1889. Fuller made several additional appearances, snatching top billing from a collection of magicians and wizards. He was praised as "the poetry of gracefulness" and his feats "elicited loud and repeated applause."[159]

Rinks soon opened in other cities, attracting large crowds, especially in Veracruz and Chihuahua City. In Mexico City salons offered skating from 10 A.M. to 4 P.M., Tuesday to Friday, for women only, allowing men to enter the rink in the late afternoon and evenings. The rinks, at least until the mid-1890s, always closed during Holy Week, reopening Holy Saturday evening. The Mexico City Cabildo issued a concession to Fernando Veragua to open a wooden rink during November and December 1895, in the Alameda. The Cabildo collected 12 percent of the profits as Mexicans rented skates and wisked around the arena decorated with wintry scenes. The franchise was extended until the end of January 1896, for matched races that demonstrated the skills of Mexican against foreign skaters. No doubt fans sympathized with Telesforo García's son Francisco, who fell during competition and was hospitalized for the removal of numerous splinters. At the end of the month, the rink was dismantled and shipped to Guadalajara. Skating continued to draw large crowds at other rinks. The vogue soon appeared on the streets and constituted such a hazard that in 1907 the chief of police prohibited skating on the streets and sidewalks, especially after dark.[160]

Strapping on wooden rollers gave Mexicans a shared experience with the Anglo-American leisure class, and residents of Mexico City continued the recreation until the outbreak of the revolution. This activity received praise along with bicycling for providing wholesome exercise for women. Acclaim went to skating as well for its "socialistic" nature, bringing together men and women, foreigners and Mexicans in healthy physical activity.[161]

With or without roller skates, Mexican gentlemen did not question the efficacy of sport. Nor did they waver in their opinion that recreation offered modern society a scientific avenue to good health. Their therapeutic view of recreation found its way into government policies shortly after the turn of the century. Its first official champion, Ing. Miguel Quevedo, as early as 1902 directed a commission (comisión de embellecimiento y mejoras de la ciudad) that devised a comprehensive plan that envisioned open places for recreation or simply fresh air in the capital city. It announced plans for additional monument squares, creating space within the city, and expansion of the Alameda and other existing parks. The committee encouraged every school to develop a small park for students and proposed city-owned sporting areas for adults, whom the committeemen believed needed exercise. Quevedo's report gave its hardiest endorsement to playgrounds, open to all youngsters, but especially planned for working-class children. The proposed playgrounds featured extensive sand gardens like those constructed in the United States and Great Britain. Chapultepac met nearly every particular of the committee's ideal park, but its location in the suburbs was a drawback because this made it the recreational center of the upper classes and distant from the working classes. The commission proposed a new park across the Viga causeway in the working-class zone of the city, so it would be easily accessible to poorer residents. Finance Minister José Limantour endorsed the proposal but could not find enough reasonably priced land, so it was necessary to locate the workers' park in the southeastern suburbs. Balbuena Park, like Chapultepec, was too distant from the poor barrios of Mexico City to attract many workers or their children. In the center of the city, where it was most needed, no park existed.

Support for playgrounds and open spaces as indispensable means to health and hygiene continued to grow among the city's technocratic officials. This movement resulted in a special Hygiene Exhibition in 1911 that featured a public lecture by Quevedo, entitled "Open Spaces and Forest Reserves of Cities: Their Adaptation to Gardens, Parks, and Playgrounds." At the time of his presentation, Quevedo was a member of the Public Health Council and chief of the Forestry Department. His lecture began with a review of the evidence that human beings need fresh air to grow, flourish, and reproduce; he cited European and North American biologists on the need for this air to be renewed and recirculated. Proof of the health-giving benefits of fresh air and open spaces, he argued, was that men from the country were always more robust and vigorous than men from the city. Similar lectures could be heard across the United States, where the Progressive reformers blended their faith in science and bureaucracy into well-intentioned reforms. The Quevedo lecture continued with a discussion of the importance of living space for city residents, beginning in the home, where he contended that each person needed twenty to thirty-five cubic meters for adequate space as well as plants that would renew the air people breathed. Space could be created, he argued, by widening the streets and by conserving spaces for parks and playgrounds. He placed Mexico City into worldwide perspective by reporting the ratio of persons to hectare of parks and open areas. His statistics ranged from the 51 persons to hectare in Meriden, Connecticut, to the highest figure reported, Mexico City's 2,500 persons to hectare, more than twice the number of London, Chicago, and Paris. The lecturer then discussed the importance of trees, calling for a reforestation program on the hills around Mexico City to improve air quality by increasing oxygen and decreasing dust, to prevent erosion on the surrounding hillsides, and to improve the quality of city life by the appearance of trees and shade near the capital. Quevedo's plans soon were ignored, as the Mexicans turned to the revolution, first destroying a government and then trying to reestablish a new one. Only in the 1920s was there a return to the playground movement and the teaching of physical education, and then in 1971 the government announced plans to reforest the hills around the city as part of an effort to improve air quality in the capital.[162]

Quevedo's committee and his exhortations did not have the results that he and other Mexican reformers desired, but the campaign for playgrounds in Mexico City shows clearly that the Porfirian gentry were well abreast of sport and recreation movements in the United States and western Europe. London, New York, and Boston had developed sand gardens and parks with play areas in the 1880s, but the great impetus to playgrounds came after the 1906 founding of Playground Association of America. Mexicans kept pace with the boosters of sport for health and crime prevention for youngsters in Chicago, Los Angeles, Pittsburgh, Seattle, and 467 other cities that by 1916 had established municipal parks and playgrounds. The paternalistic use of the city bureaucracy characterized those who had accepted technology and demanded that this modern efficiency be put to use improving society. Called Progressive in the United States, this attitude in Mexico formed another current in the Porfirian persuasion.[163]

Recreational choices reflected a growing tension in Mexican society between tradition and technology. Upper-class urban Mexicans (los de arriba) mounted their wheels for a gala trip to the countryside; country workers (los de abajo) cut off one handle on imported plows so they looked like the traditional tool.[164] The opposition of campesino and worker to technology can be found in the lower class's means of expression. Holy Saturday, the day before Easter, regularly allowed social reversals through the burning of effigies of Judas, dressed as upper-class Mexicans at.d political figures. José Guadalupe Posada, the people's artist, did one of his most famous etchings showing a wheelman on a monstrous bicycle threatening the lives of the people.[165] In traditional recreations, society was divided between those on the shady side and those on the sunny side, but the lower class was notable only by its absence at Mexico's modern sports of baseball, boxing, and bicycling. The gap between los de arriba and los de abajo had widened, helping to create the circumstances in which the 1910 revolution could overturn the Díaz regime, and accentuating this division to the point that it would prevent the revolution from succeeding until the era of Lázaro Cárdenas in the 1930s. To understand this split, we turn now to the material culture and attitudes of Mexico's traditional society.

Rocks
and
Rawhide
in
Rural
Society:
Tools
and
Technology
in
Porfirian
Mexico

The backwardness of rural Mexico astonished travelers who came to the country during the dictatorship of Porfirio Díaz (1876–1911). They expressed surprise at the poverty of the people in this supposed treasure house and shock at the dearth of tools in the homes, fields, and mines. Commentators familiar with the United States and Great Britain had an immediate explanation for what they regarded as stagnation: Mexicans lacked modern technology. Many concluded that Mexico had yet to advance beyond chipped rocks as utensils. These descriptions of Mexican backwardness during the Porfirian years demonstrate the encounter between two cultures, the industrial and the traditional, and provide examples of the symbolic inversions used to label Mexican society as stagnant, ancient, or primitive. The observers asked rhetorically why Mexicans resisted development; then they formulated answers that confirmed Protestant, Anglo-American attitudes about the tropics, Hispanic culture, race mixture, and especially the Roman Catholic Church. Their solutions created opportunities for foreign investors by requiring the panacea of the age: technology.

The Mexican countryside seemed locked in its own stone age. One traveler commented, "Clinging yet with Indian pertinacity to ancient customs, following, even in dress, traditions two or three hundred years old, they seem as removed from the pressures of changeful events as the fossil remains of another age."[1] Stones served for nearly all the tools used in the household and in the fields. Women ground the meal for tortillas, the basic item in the diet, by using a stone roller on a rectangular, concave stone sheet called the *metate* (the two looked something like a rock rolling pin and washboard), or a smaller stone mortar and pestle (the *molcajete* and the *mano*). Even long-distance pack trains carried this improvised mill, so that when the mules stopped for the night, one muleskinner could grind the corn for the evening and morning meals.[2] No steam- or water-powered village mill reduced the daily drudgery. Women ground maize, a dozen kernels at a time, then patted the *masa* (the damp flour) into a thin, flat circle and toasted it on a hot rock or pottery griddle (the *comal*) resting on the traditional three-stone cooking fire that served as stove.[3] The gentle slapping of the tortillas and their sizzle on the *comal* were the most common sounds of domestic Mexico. No stoves, nor fireplaces, nor kitchens existed. Some cooks had, at best, a shed where the charcoal fire was raised off the ground on a waist-high stone platform, with the three stones replaced by a brazier cut from a kerosene tin. A woven-straw fan whipped the fire to gleaming readiness; the charcoal did not smoke, so the Mexicans constructed no chimneys.[4]

The tortilla served as Mexico's daily bread and its dinner service. It was rolled into a scoop to dip into the beans or gruel boiling in an earthenware pot; it served, when toasted hard and called a *tostada,* as an edible plate for whatever scraps of meat or vegetable might be available. The housewife needed only a knife, for cutting and chopping, and a clay pot or two. Having cooked for centuries without iron vessels, Mexicans saw no need to change, even if they could have afforded it.[5]

Rural houses, really huts, seemed to demonstrate the same, nearly prehistoric backwardness. Quite probably these dwellings represented the fusion of Aztec and early Spanish flat-roofed styles. The most prevalent flat-roofed buildings were constructed from adobe, sun-baked straw and mud blocks. The scarcity, and consequently the cost, of lumber prohibited the construction of wooden buildings; and the price of wood, the only fuel available, prevented the manufacture of kiln-baked bricks.[6] In a few wooded mountain regions, log houses of notched construction existed. Apparently this corner-timbered style was introduced by Sudeten German miners in the 1530s in Central Mexico, and from the United

States in the second half of the ninetenth century in Mexico's far north.[7] In the *tierra caliente,* the tropical zone, the people constructed their huts out of saplings and leaves, usually stuccoed with mud. Whether adobe, wattle, or log, these one-room dwellings had no windows and no flooring but packed earth mixed with ashes. Doorways provided the only source of ventilation and sunlight.[8]

Roofs were the most costly and the most difficult part of the construction. Whenever possible, the roofs were saved and used again. In the mining camps of Michoacán, the palm thatch roofs would be carried away by the miners when they abandoned one camp for another.[9] When thatch was not used, the roofs were made by laying rows of poles across the top of the walls, then covering these with one or two feet of dirt and over the dirt a layer of pine boards. The lumber was the most expensive part of the house.[10] One mining camp superintendent from San Francisco found in Huehuepán, Durango, that it was cheaper to rent a roof than to have one built.[11]

The residents of these huts lived essentially without furniture, having as a rule neither chairs, tables, nor beds. Mats, called *petates,* served as sleeping pallets. A few rural Mexicans, slightly higher on the social scale, might have a bed frame constructed of four mounds of clay, crossed with rough boards. No one had mattresses; none had bedding. Men slept in their clothes, wrapped in their *sarapes* when it was cold. Women curled up in their clothes and covered up with their *rebozos.* Because a person usually only owned the clothes he wore, chests were unnecessary. What extra items the family owned hung on pegs or were suspended from the ceiling logs. The earthen pottery, in all sizes, served not only for cooking but also for storage. The only decoration within the house was a paper picture of the Virgin of Guadalupe or one of the saints.[12]

The houses had no heating because the cold was not so extreme as to make it absolutely necessary. In the towns of the higher elevations, including the capital city, the mornings were cool and the winter months often bone-chilling, with occasional ice and every four or five years even snow. Shivering in the cold, Mexicans did as the Italians did and went out in the sun to get warm; indoors they wrapped up as well as they could. Moreover, the cost of fuel was so high that few could have afforded to heat their hovels even if they had had fireplaces or stoves. Wealthy hacienda owners bought hearth rugs to use as saddle blankets, as they had no fireplaces.[13] What disturbed the Anglo-American commentators more than the cold was the absence of the hearth and, consequently, the family life they knew. "The home, as we understand it, does not exist," wrote H. H. Bancroft, who explained, "The absence of fire-places indicates one great obstacle to those family reunions which have so important an influence on our society."[14] These amateur sociologists concluded that without these gatherings the Mexicans lacked the family structure that served as the building block of society. Victorian conventional wisdom made the family the best hope for the preservation of moral order. The missing chimneys signified that Mexicans, without properly constituted families, were indeed primitive, and doomed to immorality and disorder.[15]

Near nakedness confirmed to foreigners and urban, upper-class Mexicans that what they saw in the country was the primitive life of ignoble savages. The vast majority of these Mexicans walked barefooted or wore only sandals. If they had *huaraches,* they made them of rawhide or plaited fibers, fastened to the foot with strings of the same material. This footwear was so easily made and repaired that every poor Mexican, no matter what might be his other occupation, was his own shoemaker.[16]

Even with sandals, some Indians remained outside the influence of Mexican society. Just as the Spanish colonial government had tried to regulate clothing, Porfirian officials unsuccessfully issued hat and pants laws.[17] Indian men continued to wear only a breech cloth and the women only a few yards of cloth that they wrapped around themselves. They wore these clothes even if they took a few days' work at a hacienda or were hired on for a longer time in one of the mining camps.[18] The first step toward acculturation by an Indian came with the decision to acquire the fashions of the Mexican countryside. What clothes the rural Mexican had were made of unbleached cotton cloth. Men wore collarless and buttonless shirts and pants with long legs that covered the feet. A twisted-fiber or leather thong served as the belt. Many observers expressed suspicion about the character of these men who wore their shirts outside their pants.[19] Each campesino had his *sarape,* the often rather brightly colored woolen blanket that served as a jacket, rain poncho, and bedding. This Mexican topped off his costume with the most expensive *sombrero* he could afford. Ignoring the turn-of-the-century maxim that one should "keep the head cool, and the feet warm," the Mexican who could afford it bought a heavy, hot, felt sombrero. If he could not purchase felt, he bought a substitute of straw. Whatever the material, the broader the brim and the taller the crown, the more admired the sombrero.[20] This fashion attitude could be summed up as "a 25-dollar hat and a 25-cent pair of guaraches."[21] The Mexican would gladly pay a hundred pesos for his hat; those who could did so.

Rural women also had a limited wardrobe. If they did not go barefooted, then they wore the same sandals as the men. Their dress was a tuniclike garment made of white cotton, with a petticoat of the same material, although brightly colored if the owner could afford it.[22] This chemise left bare the head, neck, shoulders, and legs below the knees. The costume, proper Victorian travelers declared, "commenced too late above and stopped too soon below."[23] Many women agreed and covered their shoulders and necks with their rebozos.

In place of the serape and sombrero worn by the man, the typical woman of the countryside had her *rebozo*. This shawl usually was dyed blue, and if not, it was gray.[24] The woman wrapped it around her for protection against the cold and draped it around her head as a shield against the sun and rain. Pulled low to the eyes, it offered, if not anonymity, at least socially approved modesty; during fiestas, tossed around the shoulders, it became an ornament; at night, it served as a blanket or pillow. One end could be used to flirt with a lover, the way the woman in the parlor used her fan. The mother folded one end, so it held a baby, and then wrapped it around her neck so the child hung on her chest as she went about her chores.[25] The rebozo, perhaps of some brighter color, was worn by the lower-class women of the towns and the poor districts of Mexico City, but the blue or gray rebozo marked the gender, origin, and status of the lower-class woman from the country.[26]

The life in rural Mexico—food, clothing, and shelter—seemed stone age, primitive, and backward. The quality of this existence one traveler placed well below the luxury of modern, nineteenth-century civilization and only slightly above the vicissitudes of the life of the Plains Indians. He concluded that life in rural Mexico was greatly inferior to the scarce comforts of slavery in the antebellum southern United States.[27]

This portrait of prehistoric backwardness received confirmation by the absence of watches, vehicles, and machines. Mexicans did not make watches, and virtually no one used them.[28] In near disbelief, a traveling

New York Times reporter wrote that Mexicans scarcely understood the use of the wheel. Freight, he learned, traveled not in wagons but on the backs of mules and, even more often, on the backs of men.[29] Strangers to Mexico, beginning with the Spanish conquistadors, never failed to remark on the tremendous strength and ubiquity of the native porters, called *tamemes*, seen tottering under huge loads as they lurched down the street. Mule trains reached even the nearly forgotten corners of the country, expecially if a mine were in the vicinity. Mexico City's enterprising businessmen might form partnerships with foreigners to build railroads to ship their ore and freight, but the goods destined for barter among Mexicans continued to travel on the backs of men and mules throughout the years of Porfirian Mexico.

The image of backwardness extended to agriculture as well. So primitive seemed the tools and techniques that observers remarked that Mexico had not advanced beyond the methods of cultivation used in ancient Egypt. Retarded technology characterized agriculture throughout the country, and Solomon Griffin, a New England journalist, wrote that the sight of this rural life would "prejudice some Yankee farmers forever against Mexico."[30]

No implement better demonstrated the stunted agrarian technology than the Mexican plow. This basic implement, centuries old and modeled on the one used in medieval Andalusia and probably earlier in ancient Egypt, was a long tree branch, with a crook, sometimes faced with iron, serving as the plowshare. An ox powered this one-handled implement. Mexicans hooked it to the horns in such a way that the animal pushed rather than pulled. This often strained the animal's neck muscles to the point that on occasion it could not bend its neck, and could drink only by wading mouth-deep in the water. On those ranches that did import plows from the United States in the 1890s, peons took a machete and hacked off one handle, so that the new device looked as much as possible like the traditional implement; nor did the workers alter their method of yoking the oxen, even when neck bows were available.[31]

Adjusting to the Mexican market, one Illinois farm implement company began manufacturing a one-handled plow to export south of the border.[32] This implement survived into the twentieth century. Sociologist Norman S. Hayner, as recently as 1940, reported that 95 percent of the plows used in Oaxaca were these wooden, one-handled tools, called appropriately *egipcios,* recognizing the ancient origins. Nearer the United States border, in Nuevo León, only 10 percent of the plows were *egipcios.*[33]

Other agricultural implements were unavailable or unused in Mexico. Fieldhands harvested wheat with a sickle with saw-teeth rather than a smooth blade and without a cradle to catch the grain. Once collected, the grain was threshed by spreading it in a corral and allowing the animals to trample it for two or three days. One improvement in this process was to move the grain to a stone floor where the animals were driven around and around to complete the separation of wheat from chaff.[34] Peons had to drive the sheep, goats, or mules around for hours, and when the process was completed often dirt and animal filth had become mixed with the grain. Foreigners demonstrated threshers in Mexico. One *hacendado* learned that with the machine he could replace a dozen workers and twice that many animals and thresh his wheat in one quarter of the time. The village priest came to see the machine and declared it was possessed by the devil and forbade the peons to work with it. The American owner had to ship the machine out of the region to prevent the workers from destroying it.[35] Fieldhands near Silao in the 1890s wrecked a threshing machine because of their opposition to it.[36] Other Mexican foremen and farmers objected to these machines because they left the straw whole. When animals trampled the straw, they left it ready for immediate use as fodder.[37]

Mexicans ignored what Yankees regarded as basic tools and techniques. North of the Rio Grande, milking a cow was a twice-a-day chore and was done by sitting on a stool, while the animal stood in its stall. South of the river boundary milking was done only once a day, out in the field. The milker lassoed and tied together the cow's hind legs, then squatted beside the animal and collected the milk in an earthenware pot rather than a bucket.[38]

Shovels and wheelbarrows existed in Mexico, but only foreigners used them. When excavating and moving dirt, Mexicans tied a piece of rawhide between two poles and moved the earth on this stretcher.[39] In other instances, workers used a horn spoon to scoop up earth, ore, or metal and load it into a leather bag, called a *zurrón,* which was then transported to the chosen spot. They followed these methods even when they had shovels and could toss the shovelfuls of dirt the necessary distance.[40]

North American contractors imported wheelbarrows to use in building the railroads and other projects, such as the Baptist church in the
capital city. Mexican workmen were coaxed into using them, but not in
the way the foreigners expected. One laborer working on the church
loaded his wheelbarrow with bricks, lifted it onto his head, and trudged
over to the masons. After emptying it, he replaced the wheelbarrow on
his head and returned to the brick pile for another load. Foremen reported similar actions by workmen on railroad construction crews, leaving the bosses shaking their heads in disbelief.[41]

Irrigation techniques remained simple. Often the peons dipped water
out of streams with pottery jugs and poured it into ditches. In other instances, they used a long sapling resting in the notch of an upright log as
a boom with an earthen pot attached to it to scoop up the water. These
methods remained the same as those practiced thousands of years earlier
along the Nile.[42] No farmer rotated his crops. Year after year the Mexican
cultivator continued to plant and harvest exactly the same crop he had
grown the year before. Nor did he rest his fields. Both practices were
evidence to foreigners that Mexicans did not understand scientific
farming.[43]

Mining boomed in modern Mexico, with an influx of foreign engineers and investors, but this new wave of activity resulted in few
changes in traditional mining techniques or in the use of mining or
smelting machinery. The two factors that worked against changes or innovation were the low wages of workers, meaning that owners had little
incentive to import labor-saving machines, and the isolation of most
mines, beyond the nascent transportation system, so that all goods had
to be shipped by mule. Stamp mills, for example, had to be dismantled
into three-hundred-pound lots for shipment by muleback. Nearly all
mining supplies for the Sierra Madre mines came from San Francisco,
California, by steamer to Mazatlán or Michoacán or by rail to El Paso,
Texas, then to Jiménez, Chihuahua. From Mazatlán and Jiménez, the
goods had to be packed into the mountains.[44]

The mines differed little during the Porfirian years from what they
had been in the colonial era. Workmen cut a short tunnel into the hillside
and then dug straight down. They climbed in and out of this pit on poles,
eight to ten feet in length with the bark stripped off, and notches cut for
hand and foot grips. A series of these poles allowed the workers to de-

scend several hundred feet into the pit. Long, low tunnels were cut into the side by the miners attempting to trace the ore veins.[45]

In the shaft, the drillers (*barrateros*) swung steel-tipped iron rods, instead of picks, to tear loose the ore and prepare holes for blasting. These *barrateros* comprised an elite in this underground society, with somewhat higher wages as well.[46] In other mines, steel wedges did the work of drills and blasting. Workmen used the wedges to sledge out the minerals.[47] Once the ore had been freed, carriers collected it in bullhide sacks. The miner placed a trumpline around his forehead and lifted the bag, weighing 150 to 200 pounds, onto his back, and began the ascent on the pine logs that served as ladders. Often the carrier had to steady the bag with one hand and climb with the other. This was an extremely hazardous and low-paying job.[48]

Outside the mine, the workers emptied their sacks on the dump, usually protected by a thatched roof. If the mine had no stamp mill, workmen crouched around the dump, cracking lumps of ore into powder between two flat stones. Later the crushed ore was put in a wooden trough and water poured over it. In many instances the workmen had to carry the water to the troughs, again using their bullskin bags. After the washing, the ore was sacked in two-hundred-pound bags for shipment to the smelter. This was the technique, for example, at La China mine in the tierra caliente of Michoacán. The workers earned an average of eighteen to twenty cents a day for this employment.[49]

Mines located nearer to transportation centers or with stronger financial backing often had stamp mills. At these mines, machines crushed the ore: first a rock breaker reduced it to pieces about the size of a walnut, and then a battery, consisting of iron stamps, each weighing about 750 pounds, fell about seven inches and dropped ninety times a minute to complete the work. The powder was placed in tanks of water and agitated, and then quicksilver was added to the mixture. This solution was drained off into settling pans and circulated for several hours to assist the amalgamation process, then sent through sluice boxes leading to the tailings pit. The amalgam, after being collected, was placed in a retort, connected by an iron tube to a glass retainer for catching the quicksilver after it had been freed and had condensed. The retort was heated with a good fire, vaporizing the mercury and leaving the metal (mostly silver) as a residue.[50]

One engineer estimated that using these techniques Mexican miners took away about 60 percent of the metal contained in the raw ore. Scavengers who worked the tailings recovered additional amounts of silver. These workmen also collected a fair quantity of mercury, which they resold to the mines. One traveler saw them sorting through the ore remains and reported that they worked only with their hands and a flat, shingle-like piece of wood. This same traveler saw one man with a shovel, something so extraordinary that he had to record it for his readers.[51]

The metal was melted and run into bars for shipment to the mint. Mule trains, called *conductas,* carried the bullion out of the Sierra Madre to either Culiacán, Sinaloa, or to Parral, Chihuahua. When it went to Parral, it was reshipped by stage to Jiménez and then by rail to the mint in Chihauhua City. The leader of the *conducta,* who was one of the most trusted men in the mining camp, usually took only a handful of well-armed men with him to guard the bullion and to bring back several thousand dollars in coin. The danger of robbery was slight because of the weight of the bars and the coins that made escape slow and difficult.[52]

Improvisation, rather than imported machines, served in all the mines of Mexico. Using materials near at hand, the Mexicans made what they needed. If a hoisting rope was called for, they made it by spinning a larger diameter cable of hemp, sisal, or whatever fiber they had for cordage. Bullskin bags replaced buckets, and the wooden windlass, called a *malcate,* turned on wooden axletrees by teams of horses or mules, served in place of the cast-iron steam-driven hoist used in modern mining operations.[53]

Throughout the countryside, Mexican workers resorted to rawhide to improve and repair tools. One commentator concluded that what a Mexican could not do with rawhide was not worth doing. Thongs yoked the plow to the ox, bound cargoes on the backs of mules, stitched together everything that could be laced, tied rails to fence posts, and held rafters in place. Pins and nails had no place in this society constructed with leather. What the midwestern farmboy did with bailing wire, the Mexican did and more with his rawhide.[54] But, however useful rawhide was for repairing the implements of traditional Mexico, it would not work on machinery. An insurmountable problem for those who wanted to adopt modern implements and machines was the absence of spare parts. If an imported tool or machine needed repairs, the native blacksmith could not fix it, especially if it were made of cast-iron. The implement was tossed aside.[55]

Discarded tools and the lack of machines gave mute evidence to foreigners of Mexican primitiveness. Besides the absence of machinery, the other indicators of change—which travelers so ardently believed revealed progress—registered no economic or population growth, nor political or social convolutions. This apparent inactivity indicated not a stagnant society but rather the resiliency of rural Mexico.

Although it was not apparent in short-term reports, this society, like other rural civilizations, did undergo immense fluctuations (such as population changes) over long periods and even experienced, at times, the convulsions of famine and epidemic disease. Yet what characterized this countryside was its hardshell resistance to change, effected by its ability to recover from the jolts of both windfall bounty and sudden calamity. What distinguished rural Mexico was its stability.[56] "Balance mechanisms" restored its equilibrium whenever it was temporarily or accidentally upset.[57] The essence of this equilibrium found expression in marginal existence, in poverty. The same mechanisms that helped the culture recover also prevented the improvement of living conditions. If increased food became available (because the area had suffered population loss, for example), the local community grew in numbers until it regained approximately the same level of deprivation; if famine struck the region, starvation continued until death and reduced births restored the balance. Moreover, the people of Mexico's rural society reached an accommodation with their situation that prevented any effort to change it.[58]

Faced with an apparently unending situation, rural Mexicans lost hope. They became resigned to their lot in life. Poverty was hard enough; few wanted to compound this hardship with the frustration of vain efforts to change these conditions. Those who could not accept this life escaped it by fleeing to the towns, or to work on railroads, or even across the frontier to the United States.[59] Those who stayed behind learned how to make the best they could of their lives. They coped with poverty.

These rural Mexicans still found solace and pleasure in their culture that did not expect or seek constant change. Their community rested on traditions, especially distinctive conceptions of both time and work. Here no one needed minutes or hours, when morning and afternoon, evening and night served as small enough designations. Except for Mexico City and one or two other cities that had imported clocks for their municipal buildings, the provincial towns shared the countryside's indifference to the hour. Each town had its own local time, which varied by ten or fifteen minutes from its neighbor's, so that the nation possessed a crazy quilt of time zones.[60] In sedentary communities it mattered little; traditional society had a distinctive rhythm tied to agricultural seasons and the liturgical calendar, itself derived from changes in nature.

The nonindustrial world of the countryside made no division between work and leisure. The distinction had no meaning. Work involved more than labor; it included a sense of accomplishment, pleasure in the task, and camaraderie. In this society, work helped strengthen family ties and community solidarity through shared tasks and celebrations. Fiestas seemed the only recreation for these people, but these were more than leisure activities; they had to be celebrated or dire consequences faced the villagers. The compulsion, the cost to the sponsors, and the obligation to perform the ceremonies precisely made work, not play, of these celebrations.[61] But work did not have the onerous definition of the modern world and nonwork had not become leisure. The workmen who finished one chore before day's end began another; no one rushed to finish what was a pleasurable task.

Time was money to foreign travelers, and they could not understand this traditional society that existed beyond copper wages and the clock. Those Mexicans who knew something of the other world recognized that there time meant work, and work yielded not money but only coupons or credits at the company store. Moreover, working men and women in both the traditional and the modern worlds probably recognized that producing any surplus would more than likely lead to it's being expropriated by local elites through taxation or some other form of exploitation. Working, with this in mind, prevailed over any need to hurry.[62] Rejecting this conception of time and money, they found no reason to save either.

This astonished visitors to the country. "The lack of labor-saving appliances," wrote the *Times* correspondent, "is very striking."[63] After living in the mining camp of Guadalupe y Calvo for five years in the 1880s, J. R. Flippin said that Mexicans did not care "for the new-fangled labor-saving machinery of the nineteenth century."[64] Indolence seemed the major characteristic of these rural Mexicans. Flippin remarked that the peons "often dawdle and putter in a way that would be wildly exasperating further north," and Henry Howard Harper described these people as "indigent, lazy and utterly devoid of ambition."[65] These reporters rejected the possibility that they had observed a traditional culture, one in which an accommodation had been reached with the conditions of life, including poverty.

In fact, these commentators determined that poor and backward were identical conditions. The cause for one was the cause for the other; the solution for one was the solution for the other. The identification of poverty and backwardness was the first of a series of explanations that started from the fact of poverty and grew into elaborate constructs of the culture and behavior of rural Mexicans. These formulations served to justify the presence of foreign experts and to make plausible the programs of foreign technology.

One of the earliest of these explanations turned on geography. Latitude placed much of Mexico in the tropics, and several travelers blamed the sloth of the people and the underdevelopment of the countryside on the enervating influence of this climate. Typical comments included, "The climatic lassitude infects every process" and the peons behaved as they did "by virtue of climatic and other conditions that surround them."[66] Of course, this argument came from those who had been reared in colder and therefore they believed, hardier environments.

Other common explanations followed this pattern of reasoning: neither the United States nor Great Britain was poor, but Mexico was; the difference, therefore, could be found by locating the differences between Anglo-American and Mexican culture. Three common explanations resulting from this logic blamed the system of land tenure, the heritage of Spanish colonial rule, or the influence of the Roman Catholic Church for the economic stagnation.[67] These factors certainly helped to mold the culture of rural Mexico, but they did not account for its poverty in the nineteenth century.

John Coatsworth has examined these themes and determined that not one nor any combination of them caused Mexican backwardness. The major obstacles to economic growth were the inadequate transportation network and the ineffectual economic organization (that is, the legislative and juridical environment was unfavorable to entrepreneurs).[68] The developers who confronted these obstacles were in Mexico City and were men who had refused to make an accommodation with poverty. These promoters overcame the difficulties with Porfirio Díaz's help, especially his lavish assistance to the railroads and extremely friendly legislative and juridical cooperation with entrepreneurs. Nevertheless, the explanations for Mexico's faltering progress remained unchanged.

Protestant, Anglo-American travelers, often in search of economic opportunities for themselves or to describe conditions for prospective investors among their readers, regularly blamed the Spanish heritage, the Catholic church, or the great estates for the stagnant countryside. Their descriptions demonstrate how these observers took the fact of Mexican poverty and used it to justify characterizations of the Mexicans based on opposites of the traits of Anglo-American society. Because Americans were rich (by comparison), they were also modern and progressive; because Mexicans were poor, they were also described as primitive and backward. This kind of symbolic inversion, in some instances, extended to racial characterizations, which portrayed Mexicans as "a weak, effete, mongrel, withered race,"[69] and pejorative remarks about Mexican cleanliness, which alleged they tolerated "all kinds of filth within arm's length of the door."[70] The lack of public sanitation and of personal hygiene received severe criticism and the conclusion was that "filth and stench fill their hovels and the wonder is how they survive so long the unwholesome conditions."[71]

Curiously, those Mexicans who could not be described as being dirty were pictured as depraved. These "Indians" went to ditches and streams where they washed their clothes and spread them on the banks to dry. Then men, women, and children "promiscuously" scrubbed and splashed around, completely nude in the water. Covered only by the blue sky, all these people seemed to enjoy themselves and seemed utterly unconscious of the modesty demanded by foreign observers.[72]

Whether dirty or obscene, the country Mexican appeared to lack the sobriety that Anglo-Americans viewed as the mother of industry. Cheap pulque sired the drunk peon, who was quick to anger, quicker to violence; quick to betrayal, and quicker to robbery. The rural Mexican, quaffing liters of pulque, became absolutely disagreeable and thoroughly dangerous.

Pulque was the drink of the people. This mildly alcoholic beverage, as well as tequila and mescal, came from the maguey plant cultivated in fields holding up to seven hundred plants. The mature, eight-year-old plant produced for about five months, during which time it yielded 360 gallons of pulque.[73] This liquid was poured into whole pigskins that looked like the live animals with legs dumbly kicking in the air. These pigskin bags were shipped to town.[74] What Mexicans cherished others could scarcely tolerate. Stanton Kirkham sampled it and reported, "It tastes like poor cider and smells like old cheese," while his countryman Alfred Coffin snorted, "Just liquid filth, no more, no less."[75] For personal use, Mexicans reduced the smell by adding sugar and other flavors. The owners of *pulquerías*, according to Coffin, "added a quantity of marihuana to the cask, and presto! he has the regulation Kentucky tanglefoot, warranted to kill at forty rods." This drink supposedly could make a person's eyes look two ways at once.[76] Another visitor declared that pulque looked and smelled like buttermilk with the addition of rotten eggs.[77] Howard Conkling spoke for all his fellow travelers when he said, "one must practice to like it."[78] And Mary Blake concluded, "It no doubt has virtues, but they are well hidden; and if, as they claim, one can become intoxicated by prolonged drinking, it is the sourest, thinnest, saddest means of reaching exhilaration that the mind of man ever conceived."[79] Drinking pulque was the universal habit in Mexico. The common price for this popular drink was three cents a quart. Drinking it tended to magnify the character of the people. "In the wide universe, I venture to affirm," wrote Flippin, "there is no tougher character than the drunken peon. . . . The Mexican who does not drink and get drunk is the dead Mexican."[80]

In all these descriptions we find these Euclids of ethnology developing the geometry of culture. Their logic started from an analogy between the theorem that parallel lines never intersect and the theorem that cultures acted in exactly the same way. Anglo-Americans saw themselves as sober, industrious, and honest. Mexicans were different; they were poor, so they must also be drunk, lazy, and dishonest. They were disorderly, even lawless, but the Díaz government had suppressed banditry on the national level, so these descriptions attributed thievery to the individuals of the poorer classes, who exercised this predilection especially when the peon got drunk.[81]

Developing the stereotype of the indolent peon fit into the general ideology of the United States and the western European nations intent on expansion of trade or empire or both. The myth of the lazy native justified commercial or colonial occupation as a reform of a backward society. In reality, it was those who rejected the foreign intrusion and changes or who saw little gain in hard work when the profits went to outsiders who were branded as slothful Mexicans.[82]

In working out this paradigm of Mexican characteristics, even more important than latitude or ethnic background as a determining factor was the Roman Catholic Church. Foreign travelers pointed to numerous characteristics that they argued sprang from the Mexican's religion. Protestants criticized the devotion to saints, which seemed like pantheism. Mexicans celebrated many saints' days, and it was reported that they "generally take occasion to wind up the day in some drunken orgies."[83] Medical practices also depended to a large extent on these saints. Before any sick person received a prescribed remedy, the saint had to be called upon to bless the medicine with healing power. If the patient recovered, the saint received the credit; if the patient died, the saint was never blamed; the people thought that he had been disinclined to interpose his power perhaps because he had been unappeased for some unintended affront. The conclusion from abroad was, "Where this saint worship prevails to a large extent you may rest assured that its devotees are poor, ignorant and priest-ridden."[84]

Thus commentators, both foreign and Mexican, had two parallel columns of traits that rested on the factual foundation of Anglo-American wealth and Mexican poverty. The observers then used the attributes or ideals of Anglo-American society in one column and tabulated their exact opposites to describe rural Mexicans. After describing the backwardness of the Mexican countryside, observers proposed a method of improvement, one that included what they had near at hand: technology and capital. Their depictions revealed how they took an ideal from their culture, in this case technology, and then endowed the Mexicans with its opposite. This symbolic inversion can be used to justify prejudice, lower social status, slavery, or war,[85] but in this instance it was used as the rationalization for programs of modernization that required the importation of foreign machines and investment funds.

The British first fell victim to this kind of thinking in 1824. With nothing more than the belief that Mexicans were backward, they deluded themselves into believing that all Mexico needed for development was capital investment and applied technology. They expected substantial profits and immediate success in mining. The British minister, Henry George Ward, marveled at his countrymen who had no concern for "industry, perseverance, a knowledge of the scene upon which operations were to commence—of the men by whom they were to be conducted,—of the language and peculiarities of the country, in which they were carried on." To the investors, all these considerations were of minor importance, and their investments failed almost immediately. By 1828, bankrupt British managers blamed Mexicans, "their backwardness, their infernal sloth, and popish religion." The British faith remained unshaken in capital and technology as the means to achieve profits for themselves and to accomplish modernization, definded as economic development, in the rest of the world.[86] This was exactly the same process used by the United States government experts after World War II who devised aid programs for the underdeveloped world. "The remedy," wrote John Kenneth Galbraith, "included the diagnosis. Having vaccine, we identified smallpox. Only by accident could a therapy so selected be successful. There was, alas, no such accident."[87] Nor did such an accident occur, despite tremendous efforts at providing technology and capital, in Porfirian Mexico.

Not just foreigners accepted the descriptions of Mexico as backward. Those Mexicans who sought to build their society in the image of the industrial nations accepted these characterizations of Mexican society and the technological panacea offered. When foreign technology did not re-create Mexico in this image during the Porfiriato, they concluded it must be the nature of the Mexican that caused its failure. This contributed to the national inferiority complex described by Samuel Ramos.[88] Of course, this sense of inferiority affected only the elite; it had no impact on those people who lived in rural Mexico.

Retarded agriculture, mining, and transportation were all the result of the constant repetition of ancient techniques. David Wells, writing in 1885, declared, "The fruits of the soil and the results of individual labor have been repeating themselves for hundreds of years." He continued, "Men have died, but others do the same thing from generation to generation."[89] No one was going to take major risks as long as life in the countryside for the vast majority was lived on the margin of existence. Risk involved not just one crop but survival for the entire family.[90]

These retrogressive habits would soon scatter before the "march of improvement," according to Solomon Griffin and other sons of American technology, if only Mexicans witnessed new techniques and tools in action. But, besides its unwillingness to take risks, rural Mexico had experience that provided it with great resilience. Occasionally, foreigners learned about the inner strength of this poor society.

Henry Harper made a journey in 1896 with two other prospective investors to the Huasteca region (the coastal strip from Tampico south to Veracruz) in search of promising agricultural opportunities. After a boat trip filled with delays, encounters with wood ticks and mosquitos, hardships and cussedness of both man and geography, they arrived at Tuxpam, expecting a land of promising coffee, rubber, sugar, and citrus plantations. They were disappointed. His friends gave up, but eventually Harper purchased a cattle ranch from another American who was retiring after thirty years in Mexico. Harper believed that the region needed only the application of American energy and technology to reap substantial profits. His first effort in applying his nation's know-how was to instruct this foreman to borrow the imported steel plow that had been sitting unused for years in town and plow one field for corn. Villagers, who had already planted their corn using traditional digging sticks or the centuries-old wooden plow, sauntered to the field to watch the steel implement do its work; when the plowing and planting were finished, they left without comment.

In the months that followed, Harper seemed vindicated: the corn grew quickly, soon stretching above a man's head, with the large ears almost out of reach. But Mexico would teach him a hard lesson. A summer storm blew through Tuxpam and its countryside. Heavy winds ripped up the entire cornfield, because the root system could not hold the stalks in the loose soil that had been deeply plowed with steel. The surrounding *milpas,* with shorter corn stalks sticking out of nearly rock-hard ground, suffered no damage from the winds. The hard soil, punctured only by the wooden sticks, held the roots, keeping the stalks and the seasons' harvest upright.

Harper abandoned his efforts to introduce any new techniques on his property. After this decision, he reported that he always managed a tidy profit from his crops each year until 1908, when oil was discovered on his land, and he leased his ranch to a foreign company.[91]

Careful examination of the descriptions of rural Mexico reveals off-hand comments that demonstrate the accommodation and adjustment of the people to their environment, resources, and poverty. This accommodation and, in many instances, successful adapting of what was available to them would not do for those interested in bringing the latest in technology to Mexico, but their unguarded comments reveal admiration and often praise for the adjustments of this rural society. The Mexican villages, because they had been constructed of adobe, rather than costly wood, had what William Seymour Edwards called "an air of substantial solidarity, quite lacking in American wooden towns."[92] These adobes not only looked permanent but also had other desirable attributes: they were fireproof, earthquake resistent, warm in winter, cool in summer, and highly durable. The palm hut in the *tierra caliente* had its merits, especially the way it afforded ventilation.[93]

The clothing that received such severe criticism also demonstrated the way Mexicans accommodated to what resources they had and to what conditions they faced. Going barefoot may have represented abject poverty; wearing sandals may not have. Many commentators have found sandals more healthful than shoes, especially shoes of the Mexican style.[94] The Mexican shoe, described as "an instrument of torture" with a high heel and tooth-pick toe, could hardly be more healthy than the sandal that was "cool, cheap, and did not irritate the feet."[95]

The same could be said about the cuisine and household and agricultural implements. Mexican cuisine, consisting of the pre-conquest complex of maize, beans, squash, and chiles, supplemented occasionally by the colonial additions of eggs, pork or another meat, and cheese, reflects creative adaptation. Maize preparation since time forgotten included soaking the corn kernels in water with small bits of limestone. This procedure loosens the difficult-to-digest sheath of the corn and the limestone multiplies the calcium content to at least twenty times that in the original maize. Scientists believe this process increases the availability of amino acids, extremely important given the scarcity of meat in Mexico. Beans provide protein, and squash, 90 percent water, offers liquid in this arid land and filler to create a satisfied feeling. Chiles serve a remarkable role, surpassing almost all other plants as a source of Vitamin A and offering substantial amounts of Vitamins C and the B group. They stimulate the appetite and aid digestion by increasing gastric secretions. They even help lower the body temperature because capsaicin produces sweating, with the effect of cooling by evaporation. Moreover, food scientists have shown that chiles inhibit the growth of bacteria, such as staphylococcus, salmonella, and other microorganisms that cause intestinal disorders. Preparation of the food, using few implements, reflects a similar adaptation to the scarcity of fuels. Meals included the quickly cooked tortilla and other foods prepared in small portions for fast cooking over a hot fire that required little wood or charcoal. Baking, roasting, even slow boiling of foods occurred only for holiday or elite meals.[96]

A representative comment about tools by an observer who expressed surprise at the one-handled plow went on: "The marvel is that anything satisfactory can be accomplished with such an awkward instrument, and yet these fields in some instances show grand results."[97] The manager of the *Illinois State Register,* Thomas Rees, a knowledgeable agriculturalist, reported to his readers that even though many Americans had disparaged Mexico's wooden plow, he did not think that in the hands of the Mexican peon a steel plow could do any better. Moreover, he argued that the wooden plow was better suited to Mexico, where the soil was loose and ordinarily full of stones of all sizes and shapes. The best modern plow, he explained, would quickly be cut to pieces by the rocks and soon be unfit for use. Meanwhile, the wooden plow would slide to the side of stones, take more of a pounding, and survive a long time before suffering much harm. The great advantage of the steel plow, its ability to cut deeper and wider furrows, was not needed in Mexico, where farmers only needed to scratch the field's surface. This agricultural journalist from one of the leading farm states praised the Mexican plowman, saying that once he had finished a field with his one-handled wooden implement, "it is very well done and looks very nice, and is just exactly what they want."[98]

Henry Harper went even further in his praise of the accommodation achieved in rural Mexico. He told prospective settlers in Mexico, "If you would farm successfully in Mexico you must farm precisely as they do." From his own experience Harper had learned that the outsider "will eventually find that there is one well-grounded reason for every common usage."[99] Ultimately the resilience of this rural society rested on the fact that rural Mexicans took nothing for granted; life was a day-by-day venture. This recognition, more than anything else, divided Mexican from American culture. Scrapping and scurrying for the little bit extra that could be set aside for the future made no sense to rural Mexicans, when, in light of starvation and disease, as someone remarked, "who has promised us tomorrow?" Nonetheless, Harper praised the Mexicans for the life they managed, saying they were "clever enough to make the best of conditions." Rees concurred with Harper's judgment; he explained that "when the poverty of the people is considered, they deserve great credit for what they have achieved."[100]

Workingmen were not the only Mexicans who received recognition. The women earned commendation from Mary Blake, who had traveled from Boston to Mexico City. "Are we beyond taking a lesson?" she asked, and then praised the Mexican mother's method of carrying her small children in a rebozo that placed the child's weight on her shoulders rather than her arms. Blake applauded as well the exquisitely clean streets which she believed should make any American blush with shame at the thought of the filth in New York and Chicago.[101]

Rooted in the countryside, these Mexicans during the Porfirian years had little hope for a better lot in life. Some had the experience of travel, at least in the form of a pilgrimage to Guadalupe or one of the other shrines. But these experiences, by their nature, were outside ordinary activities (called liminoid by anthropologists), like election days in the United States, with little carryover to everyday life except to strengthen the community's resiliency.[102] It was the sawed-off politician Francisco I. Madero, who traversed the nation, giving speech after speech, in 1910, that awoke the possibility of changing one's situation. In that way he was the most revolutionary of the early twentieth-century revolutionaries. But his promise of hope was fleeting, and his successors had to face the rock-ribbed resilience of rural Mexico, one in which new tools and technologies were shunted aside, whether promoted by foreign entrepreneurs or revolutionary politicians.

Everyday Mexicans during the Porfirian years found solace, even humor at times, in their traditions. The secular festivals that complemented the religious celebrations offered them the opportunity to release pent-up frustrations and parody those who wanted to destroy their way of life. The Porfirian Liberals attacked traditional Mexico by restricting the church and seizing village lands. These Mexicans under siege confronted modern life in the countryside and the city, and fought to preserve their customs through Judas burnings, Day of the Dead rituals, and Carnival. Each of these folk events had an element of humor, which anthropologist Paul Stoller calls the comedy of paradox, used to resist the influence of an overwhelming foreign culture of modernity.[103] A struggle for the nation's cultural identity ensued, which can be seen in the celebrations of Judas Day at the Jockey Club.

"Railroad Judas, 1882," a sketch by
William Henry Bishop in *Old Mexico
and Her Lost Provinces* (New York:
Harper and Brothers, 1883).

"The People's Glory": an ironic view of
the church, liberty, and democracy in
Porfirian Mexico. From *El Hijo del
Ahuizote,* April 7, 1901. Courtesy of
the Latin American Library, Tulane
University.

Hoy que es el día de los judas,
Con grande satisfacción
El pueblo les prenda fuego
A Montes de Oca y Burrón

"Hallelujah Saturday in Politics," satire of the support for Bernardo Reyes in the Porfirian regime. From *El Hijo del Ahuizote,* April 12, 1903. Courtesy of the Latin American Library, Tulane University.

FESTEJOS

Hoy.

COLEGIATA

LOS "INDIOS" DEVOTOS DE AHORA.

GUADALUPANOS.

AYER

LOS INDIOS DEVOTOS DE ANTES.

"Guadalupine Public Rejoicing: The Devoted 'Indians' of Today and the Devoted Indians of Yesterday." From *El Hijo del Ahuizote,* November 27, 1898. Courtesy of the Latin American Library, Tulane University.

"Why Ride a Bicycle?": a satirical look at cyclists. (See discussion, pp. 41–52.) From *El Hijo del Ahuizote,* January 23, 1898. Courtesy of the Latin American Library, Tulane University.

Judas
at
the
Jockey
Club

Jockey Club members, shouldering their Judas tableau, followed mounted policemen who used the flats of their swords to force a path through the pushing, shouting crowd to the center of San Francisco Street, where they hoisted the cardboard and gunpowder float to first-floor level on ropes strung from the balconies of the clubhouse and the building across from it. Howling and shoving to gain a better place for the events to come, the men and women in the expectant mob saw the most elaborate and ornate Judases ever commissioned by the Jockey Club. The papier-maché grouping comprised a hot-air balloon, covered with coins, with a gondola carrying four Judas figures. The Judases represented a mulatto, a butter salesman mounted on a pig, a singer sitting cross-legged playing the guitar, and a beggar. The first two figures, criss-crossed with sausage strings, glittered with old-style coins, *reales* and *pesetas;* the other two effigies sparkled with silver *pesos,* the symbols of Mexico's wealth.

Crashing bells shattered the silence of three days and marked the end of Lent and the exultation of the Resurrection. These sudden bells burst forth with the official church announcement of joy; the popular secular celebration followed immediately as the Jockey Club members ignited the fuses of their effigies, and within seconds the gunpowder blew the cardboard balloon and Judases in all directions above the crowd, who clawed and snatched to grab coins, clothes, and sausages from the dismembered figures. Simultaneously across the city, other Judases were ignited and exploded over crowds gathered wherever a Judas hung above the street. For the next hour, celebrating mobs continued to explode the sham Iscariots.

These Judas burnings and other festivals such as Carnival and Day of the Dead celebrations were linked to the feasts of the church, but none was conducted under clerical auspices or supervision. Mexico's popular classes seized official celebrations for spontaneous merrymaking that exhibited their festival spirit through discrete forms of ritual spectacles (Holy Week pageants and passion plays), comic verbal compositions (mock epitaphs and calaveras), and various genres of billingsgate (curses and oaths, especially *los chingoleses*). Together these forms and festivals constituted the popular humor and folk culture. They gave authentic expression to an archaic European tradition that extended back to the Middle Ages and represented a vital heritage shared by the common people.[1]

European Origin and Latin American Examples of Judas Festivals

The burning Judas ended Lent, the period of fasting and abnegation that precedes Easter. Linked to liturgical holidays, Judas celebrations on Holy Saturday (or Little Resurrection Day) shared many elements of Shrove or Fat Tuesday festivals, which mark the advent of Lent. The origins of these festivities probably have been intertwined in Roman Catholic folk culture. Carnival seems to have evolved from the Roman Saturnalia, surviving as a folk celebration and gaining popularity when Pius II (1464–1471) extended papal sanction.[2] This festival often featured a king of the occasion, whose effigy (sometimes called winter) was burned to conclude the merrymaking that included rich food and drink, inversion of social roles, and suspension of rules before Lent's forty days of fasting. Marking the end of these Lenten restrains and the rejoicing in the belief in the Resurrection, Judas Day celebrants burned effigies and enjoyed this riotous opportunity to turn the world upside down and set aside customary rules of social hierarchy and decorum. When this practice began remains unclear. Several early descriptions exist along with a few suppositions about the origins of the popular festival in the context of other Euorpean Easter celebrations.

In parts of central Europe, especially Germany, celebrants as early as the Middle Ages burned Judas effigies in an Easter fire on Holy Saturday. They saved the ashes of the straw figures and planted them on May Day as a preventative against the blight. In Upper Bavaria, peasants burned Judases in the belief that it would prevent damaging hailstorms. Men and boys (women were excluded) raced with tapers lit from the holy candle in the church to ignite the effigy. Women, on the following day, rewarded the winner with Easter eggs. Practices reminiscent of Mexico's Judas burnings existed in the Mediterranean region. The islanders of Corfu symbolically stoned Judas on the eve of Easter Sunday by throwing old crockery into the streets.[3] In Italy, throughout Tuscany, the people celebrated Sabato Santo (Holy Saturday) with the Gloria Mass and a popular *fèsta*. Florence for centuries has held a religious procession ending with fireworks after the mass. An ancient family, the de'Pazzi, contributed a splendid, explosive-filled car, so that this event has become known as the *Scoppio del Caro*, the explosion of the car. The fuse for many years was lit by striking a piece of flint against a piece of the Holy Sepulcher brought to the church in Florence by a returning crusader. More recently, the explosives in the wooden car pulled by white oxen are ignited by rocket. A guide wire stretches from the altar to the explosives. At the conclusion of the mass, the priest lights the rocket, which runs down the wire to set off the fireworks. Florentine farmers hold to the belief that if the rocket works right, the harvest will be abundant; if the rocket fails to ignite the fireworks display, the crops will be poor.[4]

Both Spain and Portugal have the tradition of celebrating Holy Saturday, and in some towns of destroying straw or cardboard figures. In one Portuguese tradition, townsmen took a straw Judas and paraded the figure through the streets on Holy Saturday, and then drowned, burned, or hanged the figure. The popular character of the celebration appeared when people made the Judases in parody of elite persons. This seems to have developed as a secular or mock *auto-da-fé*, the public punishment of those the Inquisition had found guilty of religious crimes, with a Jew as the victim. With the departure of the Jews from Portugal or their conversion to Catholicism, the effigy became Judas.[5] In Spain during Lent, often a grotesque figure was hung in public view until Holy Saturday when it was destroyed. This custom, sometimes called "Partir de la Vilga," was replaced in many towns by "El Pelele," the scarecrow or Judas.

Either Good Friday or Hallelujah Saturday was a time for the execution of Judas, either by burning or exploding effigies filled with gunpowder.[6]

From the Iberian Peninsula this practice spread to the New World during the colonial period, although no specific descriptions have yet been discovered. Judas executions were widespread during the nineteenth century. Ricardo Palma and other authors have described the burning of Iscariots on Holy Saturday in Lima and other places in Peru. Cubans also practiced the custom.[7]

Venezuelans burned Judas effigies with gusto on Easter Sunday afternoons. The 1858 celebration drew Richard Bingham, the British chargé d'affaires, as a spectator, and the Britannic nabob believed he saw a caricature of himself destroyed. He protested to the Venezuelan minister of foreign affairs, who replied that the government neither organized nor condoned the celebration, so obviously knew nothing of it. The foreign minister assured Bingham that he would launch an investigation and that no means would be spared to protect the honor of representatives of the British government. Nothing came of the investigation, and the people continued to execute Judas. In the twentieth century in the old neighborhoods of Caracas and neighboring towns, the celebrants make a kind of scarecrow from an old suit stuffed with firecrackers that they parade on burroback before they hang or burn it. This popular custom found artistic expression in the successful 1964 play (later a movie) *La quema de Judas*. Román Chalbaud, the playwright, used an actual murder in one of the poorer barrios of Caracas to construct his plot leading to this dramatic people's celebration.[8]

Even the Emperor Dom Pedro II took part in the fiery destruction of Judas in Brazil. Pedro donated the fireworks used in the effigies exploded at the Brazilian court. Other segments of the society held their own Judas burnings: shop clerks hanged effigies resembling government officials and distributed parodies of the last will and testament of local dignitaries; blacks held their celebrations with black devils torturing the white Iscariot. This has been interpreted as a form of dual retaliation in which the white betrayer of Christ receives justice from black men. The celebrations became so raucous and the representations so specific at mid-century that in 1863 a law with a stiff fine as punishment prohibited Judases resembling prominent personalities. Until at least 1929, the practice of burning or hanging these straw figures continued in Brazil.[9]

Burning of other effigies appeared in Ecuador and Guatemala, where the burning of the devil and the burning of the old year both became popular purification rituals associated with new beginning represented by the new year. The interplay between the forces of good and evil, according to Celso A. Lara, provided sentiment to everyday life.[10] However widespread the practice of burning straw and cardboard figures, Mexico became the locale for the most enthusiastic observance of the destruction of Iscariots.[11]

Judas in Mexico

Celebrations combining religious and secular activities reached Mexico by at least 1538 with the presentation of dramas and dances from Corpus Christi Day, June 20, to Saint John the Baptist's Day, June 24, in Tlaxcala.[12] Quickly other sacred and profane fiestas appeared, probably including the burning of Judases. The handicraft of making fireworks displays, especially toritos, castillos, and pasteboard Judases, seems to date from these early decades of the sixteenth century, but when the first burning of Judas effigies occurred has not yet been determined.[13] Luis González Obregón discussed the event during the colonial epoch and mused that the practice may have developed when youngsters imitated the Inquisition's practice of burning effigies of absent heretics. Genero Estrada, in *Visionario de la Nueva España,* discussed in general the boisterous Holy Saturday celebrations of the late colonial years in Tacuba and San Francisco Streets, which included the sounds of metracas (wooden rattles), the cries of vendors, and the exploding of pasteboard Judases.[14]

The earliest specific account so far located comes from the German businessman and diplomat C. C. Becher, who witnessed Holy Saturday, April 22, 1832, and described the people crowding the capital's main streets, where they hanged and burned countless effigies of Judas.[15] Fanny Calderón de la Barca next reported this most curious and most Mexican of celebrations in 1840. Following Calderón many observers, including foreign travelers, attended this popular spectacle. From 1832 to 1983 the descriptions range from accounts by Guillermo Prieto and Marcos Arróniz to those by Erle Stanley Gardner and Paul Vanderwood.[16] Comparing them provides a document of the changes in the celebration and registers the responses to social developments, especially during the 1890s. These observers also provide a glimpse of the spirit of Mexico, because, as folklorist Frederick Starr commented, this was "perhaps the most popular celebration of the year."[17]

Throughout Holy Week, Calderón saw vendors selling hundreds of effigies of the arch-traitor. Their representations came in all sizes, from doll-like to larger-than-life; all were "hideous" papier-maché figures filled with fireworks. Several smaller Iscariots were tied together on long poles to be ignited above the heads of what Calderón called the "mob." Although she did not go to the Zócalo to see the celebration on the morning of the Sabado de Gloria, she did listen to the "hissing and cracking of the fireworks" that reported the demolition of one after another "ugly misshapened monster" that represented the most execrated villain in Christian religion and Mexican culture.[18]

These Judases from the beginning contained fireworks and by midcentury sometimes also contained live cats, lizards, or frogs that gave the people a delightful fright. Other Iscariots were stuffed with food items, especially bread rolls or sausages.[19] In 1832, the ritual occurred in the capital's center, its main plaza, and nearby Tacuba and San Francisco streets. The people continued celebrating the destruction of Judas in the streets bordering the Zócalo until the early 1890s;[20] then city authorities prohibited the fiesta in the downtown area. In 1899, Starr found the celebration had moved to the poor suburbs, where the people strung Judases across the streets or hung them at street corners. Often these decentralized celebrations found sponsors among neighborhood shopkeepers, especially the owners of pulque shops, who commissioned Iscariots that contained meat, soap, candles, bread, and clothing, to be scattered over the crowd when the effigies exploded.[21]

Judas Burnings and Holy Week

Judas Day events fit snugly with the other activities of Holy Week, particularly in conjunction with the symbols of Holy Thursday, when the people and the church commemorated the crucifixion of Christ by shrouding all the altars and removing all images of majesty and joy, displaying only the figure of Christ on the cross until Saturday. From Thursday until the conclusion of Saturday morning's Gloria Mass, indicating the resurrection, neither the priests nor the people used bells. This brought an intolerable silence that had to be shattered.

During regular times, in Porfirian Mexico, hundreds of bells provided constant and reassuring sounds in Mexican communities. Foreigners found it an incessant, numbing noise. The bells, which did not have clappers, were sounded by the strike of a hammer, producing a continuous din.[22] The national cathedral had forty-eight bells that rang regularly. The booming was the most important sound in daily life, reckoning time, announcing religious services, signaling alarms. Bells had a sacred character that protected the community from the evil that could penetrate silence. Making the sounds of holy sanctuary and friendly community, the bells became so familiar that the people gave them names identifying their tonal personalities or dedicating them to saints or martyrs of the church. Residents of the capital listened for the voices of Santa Maria de Guadalupe (thirty-six feet tall) and Doña Maria (weighing fourteen thousand pounds) from the cathedral.[23] Without these sounds the community imagined imminent harm in the silence.

During the dead period from Thursday afternoon through Saturday morning, the priests used rattles to replace bells in the mass. The people dreaded the silence, and their presentiment of lurking evil led to the creation of noise with whirligig rattles called matracas. These produced a grating, jarring sound (something like dragging a stick along a picket fence) that replaced the oppressive silence. The priests with rattles and the people with matracas made sounds that held back evil. Individual involvement, like whistling in the dark, seemed necessary to many until the bells returned. Those who felt no superstition often bought and exchanged fancy, even silver matracas as gifts. By the turn of the century, the matraca had acquired the additional meaning of gift or tip. Beggars asking for coins during Holy Week would ask for a matraca. The word also became a colloquial term for a jest, especially a contemptuous joke.

Printed jests called matracas appeared on business-card-sized handouts and in the newspaper. One example from the satirical opposition press comes from *El Hijo del Ahuizote,* in which a writer reported that a friend had told him about several matracas (although he was uncertain about who was to receive them). One was a flat piece of iron, blunt with two very clean, smooth sides, on which one could read "I serve my master" and on the other side, in letters made by artistic casting, one could read "The Bully"—the nickname given the Porfirian regime.[24] Satirical jokes such as this and other jests and gifts represented the popular balance to the overwhelming solemnity of the period. The noisemakers contrasted with the silence; the profane joke with the sacraments.

The end of this dangerous interlude came after the Hallelujah Mass on Saturday morning with the thunderous tolling of all the church bells. Joyous peals marked the Resurrection, the salvation of the believers, and the restoration of ordinary activity. The people personally marked their escape from danger with sounds of their own. The bells expressed community; fireworks spoke for individuals. The Judas figures carried the crackers, rockets, and squibs to fill the air with joy. These explosions indicated the end of danger, silence, Lenten prohibitions, and the beginning of a celebration. The exploding cacaphony traditionally indicated a fiesta.

Fireworks marked the transition in the Holy Week rituals from the official, serious, severe observation of the Gloria Mass to the popular, humorous, unrestrained practice of exploding Judases. Tolling bells sounded sacred time; exploding fireworks announced a transitional time, not sacred, not secular, but simultaneously combining both with the elements of festival. This is the customary use of fireworks in Mexico's cycle of religious and civic festivals. A dozen rockets bursting in the sky signaled a cockfight or announced a public dance, or the temporary suspension of rules and hierarchy during Carnival or Judas Day. Skyrockets, symbols of nature, especially thunder and lightning, brought those who heard the exploding Judases (whether attending the event or not) down to earth from the ethereal stations of Holy Week. They announced the commencing of the profane complement to the sacred observance that until the 1890s together formed Holy Saturday's ritual.[25]

Because the Judas burnings were not officially sanctioned by either church or civil officials, this festival had a spontaneous and creative character. These celebrations, without official approval or support, remained outside the prestige system and manipulation of even the confraternities (Catholic lay brotherhoods called cofradías) associated with many religious devotions and civic holidays. When a shopkeeper, a merchant, or the Jockey Club exploded a Judas it did so without a bureaucracy, without creating a Judas Day committee (except in 1893), and without giving prestige to the person who hosted the burning. The informality of the celebration emphasized the extra-official character of the event that became the freedom of action of the people who rejoiced at the end of Lent.

Moreover, the lack of recognized individual or organizational sponsors reversed the elaborate religious and political system of the confraternities; the absence of designated sponsors reinforced the principal character of Judas burnings, that is, turning the world upside down for the entire society.[26] The Judas characters tell us about the people who purchased the effigies because they were guided only by whim informed only by the unconscious.

All those who witnessed the destruction of Judas or who heard the explosions were involved. None remained aloof. Understanding the ritual requires that the people be seen as united participants rather than divided into actors and audience. The entire ceremony comes from the centuries-old tradition of carnivalesque humor handed down by oral instruction and watchful imitation. We have only one complete description of this tradition, the classic *Gargantua and Pantagruel* by the French literary giant François Rabelais (1494?–1553).

Tradition and Folk Celebrations

Rabelais mapped this tradition, captured its humor, and described this alternative to the serious, sedate life of the medieval and renaissance era. He identified the duality that balanced social hierarchy and spiritual solemnity against individual equality and raucous profanity.[27] Moreover, this humor portrayed an exaggerated ambivalence that captured the sense of death and conclusion at the same instant as birth and beginning. The destruction of Judas was literally accomplished at the same time life sprang forth literally on those occasions when the effigy contained cats, other frightened animals, or life-giving bread and meat that was strewn above the crowd. Thus the death of Judas provided life and abundance.

Equally important, the meat or bread or soup was for everyone who would scrap for it. No title or profession had precedence in the scramble. This sense of abundance, of food for all, is one characteristic of the festival expressed in feasting or at least including food in the celebration. It provided the sense of plenty that reversed the everyday world.

For a society enraptured with progress and capital, the symbols of abundance needed expression in currency. During the 1880s, often the Judases had coins attached to their clothing, which were scattered as the effigy exploded, and it became the custom for observers in the buildings lining the streets to shower the mob with coins. The Judas burnings outside the Jockey Club became especially well known because the gentlemen members tossed handfuls of coppers to the crowd.[28] This reversed the world, temporarily offering abundance to all. Moreover, it portrayed the utopian time expressed in parables; the people could visualize the arrival of the time "hasta que los ricos amen (when the rich loved others) and "hasta que los pobres tengan (when the poor had something).

In many other ways, this festival captured the medieval-renaissance spirit of popular life. Judas figures might be made as hideous figures, as ugly as sin—which, as one observer noted, they were supposed to represent.[29] In destroying these grotesque and horrible figures, the people mocked their fears they had felt during the previous two days. Devils, demons, and fantastic horrors became comic Judases that writhed in destruction.

The control of anxiety through the burning of effigies dates from as early as the Saturnalia, and has continued through later religious celebrations such as Carnival. Significantly, beginning with the medieval era, it was often man's invention, gunpowder, that destroyed evil; thus man's knowledge held back the unknown and the horrible. In Mexico, this aspect of the festival was manifested in the manufacture of the Judases, because the gunpowder guild, living in its own section of Mexico City and Guadalajara, had seasonal employment as they produced the Judases.

Debasing Judas provided one of the occasions when Mexicans engaged in social reversals. This fiesta became, in Octavio Paz's words, "a revolution in the most literal sense of the word."[30] This occurred in much the same way that Mexicans inverted society on the Day of the Dead. In this latter celebration, which is well known to those interested in Mexico, sweetmeat and bread skeletons and skulls are sold (bringing life to the dead) and mock epitaphs composed for the well-to-do and local politicians (again reversing the living and the dead). The penny press, beginning in the 1880s, started publishing sardonic postmortems as a way of upsetting the social hierarchy, and José Guadalupe Posada began illustrating these rhymed obituaries. Both the jingles and the sketches have become known as calaveras; both offered the common people the opportunity, without fear of censure or reprisal, to express their dissatisfaction with political and social leaders and to define their grievances, real or imagined.[31]

Study of social reversals is part of a growing interest in the festivals that reflect and shape culture and society. This increasing attention focuses on complex societies and is perhaps most closely associated with the work of Victor Turner, especially his *Dramas, Fields, and Metaphors: Symbolic Action in Human Society*.[32] Despite this growing interest, little study has been made of the urban popular festivals, even of the best known, Rio de Janiero's Carnival. To understand these events, Robert H. Lavenda argues, "it is necessary to recognize their essentially interpretive self-reflective natures, and see them as complexly layered media of communications.[33]

The Judas festivals dramatically demonstrate social reversal. Social inversions fulfill several functions; they serve as rebellious rituals, role reversals, and institutionalized clowning. Recent anthropological studies have found that these reversals are not limited to seasonal celebrations, occur not only within established and unchallenged social orders, and are not confined to primitive cultures. Rather, they can be broadly defined as "any act of expressive behavior which inverts, contradicts, abrogates, or in some fashion presents an alternative to commonly held cultural codes, values, and norms be they linguistic, literary or artistic or religious, or social and political."[34]

Several Holy Week rituals or inversions that were known in the nineteenth century climaxed in the celebration of Judas Day rather than Easter Sunday. All week long the shops were closed, the churches were shrouded, and the people celebrated in the streets. From Wednesday through Saturday's Hallelujah Mass, no horse or wheeled transport was permitted in the city. Viceregal regulations from the late colonial period permitted only pedestrian traffic and restricted other behavior that detracted from the Holy Week solemnity.[35] One traveler reported that "servants and laborers of every sort refuse to work; you can neither do anything nor get anything done. The only recourse is to spend your time in the streets like the rest." Throughout Holy Week, the people performed "curious ceremonies, not to be witnessed at any other season,"[36] that included the "washing of feet" and passion plays.

Washing of feet took place in the cathedral. Twelve seats were placed inside the altar railing for a dozen old men selected from the city's beggars. Great curiosity racked the pueblo to know who would be chosen. As Julia Jackson described it, "the crowd gathered to witness this spectacle was composed chiefly of native Indians. It was dense, eager, and perspiring."[37] She further described the actions of the priests dressed in gorgeous vestments, the most resplendent of whom "was relieved of his outer robe and with a towel on his arm, and accompanied by another priest bearing a small silver basin of water, he passed from the first to the last of the beggars, placing on one foot of each a few drops of water which he immediately wiped away with the towel; after which he stooped and *seemed* to kiss the spot thus washed. He looked glad when it was over, and I have small doubt that he was."[38] This same ritual occurred in Puebla as early as the 1820s, and the town's leading men undertook to provide new clothes and sustenance to each beggar for the year.[39]

On Good Friday the best-known passion play was performed at Tacuba, a little town easily reached by tramcar in the 1890s. The actors presented the drama in pantomime, with a priest explaining the scenes as they appeared. All the performers were Indians and the performance solidly realistic. The crowd became oppressive. Jackson sketched them as a "beggarly, dirty, ill-odorous mass of dark-hued humanity surging now one way, now another. . . . There may have been religious feeling there; but if so, it was just about as apparent as it is in a second-rate circus in a country town in the United States."[40] Those who played the Roman soldiers were actually stoned and beaten by the audience after the performance.

The Saturday morning following Good Friday was devoted to Judas Iscariot. Jackson reported that she had "never seen any hero of history more thoroughly celebrated. . . . Extensive preparations were made, and for many preceding days the streets were grotesque with images of him. Every little child seemed to be running about with its hands full of toy Judases. These effigies present great variety of size and style, from an inch in length to the crudest clown."[41]

In these Judas celebrations, every Mexican from the lowest classes in both the urban districts and the countryside, used representations of Christ's betrayer to invert social relationships that mark carnivalesque celebrations. In the first known description, Becher reported that "here and there among the Judases the people hanged and burned the unmistakeable figures of the public officials that they hated."[42] The most obvious social reversal came in the costumes. Starr in 1898 identified "male Judases and female Judases! . . . fine gentlemen, dudes, ruffians, ass-headed beings, devils." Later he cataloged fat and lean Judases in charro suits and military uniforms.[43] Often the clothing exaggerated the gaudy fashions and conspicuous consumption of well-known local dandies. One Judas in 1890 wore bright blue trousers, a gray coat with huge buttons, and a flaming red tie. A second figure in the same celebration sported pale pink trousers, yellow coat, and polka-dot vest.[44] The effigies often had the likeness of some living person, as a parody of some bigwig, or they caricatured a physical attribute known to the people, such as the wine drinker's bibulous nose. No matter how garish the costume or how outlandish the features, the Judas signified his membership in the aristocracy by wearing a top hat.[45] The people found great pleasure in burning an effigy all dressed up as someone whom they could not but obey in real life: Judas policemen often exploded in these fetes.[46]

During the celebration, these life-sized or larger figures, stuffed with fireworks, were often treated somewhat like piñatas. In fact the tendency to use Judas to parody high society was carried over in a general way to piñatas.[47] Crowds used sticks to torment these Iscariots that hung above their heads. When the excitement reached a fever pitch, the owner ignited the fireworks by the fuse that trailed near the coattails. Exploding firecrackers and skyrockets destroyed Judas.

Social inversions, which Rabelais identified as such a vital part of folk culture, seem to occur with great frequency and intensity during times of particular tension and paradox. In Spain, for example, world-upside-down broadsheets greatly increased during the economic and social dislocations created by New World silver and gold during the sixteenth century.[48] At present, we know little about the number of effigies burned and the intensity of participants in Judas Day and other similar festivals during the nineteenth century in Mexico. We do not know if they increased during the struggles for independence, during the Wars of the Reform, or during intervention by foreigners.

Although we have only glimpses of these Judas festivals, there is some evidence that indicates the ebb and flow, the trends, of popular celebrations, especially for the years between the fall of Maximilian and the revolution (1867–1911).[49] Tantalizing hints appear here and there. Becher's 1832 description comes from the era of Santa Anna's first campaign for the presidency.[50] At mid-century, in the first year of Santa Anna's last dictatorship, the governor of the Federal District, Colonel Miguel María de Azcárate, issued a Holy Week decree, March 17, 1853, to preempt holiday abuses. "In the salute of the said Saturday of Glory," he ordered, "no fireworks shall be thrown by hand, neither shall any kind of firearms be discharged; nor shall there be burned nor sold those figures commonly called Judases, if they have any dress or sign with which to ridicule any social class or special person." The governor set penalties of one-to-five-peso fines and five to fifty days in fetters. Another example comes from the era of Maximilian after the imperial army suffered several defeats in 1865. Rumors crisscrossed the capital city that the people planned to burn Judases of the imperial officers to celebrate Liberal victories. The chief of police reacted to this prospect of disorder with a decree forbidding all fireworks and prohibiting the sale of the "effigies known as Judas" with a fine of twenty-five pesos and confiscation of goods. The Liberal newspaper *Orchestra* parodied this police chief, whom the editor reported had granted an indulgence to Judas.[51]

Other festivals became more popular in character and more extravagant in celebration during the hectic years immediately after the fall of Maximilian. The Day of the Dead feasts of 1867 distressed polite society when the people's unusually spirited exhilaration became a "vulgar show" of "Gothic and Vandal theater" by the same crowd whose major interests were "gingerbread shows, dulces, and idleness." Carnival the following year reflected the same changes and the continuing political tensions. Once a rather exclusive holiday in which high society attended masked balls in the main theaters, Carnival became an event for the common people, who began holding piñata balls with cheap admission at lower-class halls. In 1868, "nearly everyone as well as Nobodies went to balls." Maskers and spectators crowded the popular Iturbide and Principal theaters, the Chiarini Circus, and nearly every street corner of every neighborhood. All the "nobodies" wore masks and many dressed as bears, monkeys, and baboons,[52] costumes that reversed nature's hierarchy by putting animals in the places of the bon ton who usually attended masquerades.

Popular participation in other festivities apparently increased. Rowdy behavior during these religious and civil celebrations prompted polite society to act in 1871. The respectable people planned to rescue Carnival from the common people. Preparations included private balls and public celebrations without the mask and domino (the loose cloak worn with a mask) that was so often used to cover "bad manners and improprieties."[53]

In another example, the council directed the Junta Patriótica, in charge of festivities, to restore city order to Independence Day. As a result, the committee announced there would be no fireworks on September 16. Instead, the junta proposed to distribute the $1,000 pyrotechnical fund to the beggars who swarmed the city's streets. Moreover, in 1872 there was a general request, which went unheeded, for a subdued celebration of Carnival so as not to excite disorder during the tense times of Díaz's La Noria revolt.[54]

The restoration of order following the failure of the La Noria revolt in 1872 resulted in a reduction of popular celebrations. Carnival festivities declined so much that costumes scarcely appeared at all in 1876. The city's elite ignored the celebration and departed for the suburbs, especially Santa Anita, south of town along the Viga Canal. During Carnival and Lent, military bands played daily beside the canal and city police circulated through the crowds to keep order.[55] The Paseo de la Reforma was abandoned and masked balls disappeared, so that the observance of Carnival seemed to be nearly a thing of the past.[56]

Popular festivals returned with renewed vigor in mid-1876 with the political uncertainties created by Díaz's Tuxtepec revolt. The relationship between popular celebrations and rebellions appeared in the report that one of the Porfirian leaders in Veracruz was "a *woman*."[57] This kind of bottom-to-top reversal of social roles reflected the world-upside-down character of Carnival and Judas Day. The report of a woman commanding men signaled the equality and utopian feelings of carnivalesque celebrations. This report, even if apocryphal, related the Díaz movement to popular rebellions of sixteenth-century Europe in which leaders sometimes dressed as women to display the toppling of hierarchy.[58]

We do not know if these popular celebrations, especially Judas burnings, increased during these years in relationship to the expansion of railroad right-of-way, as was the case with agrarian resistance.[59] One 1881 account provides a tantalizing description of a Judas fiesta involving the railroad. A British visitor traveling from Veracruz to Mexico City first saw the celebrants when the train stopped at the Apizaco station, where the rails from Puebla joined the main line. While the locomotive screeched to a halt, a crowd celebrating Holy Saturday and carrying several Judas effigies engulfed the train. The crowd strapped one effigy, dressed as a peasant with a straw sombrero and cotton manta drawers and shirt, across the headlight of the engine. After much shouting and revelry, they ignited the fuse. The engineer blared the whistle as the campesino Judas exploded.[60] Here the betrayer symbolized the peasantry confronted, then was overwhelmed by rapacious technology, symbolized by the railroad. The Judas represented the people destroyed by the locomotive and it offered a graphic projection of the sentiments also expressed in the corrido that the railroad had destroyed the poor man's corn.[61] These attitudes were firmly grounded in the beliefs of the people, who had tried to protect their fields by armed resistance against predatory speculators seizing their corn patches for railroad right-of-way.

A new outburst of popular celebrations followed Díaz's seizure of power in 1876 and continued until the mid-1890s. An excellent example occurred in 1886 in Mazatlán. The town's society was in an uproar over wild rumors that some 600,000 Chinese workers had been diverted from Portland, Oregon, and were on their way to settle on Mexico's Pacific Coast, especially in the Mazatlán region. Persecution of the Chinese in Mazatlán increased immediately, especially by members of several artisan mutuals and by teenage boys. During Holy Week, this persecution and apprehension resulted in the manufacture of dozens of Chinese Judas effigies. The police interfered and confiscated all of them to prevent the possibility of violence. Although the Díaz government kept the lid on the anti-Chinese hostility, in 1911 the revolution offered an opportunity that resulted in the massacre of Chinese residents of Sonora.[62]

Besides providing an opportunity to reverse society's order, the Judas festivals in the 1880s offered an opportunity for the masses to display their good humor. The marketplace exhibition of folk humor was a tradition that Mexicans inherited from medieval Europe through Spain. This heritage contrasted sharply against the serious, official, ecclesiastical, and political ceremonies, offering instead a secular and light-hearted element to the world and human relations. Events such as the Judas burnings allowed the people to construct a second world and a second life that was based on humor.[63]

The humor which gives form to the carnivalesque rituals frees them completely from social and ecclesiastic dogmatism, and often parodies church cults. These occasions are not spectacles seen by the people; the people live them, and everyone participates because the drama embraces all the people. During the ceremony, life is subject only to the ritual's own laws, that is, the utopian realm of community, freedom, equality, and abundance. Carnival laughter had a complex nature. First, it was above all festive laughter, not the individual reaction to some isolated "comic" event but the laughter of all the people. Second, it was universal in scope; it was directed at all and everyone, including the participants. Third, this laughter was ambivalent, both gay and triumphant, and mocking and deriding. It asserts and denies, it buries and revives; it gives and takes away. Most of these characteristics of folk humor have been ignored. Most analysis today presents merely gross modernizations, explaining it either as purely negative satire or else as gay, fanciful, recreational drollery deprived of philosophic content. The feature most often ignored is folk humor's ambivalence.[64]

The characteristics of folk humor figure prominently in the Judas festivals of this period, especially in the 1880s. Carl Sartorius remarked as early as the 1850s on the humor that Mexicans found in the burning of Judas effigies. He observed the figures, filled with crackers, squibs, and rockets, and often with live cats, frogs, or lizards. When the bells signaled the time, these paper creations burst with exploding fireworks, the cats bounded away or the other creatures scattered into the crowd, providing a delightful fright for the throng. Sartorius reported that all of this — the figures of Judas, the exploding fireworks, and the bounding cats — resulted in an uproar of shocked and excited laughter.[65] Another observer caught the same spirit of laughter, describing the people's derisive mockery and their curious good humor. The crowd displayed no ill feeling nor abhorrence toward Judas, nor did they shout any execration. They simply turned the affair into ridicule and the performance into a humorous romp.[66]

Others watched the celebration expecting to see the people heap contumely, derision, and dishonor on Judas, and found instead a festival more closely resembling the Fourth of July in the United States. Everyone was elated. Women and children as spectators clapped, cheered, and laughed as the larger effigies exploded — first an arm, then a leg, then the torso detonated. In Guadalajara, the explosions of the large and small Judases continued for over an hour in the central plaza. This event was called a "queer, strange piece of ludicrous mockery, ending as a good-natured annual frolic."[67] The description reveals another message on display in the ritual: the events allow social reversal and they reinforce male and female roles. In this fiesta, the señoras and señoritas crowded the sidewalks and balconies to watch the señores ignite and torment the Judases. Small boys had their own small Judases to light in imitation of their fathers. Here, as in so many ways, the Mexican male performed actively and the Mexican female participated in a passive way, but they are linked in this celebration, not divided into actor and audience. They are not separated by footlights; they are equally involved as they are in life, but with clearly defined roles.

The involvement of men and women and children revealed the universal character of the celebration. It included everyone. For this reason its disorder was shunned, then opposed by the upper classes, the church, and the government, especially the city council in Mexico City. The Jockey Club at first supported the fiesta, then dropped its participation.

Judas burnings displayed as well folk humor's ambivalence, especially the way it combined gaiety and derision. Most effigies parodied the rich and powerful, but on other occasions they mocked the poor themselves, or the champions of the poor—with effigies in the revolutionary years of Villa and Zapata, and later Cantínflas.[68] The explosions often scattered coins or goods to the crowd, who might be injured in the wild scramble to possess them. This ambivalent "giving and taking away" sometimes was explicit. Several times during the 1890s heated coins were tossed to the crowd, so that the lucky ones who grabbed them also burned their hands.[69] Storekeepers tossed handfuls of candies to the crowds. On one occasion the sweets had been laced with chile powder, making them too spicy to eat. Good and bad fortune appeared together during these celebrations. One woman, Zeferina Casas, trying to secure a Judas above the street, fell headfirst into Merced Street. Her misfortune was balanced by her luck of receiving only minor head and leg bruises, all to the merriment of the crowd.[70]

The popular character of this celebration came as well from the fact that it was the special day of water carriers. These aguadores served as the principal communications link in communities, as they made their rounds delivering water from the fountains and gossip from the neighbors. Described as latter-day descendants of water carriers from biblical times, the aguadores played an essential role in the community, not simply for the water they delivered, but for the news they brought. The aguador was recognized as the one man in the neighborhood who knew everyone and what he was doing and why. The profession was called by some "the noblest part of proletarianism, and the boundary-line of vagabondism." On Holy Saturday, the aguadores strew flowers on the water of the fountains and burned an image symbolic of their trade. Their identification with Holy Saturday and the burning of Judas made it especially a day of the people.[71]

The location of the celebrations also indicates its popular attributes. Although Fanny Calderón reported that the burning of Judas occurred in the Zócalo, by the 1890s it had been forced out of the central plaza and moved to the streets, usually in the poorer neighborhoods. The same shift has continued to the present, to popular neighborhoods and to homes.[72] The changing location of the Judas burnings graphically displays the struggle in Mexico between two segments in society. Mexico's traditional culture which prevailed from the conquest until the 1870s represented the Spanish medieval heritage of authoritarianism and Roman Catholicism embellished by exigency with indigenous practices. This tradition was shouldered aside by the emergent culture of capitalism and material development that promoters called Progress. This Porfirian variant of Positivism had a genealogy stretching back through Benito Juárez's reform and José Luis Mora's Liberalism to the Spanish sons of the Enlightenment. These Porfirians, flaunting their modernism, rejected long-established customs as backward, even primitive habits slowing inevitable progress.

The pueblo in city barrios and mestizo villages preserve a living remnant of the Middle Ages. This medieval inheritance had an unofficial religious character often expressed in devotion to the Virgin of Guadalupe or some other image of the Holy Mother. Pilgrimages and daily homages demonstrated the Virgin's symbolic power.[73] The Marian example taught passivity to Mexican women in this male-oriented society.[74] The pueblo revered the Virgin, but the medieval folk tradition had an unofficial, unapproved character that could not survive government tampering. In the mid-1890s, the Guadalupine symbolism suffered somewhat when it received official sanction as both the Porfirian government and the pope endorsed the 1895 coronation of the Virgin.[75] This change became immediately apparent when several delegations from Indian villages were turned away from the ceremonies, and only allowed to enter the sanctuary the following day.[76]

This folk culture found less hampered expression in the Day of the Dead rituals, Carnival, and Judas burnings. These festivals were linked superficially to feasts of the liturgical calendar but were celebrated in public places without religious supervision or government approval. Judas burnings were often sponsored by the owners of pulque shops. Proprietors announced the time of the execution, so that large crowds gathered for the event. Arriving spectators often received banners with advertisements for nearby shops. They waved these at the Iscariot that dangled above them. During the 1880s and the 1890s, merchants in lower-class barrios often purchased specially made Judases, filled with their goods. Bakers, for examples, would have an effigy stuffed with hard rolls; butchers had the figure filled with chunks of meat; soap makers had it jammed with bars of soap. Shopkeepers who peddled bulky or valuable goods usually provided only one sample for the celebration. Outside a cobbler's shop Judas might be suspended holding a new pair of shoes. A haberdashery's owner gave a fancy sombrero for Judas to hold or a clothier contributed a colorful shirt that the mannequin grasped until his fiery demise. Judas, dressed as a dandy, was suspended until it shattered under the blows of the rods and the exploding fireworks, permitting the mob to scrap for the valuables strewn over them.[77]

The Jockey Club Episode

The decline and shifting location of Judas Day and other celebrations in the 1890s demonstrated that the elite had broken with these traditions. Calm, satisfied, and secure, these Porfirians opposed displays of disorder. The destruction of Judas was a traditional, literal exhibition that both the Díaz government and the church saw as a challenge to propriety, with the potential for disorder.[78] As in western Europe, leaders attempted to regulate these festivities by making them trivial, on the one hand turning them into officially sponsored displays or processions, and on the other consigning them to the home where they became children's activities. Both government and church in 1895 had forced Judas burnings into the city's neighborhoods associated with crime and poverty, and into the countryside. Privileges formerly allowed were more and more restricted in public places.[79]

Steps in this direction began when polite society no longer retired to the suburbs during Carnival, Lent, and Semana Santa. Beginning about 1888, high society started to remain in the capital during this season. The Jockey Club took up Judas Day briefly, sponsoring numerous effigies with coins pasted on their clothing, or holding bags of centavos that were hung outside the Casa de Azulejos and exploded so the members could enjoy the spectacle of the mob scrambling for the coins. Each year the crowd increased and so did the disorder and the injuries from the explosions and the scramble for coins.

Jockey Club Judases at first were purchased from anonymous street vendors exactly as the masses purchased their effigies for the celebration. Only for a year or two did the club members commission specific mannequins. In 1890, the club entered into the general spirit of the day and strung Judases from its rented rooms across San Francisco Street to the Iturbide Hotel. Porters and street urchins gathered beneath them to scrap for the coins and items of clothing on the effigies. After the figures exploded and the jostling for coppers and goods had subsided, some Jockey Club members renewed the scramble by tossing handfuls of small coins to the crowd. The uproar continued for over an hour until mounted policemen arrived to clear the dense crowd that blocked the street.[80]

The following year, the club, still awaiting its move from rented rooms to the Casa de Azulejos, contracted with artisans for a "first-class Judas," attired in a valuable sombrero and other useful and valuable personal effects. The effigy was placed in the middle of San Francisco Street. A huge mob collected to see the burning and to scramble for the clothes and the handfuls of coins the members pitched from their windows. For about an hour, San Francisco Street took on the appearance, according to one reporter, of a "bear [*sic,* beer] garden, with 'the people' yelling, scrambling and fighting below and the lights of the Jockey Club above, beaming like so many Gods on the scene they had stage-managed so well." Injuries and accidents resulted from the melee. One *lépero* (a street person) was badly burned by the exploding gunpowder and another was kicked by a horse that had become unmanageable during the explosions.[81]

For the Hallelujah Saturday celebration in 1892, the Jockey Club spent 3,000 silver pesos for Judases and decorations and faced another assessment for damages to nearby shops after the event. Although the Jockey Club hosted the largest event, the festivities continued for a longer time on Dolores Street, where the burning of cardboard and gunpowder Judases continued until one o'clock in the afternoon.[82]

The stage for the 1893 Jockey Club event was set by the editor of *Siglo XIX,* when he wrote, "According to what we can observe today, it seems that the ridiculous farce that Catholicism taught our elders is fading away. Burning cardboard mannequins imitating Iscariot no longer diverts even young boys who enjoy little hell fires; the rancid custom is disappearing."[83] However hopeful this spokesman of modern Mexico, how wrong he spoke.

The following day the Jockey Club sponsored the most elaborate Judas burning yet seen in Mexico City. *Siglo XIX* carried an extensive story of the celebration. For weeks the members had debated, argued, discussed, and rediscussed what kind of Judases to have on Holy Saturday. Finally, they agreed to combine nearly everyone's suggestions into an Iscariot tableau comprising an aerostat whose balloon was covered with coins and whose gondola carried four Judas figures, a mulatto and a butter salesman mounted on a pig, both crisscrossed with sausage strings and covered with *reales* and *pesetas,* a singer, seated with his legs crossed and playing a guitar, and a beggar, both resplendent with *pesos.* This enormous display propelled the sarcastic pen of the editor of *El Universal,* who mocked the clubmen who had worn themselves out creating this float. "They have truly spent Holy Week in Judas's company," he sneered, as he commented on their efforts to make everything perfect. "With gloved hands, they glued coins on the figures. But there was not one who made the sacrifice of scraping out his own pocketbook to have the glory of blushing at such meritorious behavior. Puffed up with pride, full of arrogance and filled with satisfaction rarely seen, the trim, elegant gentlemen of the Jockey Club themselves escorted their creation into the street." Mounted police cleared their way to the center of San Francisco Street, where they directed the balloon's ascension to its place of detonation above the heads of the yapping crowd, which was described as being as "rabid, soulless, and maddened" as the event itself. When the bells rang out the hallelujah, the Judases exploded and scattered as the "rushing, clinging, trampling, growing crowd became a mob, hurling itself on the Judases to grab everything of value." "And the CLUBMEN," reported the editor, "burst out in laughter and enjoyed to the fullest this savage and brutal fight that resulted in bruises, breaks, sprains, and punctured eyes. Compared to this pleasure, pugilism is a virtue. This is contemptible; it is wicked; it embarrasses all cultivated society." He demanded to know, "Why has not the government of the Federal District prohibited it? A year ago, the commercial class raised a protest against such savagery. Why should the poor have to serve as recreation for the distinguished?"[84]

This celebration embodied events and emblems that offer windows on both elite and everyday society in 1893. It becomes a metaphoric melodrama of Mexican life, in which the action and plot predominate over the characters, who after all superficially are only effigies. Of the various Judas burnings mentioned, only this 1893 affair reveals the unconscious interests of the elites because they consciously sought out the artisans and commissioned specific Judas figures.

The display provides the first level of clues about this social performance. The balloon and its gondola expressed the latest in modern technology brought to Mexico to share the most fashionable foreign knowledge with humble Mexicans eager to improve their society. The hot-air balloon arrived in the spring of 1892. Professor Ivy Baldwin of Quincy, Illinois, announced a "Grand Balloon Ascension and Parachute Leap" the Sunday before Easter at the Hacienda de la Castaneda. Special train cars were scheduled to carry spectators from the capital to the hacienda. A rip in the balloon, unfortunately, prevented the performance, but it was rescheduled for Easter. The crowd of acrobats on hand in case of another equipment failure proved unnecessary. The following year the Baldwin brothers, aeronautical engineers, began offering regular trips to the clouds and back aboard the "City of Mexico," a captive balloon (that is, a hot-air balloon) at the Tivoli del Eliseo. The engineers Baldwin carried over a thousand spectators aloft in March 1893, affording them a "magnificent panoramic view of the city, the valley, and the surrounding villages," for the round-trip price of three pesos for adults and half price for children. For the faint of heart who only wanted to watch others ascend, the engineers charged twenty-five cents admission to the grounds. The "City of Mexico" captivated the public, even though problems between the balloon's owners and heavy wind forced an end to the balloon rides on Easter Sunday, April 2, 1893.[85]

The Jockey Club's display thus offered the common Mexicans (the

Judases) a ride into the sky and the future. The balloon served as another symbol as well. The "globo cautivo constelado de monedas," the hot-air balloon covered with coins, suggested that the entire world was concerned with money. Greed propelled everyone—a conclusion that would have found few in disagreement in the crowd howling for the display to explode and in the capitalist clubmen watching the melodrama they had staged. The Porfirian elite had no doubt that wages could uplift the meanest lépero from the backward Indian life. The mixed-blood, the three-penny tradesmen, the wandering troubadour, and the shiftless beggar all would be uplifted through progress. Just as surely this display demonstrated that those who progressed through capitalism and technology should not go beyond their place; the characters in the gondola could not aspire to the same level as the Jockey Club (the tableau was hoisted to the second-floor level of the clubmen spectators) without danger; those who reached above their station were exploded: a clear statement against the pretension of the socially mobile working classes.

The characters warrant special attention. The mulatto appeared in the gondola with the other outcasts. They were looked down on by frock-coat society because the ruling elite (all of whom were represented in the Jockey Club) in the 1890s was in the midst of a general effort to demonstrate the Western, modern character of Mexico. This attitude had effected by 1893 several city ordinances that regulated fashions, showing that appearances, especially clothing, made the man. These laws ordered that all males wear trousers and that various groups of employees such as hack drivers and newspaper boys adopt uniforms; moreover, they tried to replace the traditional sombrero with custom-made hats for gentlemen and caps for service employees such as porters.

The vagrant lower classes were the target of these laws. Normally this class was referred to as Indian, although obviously it included all the non-Europeans, and all the mixed peoples, including blacks. As part of this dangerous element holding back progress, they represented to the elite a betrayal of modern Mexico.

The selection of a mulatto Judas was made for two additional motives. The black person represented a lucky symbol in Mexico. Rubbing the head of a black person or touching him gave luck. So the mulatto as a symbol had an ambivalent, negative and positive, character so typical and so necessary in folk celebrations. Finally there existed the possibility of another subconscious concern. Mexico's prosperity in the 1890s rested squarely on its position as the world's leading silver producer. Numerous epigrams praised silver for the progress it bought (for example: Mexico's progress travels on silver rails; the Díaz government runs on silver peso wheels). This prosperity in 1893 was betrayed by silver itself, with the collapse of the international market and the conversion by many of the world's governments to the gold standard. Anxiety over the profitabilility of silver racked the minds of the native elite. *Mulato* was a Mexican term for silver ore of a dark green color and unusual high grade. The mulatto Judas as silver threatened to betray Mexican prosperity.

The butter vendor may have seemed an unusual impostor to include in the balloon's basket, but Mexicans immediately recognized him as a folk character nearly as familiar as the China poblana and the charro. He represented the small folk tradesmen, who sold or bartered life's necessities, such as salt and lard, to those who grew their own corn and beans. The butter represented the basic commodity of Mexican cooking. Lard, that is, mantequilla de cerdo (pig butter) was the essential ingredient in Mexico's traditional food preparation, so that it symbolized the common, everyday way of life that many of the elite saw as backward and retrogressive. Moreover, butter represented the end to the Lenten restrictions, especially not eating meat. In folklore, people were deceived into eating meat during Lent, when it was disguised as lard or butter.[86] Thus the butter salesman had an image as a trickster or deceiver.

The pig represented abundance as well and gluttony. This symbol extended from the Middle Ages, when it was customary to present the Seven Deadly Sins in processions as people riding different animals. The pig served for gluttony, and also indicated sloth. Reckless greed and incorrigible sloth expressed the elite's conception of lower-class behavior.[87]

Symbolic as well as valuable were the decorations on these images. Both the butter vendor and the mulatto were looped with ropes of spicy chorizo sausages. These ancient symbols of abundance represented the essence of folk celebrations, reversing the social order of hunger and deprivation. Of course, they gave clear demonstration that the time of fasting, especially the restrictions against meat, had ended with the conclusion of Lent. *Chorizo,* moreover, served as the slang term for rolls of coins, doubling the symbol of abundance and stressing the capitalists' interest in money.

The coins pasted to the clothes of the Judases contributed to the symbolic abundance, and for a self-consciously capitalistic community, nothing symbolized wealth and success as well as money. The choice of coinage was not accidental. In the 1890s Mexico was compelling an end to the old confusing but popular coinage that combined Mexico's decimal system and the old Spanish system of pesetas and reales (divided into eighths). The old Spanish coinage remained especially popular with the lower classes—therefore the identification with the mulatto and the tradesman. The common wisdom held that all the shopkeepers and vendors were Spaniards. Thus, adorning any Judas as a Spaniard delighted everyone, whatever his class, unless he was a Spanish merchant.

The troubador with his guitar, another of the mannequin symbols, expressed lower-class slothfulness, clearly a projection of the elite's belief that there existed the proclivity among the lower classes to avoid work and slip into the n'er-do-well life of the musician—or equally as likely that of a beggar, the fourth and final figure. Unlike the other two, these characters appeared as native Mexicans, covered with pesos and coins of Mexican denominations. Metaphorically this made a statement of nascent nationalism for the emergent businessmen about the lower classes in Mexico: that the lazy poor were both shiftless and happy. Moreover, this character testified to the gaucheness of the lower classes, in that the singer played "con cuatros," the four-fingered style of the Andalucian gypsy, a straightforward reference to this crowd of outcasts. This also referred to "cuatro" a Mexican term for the crude and inappropriate use of Spanish by "Indians," who spoke Castilian as gibberish. Covered with pesos, these two figures became *peseteros,* a term used to describe someone engaged in paltry or worthless business endeavors. The Jockey Club thus discounted musicians and mendicants in the new world of industry.[88]

This Judas burning was the last sponsored by the Jockey Club. Newspaper editors grasped immediately that, for all its outward appearance as a popular folkloric celebration, it was not one. The elite of the Jockey Club had taken the form but not the spirit of a carnivalesque event. In earlier years the Jockey Club had celebrated with the event, but once they began to commission Judases they no longer had the spirit. At one time they had participated in a ritual of mutual benefit by tossing coins to the crowd below. This tradition characterized other beginnings, such as births and marriages, when the bride's or child's father tossed coins to children as a measure to ensure good luck and abundance for the new life or the new marriage. But the symbolism quickly atrophied under the direction of the Jockey Club. Mean-spirited members tossed coins only to make sport of those who scrambled for them.

Aftermath

The Jockey Club by 1895 abandoned its part in the celebration and began participating in flowery wars and bicycle parades. Flowery wars were parades, often at Easter, in which society decorated its coaches and horses and promenaded on the Reforma. This tradition was an imitation of the flower parades held in Nice and brought from France by travelers.[89] Government and social leaders reordered Carnival by organizing a bicycle parade with $5,000 in prizes for the outstanding costumed riders mounted on decorated wheels. This parade continued to grow in popularity over the next several years. In 1900 the city council went a step further and ordered the police to prevent Judas burnings, citing them as both a fire hazard and a cause of public disorder. These regulations successfully blocked the celebration for the next several years within the city limits, although in the countryside the people still burned Judas effigies.[90]

The Judas fiestas returned with great enthusiasm to the capital city in 1908, despite prohibitive ordinances. The outbreak of celebrations came at a time of great tension throughout Mexico in response to the 1905 world economic depression, which, in combination with poor harvests and higher food prices, ground down everyday Mexicans in 1907 and 1908. Political tension was also building as the old dictator and his administration entered their fourth decade in office.

The most enthusiastic Judas burning in 1908 occurred in the capital's neighborhood of Santa Julia, a settlement that today would be called a ciudad perdida. Located to the northwest of the city, the colonia technically formed part of the municipality of Tacuba, although it was twice its size. Tacuba could not police this district and Mexico City did so only spasmodically.[91] This suburban shanty town, located near the railroad tracks, was built of cast-off lumber, tin, and cardboard. Infamous as a sanctuary of pickpockets, robbers, and sneak thieves, it hosted the most enthusiastic Judas celebration of the season. Newspapers reported other

Judas burnings in the capital, but none as crowded or enthusiastic as the one in Santa Julia. The huge crowd, described as Indians in holiday attire, jammed the prolongation of Calle Guillermo Prieto which served as a main street. Above the heads of the crowd were numerous Judases suspended on ropes held by persons on the roofs of the ramshackle buildings. These Iscariots could easily have populated Dante's Inferno. Hacendados, peónes, poblanas, policemen, and ugly-faced hags dangled above the crowd. The three largest figures portrayed a larger-than-life devil, a wild boar, and a huge billy goat that seemed to buck and kick as it was detonated.[92]

These three figures offered symbols of popular discontent. The devil, a figure that oscillated with that of Judas so that it clearly was Judas and just as clearly was the devil, represented humanity, in the sense that Christians believed God had created both Satan and man in his image, and both had fallen from grace. The figure symbolized as well worldly disorder and backsliding, retrogression from perfection, and even rebellion in reversal of the Porfirian slogan of Order and Progress.[93] The political concern manifested in this social reversal subtly reflected perhaps the most common of all Mexican proverbs, expressed by the devil figure and extended to Díaz because of his age and guile. The people said, "Más sabe el diablo por viejo que por diablo"; the devil knows more by being old than by being the devil. The concern about Díaz's age — he was nearly 78 in April 1908 — and discussions about his successor in the 1910 elections had percolated down to the capital's outcasts, who accepted the view that Díaz knew more by being old than by being president.[94]

The wild boar expressed gluttony, the opposite of the Lent observance and of the months of deprivation caused by the nation's bad harvests, rising prices, and reduced food imports. The boar served as the emblem of lechery, considered the most vicious kind of sensual greed. Lascivious behavior characterized not only the Holy Saturday celebrations but other folk events as well; so the boar performed as a rallying symbol for the enjoyment of pleasures ordinarily under strict regulations. At the same time the boar represented vulgar masculine aggressiveness and wrath.[95]

Many metaphorical meanings represented by the boar were attached to the goat as well, but with a paradoxical counter-meaning of the masculine symbols, because the cabrón was the symbol for the cuckold. the antithesis of the macho. Using the fingers beside the head to make horns was another popular way of making a goat or accusing someone of being cuckolded. The more virile a man, the more he risked to the prospect of cuckoldry. The old cabrón Díaz, the most powerful, the most virile Mexican, by 1908 had begun to show weakness that provoked metaphorical accusation that he had been reduced to a cuckold. The celebrants redoubled their laughter at the billy goat, mocking this emblem of their president which allowed them to laugh at their difficulties; moreover, projecting their sexual anxieties onto the Judas figure reduced these uncertainties, making them disappear with gunpowder.

The significance of sexually charged symbols in the Judas burnings extended from the shadowy life of the subconscious to reality's melodrama. In fact a Mexican proverb declares that "la cama es la ópera del pobre," the bed is the opera of the poor.[96] A poor man's pride, daring, strength, tenderness, and creativity had little opportunity for expression beyond the bed. Artisans had their crafts and agrarians had their relationship to the land and crops, but Díaz's modernization attacked both these outlets as backward. For the factory worker, porter, or hack driver, sexual relations provided the melodramatic reality that gave pungency to everyday life. The sexual symbolism of Iscariot figures reversed the world, extending the life of the everyday Mexican to the elite. These figures most directly expressed the carnivalesque folk tradition that extended back to medieval Europe.

Judas burnings continued, especially in neighborhoods like Santa Julia, throughout the revolution that began in 1910, sporadically occurring up to the present. During the most vicious years of revolutionary fighting, when first Victoriano Huerta and then Venustiano Carranza controlled the capital city, residents burned Judases representing the twin scourges Pancho Villa and Emiliano Zapata. The incineration of mannequins in effigy of the Centaur of the North and the Cossack of the South became so popular that in 1915 when Roque González Garza captured the city in their name, he prohibited the Holy Saturday celebrations. In the next decade the shift to more popular, more crime-ridden neighborhoods continued. In the 1920s, the festival centered in the barrios of Tepito, la Colonial del Valle, and especially La Merced. It continued there through the years of World War II.

Other than in these barrios, the burnings took place in private homes and became a children's activity (much like the Fourth of July in the United States) with youngsters igniting the toy Judases in the patios of their homes.[97] Family celebrations that destroyed Judas figures gave the celebrants a chance to fill the figures with gifts, much like piñatas, and to reinforce family religious unity through the desecration of Judas. The family celebration of this event was typical of some areas of Mexico. For example, Judas burnings, like piñatas, were largely restricted to the patios of homes or the streets immediately in front of private houses throughout the nineteenth century in the mining town of Guanajuato. A Colombian visitor to the mines, Doctor Federico C. Guilar, wrote the editor of Bogotá's newspaper *Pasatiempo* in 1883 to describe Holy Week there. He found that during Holy Friday the people purchased Judas effigies of all sizes and characters, stuffed with rockets, that they exploded at their homes the following day.[98]

In the capital, the celebration has continued to the present day in Tepito and La Merced, and in the shanty towns on the outskirts of the city limits, but the great effigies of the past have disappeared. Folklorists Florence and Robert Pettit could not find a single Judas in 1977.[99] The Judas figures have changed in recent years from human and animal figures to surrealistic, dreamlike horrors that the originator, Pedro Linares, called *alebrijes*. These grotesque dragon monsters are still exploded in a flash of fireworks. The traditional Judas figure has become a popular curio dangling from car aerials—a folk piece d'art and a tourist item.[100] In the suburb of Iztapalapa, one community leader, Antonio Guerra Juárez, lamented, "We have lost the celebration of Easter, the burning of Judas, and even of Carnival."[101] However, even as he decried the loss of the popular celebration exploding the Iscariots, across the metropolitan district in San Ángel, the Bazar del Sábado presented a special Easter exposition of twenty-four Judases by Pedro Linares. The director of the show, Ignacio Romero, declared it was his intention to rescue one of the country's traditions and to present the creations of Linares, one of the nation's outstanding folk artists.[102]

Mexico's national Indigenous Institute maintains a permanent exhibition of handicrafts and toys in its Museo Nacional de Artes e Industrias Populares, located within a block of the Alameda on Juárez Avenue. All of the pottery, wood, tin, cloth, and paper folk artifacts in this display are carefully identified for the visitor, except for some unusual items covering one wall in a small landing between the larger salons. These unidentified representations include a life-size papier-maché figure painted as a skeleton and covered with fireworks, another life-sized comic charro with fuses indicating that it is stuffed with explosives, and over a dozen grotesque figures made of clay and paper, from doll-size to about an inch long, portraying fanciful monsters and hideous devils. No labels explain these figures. Perhaps the museum curators believe anyone interested will recognize them as the effigies of Judas that once played a principal part in one of Mexico's most popular and least-known celebrations. What remains of the celebration has been reduced largely to a children's holiday. This is the fate of many world-upside-down phenomena: they become children's cartoons that are caricatures of folktales.[103] The result is that most recent descriptions of the Judas effigies appear in studies of handicrafts and toys.[104]

Mexicans produce a great assortment of beautiful, grotesque, and humorous toys. Many are seasonal, especially made for the Day of the Dead and for Holy Week. For the Easter season there are many wooden rattles and especially the Judases. Frances Toor provided a sketch of one such toy, a character that looked like a court jester, with a long floppy-eared hat and polka-dotted costume.[105] More and more the effigies have become just seasonal piñatas for children.

Judas ceremonies leaked into the Easter celebrations of indigenous villages. Some of these practices still continue. In Tarascán hamlets, two or three villagers, playing Judas, served as religious sheriffs throughout Holy Week. These characters, dressed in masks and costumes, ridiculed or levied fines on anyone violating the prohibitions of Lent. After mass on Holy Saturday in many villages, grown-ups announcing that they acted in the name of the betrayer lifted children by their ears to help them grow. Other adults, in a playful trick somewhat like pinching someone not wearing green on St. Patrick's Day, also tried to surprise their friends by grabbing their ears and shouting, "Here's your glory, Judas."[106] The most common and most significant event in the countryside, especially in indigenous villages, came on Holy Saturday when the people ritually killed Judas.

The Yaqui Indians in northwest Mexico have an effigy of Judas for their Holy Saturday, or Little Resurrection Day, celebrations. Erna Fergusson saw one of their celebrations held in Tlaxcala, where Yaqui soldiers were garrisoned. The effigy was an eight-foot figure, with a mask on top and hung all over with dolls, toys, stuffed animals, metracas (rattles), a banner of the prevailing political party, a tin pot or two, a cravat, paper flowers, and a long gourd. By eight in the morning the yard was filled with people and the women blossomed in their most colorful dresses. Full skirts of salmon pink, magenta, or orange with shawls of every contrasting shade: green, yellow, electric blue, and lavender. At about 9 a.m. Judas went up in smoke with a few popping firecrackers to mark his doom, but not much excitement. At the other end of the yard, dancers were prostrating themselves, one by one, before their cross and taking their swords and spears for the dance. Every mask now was topped with spring green—fresh leaves or paper—and the men in black had bright silk handkerchiefs tied around their arms. Other dancers gathered. Near the altar was a serape piled high with confetti and flower petals. Everyone in town had come, and many strangers. The cooks continued to cook. Everyone else waited, tensely. At ten o'clock it came. He is risen! Everything went off at once. The air whirled in a cloud of flowers and confetti.[107]

This Judas celebration has also been taken over by other indigenous communities in the most remote extensions of Mexico, both the northern and southern extremes of the nation. From coastal Oaxaca comes an interesting description of the ceremony in the Mixtec village of Pinótepa de Don Luis, taken partially from the Judas burnings of neighboring Mestizo villages. The Judas effigy stands slightly less than adult size, made of old Mestizo-styled clothes stuffed with straw vegetation (called paxtle). The head and the hands of the figure are carved in wood and painted with commercial oil paints. These are kept from year to year. In addition the bladder of a slaughtered animal (usually a pig) is filled with the blood of this animal and inserted into the figure's upper body. Judas is made to ride a mule, with a live rider behind it to manage the animal. He is led to prison (the local juzgado) and incarcerated there, "*mule and all!*" After an appropriate length of time (about an hour), Judas, still on the mule, is led to the cemetery. There he is untied and propped against a rock. The men take aim with their pistols and shotguns and fire. In a lifelike manner the effigy spurts blood as it jerks in the spasms of death caused by the impact of bullets. Cayuquí Estage Noel, head of the Institute for Indigenous Theater in Oaxaca, regards this as an example of living indigenous theater.[108]

The Judas killing by the Tarahumara comes directly from the syncretic techniques used by the missionary priests to introduce religion among these people of the barrancas of Chihuahua. The festival, the last three days of Holy Week, resembles the Matachines dances used by other indigenous peoples to celebrate various religious holidays. During the Tarahumara festival, the men are divided into two groups, the warriors, dressed as typical Tarahumaras, and the Pharisees, dressed as rancheros (that is as mestizos) wearing sombreros decorated with a feather, and their faces (and sometimes their bodies) painted white. During the 1950s, when Erle Stanley Gardner witnessed this ceremony, he identified the two sides as the Moors and the Pharisees, dressed as they have just been described. The competition for the privilege of killing Judas proceeds through the dances—complicated maneuvers similar to marching drills—and culminates in a wrestling match, Tarahumara style, between the two sides. The men pair off and, in the middle of a plowed field, engage in a heaving contest, similar to Japanese Sumo wrestling. This can result in great hilarity if in the struggle to toss his opponent, one happens to pull away the other's loincloth. The loss of the loincloth does not cause any concern, as the wrestling continues without it. If the warriors win the match, they use their assortment of shotguns and other weapons to shoot Judas, then bury him. If the Pharisees win, they gleefully introduce themselves to the life-sized Judas dummy, stuffed with brush, then suddenly condemn him for his treason. They retreat and begin shooting arrows at the effigy, and as soon as the first arrow strikes him, the Pharisees rush the figure, dismember it, and set it afire. The Jesuit priest Juan Manuel Martínez, called Father Tramps, explained the ceremony to Gardner. "In order to make Christianity meaningful to the savage mind," he admitted, "it had been necessary to permit a certain primitive symbolism which would appeal to the Indians in terms they would understand."[109] John G. Kennedy recently has turned an anthropologist's searchlight on this Tarahumara ritual.[110]

In the cities, even though the folk tradition became trivial and childish, it received new vitality in the popular culture created by newspapers (and later radio, movies, and television). The humorous opposition newspapers first claimed this sarcastic oral tradition. The madcap epitaphs and witty comments, called *calaveras,* used to celebrate the Day of the Dead soon appeared in the press, with illustrations by engravers such as José Guadalupe Posada. The people's humor of Holy Week soon found newspaper expression as well. *El Hijo de Ahuizote* carried a report on what the editor called "Semana Santa Tuxtepecana," or the Porfirian Holy Week, with a discussion of the Iscariots. "For thirty coins, Judas Iscariot, the Soul of a Spaniard, sold his master. For a regeneration joke and a kick in the pants by Napoleon, the loud laughter of Bazaine and Forey, and the nickname Bigwigs from their royal masters, the contemptible clergy sold Mexico. Don't envy them when you hear their Judas purses sound completely full! They are full of bombs, clear to the bottom!"[111]

Cartoonists took the folk tradition and worked it into their craft. The close relationship between the archbishop of Mexico and the dictator provoked a 1901 cartoon that decried the loss of democracy and liberty through the church's alliance with the state, by depicting a Judas burning. A Judas figure dressed as the archbishop explodes above the heads of everyday Mexicans (apparent by their dress), blowing democracy and liberty in every direction. The caption read, "The People's Day of Glory." Another political cartoon that adopted the Judas ceremony to express political views had the title "Saturday of Glory in Politics." The cartoon was a parody of the political activity of two Porfirians, Barrón and Montes de Oca, portrayed as two-faced, because of their support then their opposition to the vice-presidential ambitions of General Bernardo Reyes.[112]

Judas's last will and testament became a popular broadsheet form printed by newspaper publishers. Ephemeral as they were, few examples survive. One testament that illustrates the humor remains from a somewhat later period (the mid-1920s), but demonstrates a printed Judas Day jest.

Testament of Judas Iscariot
To special and political friends
I leave the following property:

. . . .

To my friends at the public market
I leave in the care of each one
an umbrella to protect against the rain
that comes through the municipal market roof.

. . . .

I leave to my friend Lupe
an estimable person
my hat and my cane
in order to be able to attend
all the little meetings of
the great federal government.

. . . .

To my friend Chico Luis
commissioner and impresario
I leave my old wardrobe
in case he becomes a consul
or secretary in his country
or in mine.[113]

Broadsheets such as this and other printed forms of the Judas effigies preserved the tradition, giving renewed vitality to the sarcastic voice of the people describing the government bureaucrat, the government's activities, and the merchants.

Popular culture in Mexico has a strongly conservative nature as it echoes the folk tradition that might otherwise disappear. Separating the folk heritage from the consciously manufactured popular media seems a feckless enterprise; remembering that the carnivalesque humor has been embedded there gives tribute to its resiliency. These celebrations are remnants of the events that once had such great followings in the cities, especially the capital city. At the turn of the century, all of the characteristics showed clearly that the Judas festival was a Mexican expression of the tradition of folk humor, of grotesque realism, and of carnivalesque spirit that was a heritage of medieval society transported to Mexico. It was a popular heritage that was the antithesis of modern life.

This world portrayed so vividly by Rabelais appeared vulgar, rude, and threatening to the Mexican elites, schooled in the Enlightenment, then Liberalism, and finally the Progress adumbrated by Positivism. Folk humor appeared to be nothing more than mockery, its playful ambivalence nothing more than disorder. The social reversals, through impudence and parody, threatened both the order and the progress demanded by modern Mexico.

If Judas effigies and figures could not be totally eliminated, they were at least diffused, both literally and figuratively, by making them into toys; the festivities were almost completely reduced to quaint displays for tourists or relegated to the countryside in indigenous communities. The upper-class Mexican beginning in the 1890s celebrated the end of Holy Week with bicycle parades, the individual's appropriation of technology, and with baseball games, the leisure activity for the modern spectator. The folk tradition, represented by the Judases, could not stand against modernization and its components of technology and leisure.

Changing Holy Saturday from a Judas festival to a bicycle parade dramatically illustrated the insistence in Porfirian Mexico on order. The city council's gratuitous concern about the fire danger caused by Judas burnings revealed apprehension about the dangerous individualism of festivals. A parade expressed order, discipline, and regimented behavior that displayed society divided into ranks and responding immediately to authority. Judas burnings and other traditional fiestas stressed temporary freedom of action, dress, speech, and assembly in a kind of theater of civil rights and social equality.[114]

Afterword

Judases and bicycles served during the Porfirian years as the most powerful symbols of the traditional syncretic European and indigenous culture
that emerged during the colonial period and of the self-consciously Positivistic culture of progress. Caught in the middle were the old Liberals
who had emerged in mid-century Mexico and had fought against the dictatorship of Antonio López de Santa Anna, the French intervention, and
the extensive influence of the church. These Liberals, typified by Benito
Juárez, had planned to acculturate the rural, essentially Indian population with a secular, capitalistic, and *Mexican* civics. These men had not
envisioned the Porfirian dictatorship. Those who wanted the survival of
these Liberal ideals rejected the Díaz system built on foreign capital,
foreign philosophies, working arrangements with the church, and self-
rationalizations for profits and huge estates. Few other Mexicans cared or
listened to Liberal grouching, but before their disappearance the Liberals
rebuked the changing society of Mexico with satire of both the traditional
culture and the emergent one. They believed in the power of the press
and the good sense of literate men, so much of their critique appeared in
newspapers, such as *El Hijo de Ahuizote*.

Pilgrims to the Guadalupine festival of 1898 appeared in one newspaper cartoon. In one panel Indians in native costumes danced along the
path to the basilica above the caption "The Pious Indians of Old"; "The

Pious Indians of the Present" showed a group of Porfirian bicyclists, with top hats and caps, waxed moustaches and combed beards, on the same road to the shrine. Both groups affirmed an allegiance to the church, opposed by the Liberals, by their participation in the festivities of Mexico's most revered holy image.[1]

Other cartoons and stories mocked both the indigenous population and the modernizers. An unsuspected perspicacity appeared in a series of cartoons attempting to identify Porfirian modernization as a policy leading to the emergence of women in new roles in society. These sketches tried to make oblique hints at an effeminate regime because it fostered female activities. Many of the parodies correctly connected the bicycle with the changing dress, behavior, and outlook of women, while attacking women's continued dependence on the church and the man of the house. "Did you know, Juan," asked one jest, "that the Pope has permitted priests to use bicycles?" "Don't tell me man!" "Exactly." "Well, I'm not going to allow my wife to make confession."[2] The association between the bicycle and the modern woman clearly accounted for the snap decision to keep the wife from confessing. Other jeering comments reflected the same association. In cartoons of the 1890s women riders are almost always drawn with short, knee-length skirts and long socks, revealing the exact form of their legs and ankles, a view that modesty would not allow even though the legs were covered. One such cyclist said, "This bicycle cost me 250 pesos. Do you think, neighbor, that there might be a cheaper one?" "Yes, neighbor, the one that your boyfriend buys you, because it will be free."[3] Still another cartoon, entitled, "What Will Probably Happen in the Twentieth Century — The Emancipation of the Woman Will Probably Be a Reality" revealed what was a dreaded prospect: the cartoonist drew a woman dressed in an army officer's uniform and carrying a cigarette.[4]

The possibility of women moving out from the home into greater public visibility provoked satirical comment that females might enter male occupations. In the 1890s, a woman bullfighter appeared, resulting in a cartoon describing her activities on the day of the corrida: the matadora sewed children's clothes, went to the market, dressed for the bullfight, fought her three bulls, was hurt by the last one, but managed to recover, and in the last two panels, dragged home the last bull and made bull-meat tamales. The cover of this issue of *El Hijo de Ahuizote* showed a successful woman bullfighter who received the crowd's acclamation as it showered her with cooking pans, a sewing machine, and other household goods.[5]

The Porfirian modernism represented by its bicycles, which offered only one of several new opportunities for women, called forth criticism from the Liberals, who parodied the dictator's regime by mocking its symbols. "An End of the Century Duel" showed two dandies fencing from the seats of their bicycles. One finally claimed victory after a series of thrusts and parries by the quick stab that punctured the other's front tire.[6] In the same sarcastic manner, another caricature listed the benefits offered by the bicycle to Mexican citizens. One should ride a bicycle, according to the artist, for enjoyment, for the amusement of the people in the streets, to become thinner, in order to pay the wages of a quack pill pusher, to pay a debt at the end of the month (by giving the creditor a ride), for love, and for the enjoyment of children.[7] Not one of these reasons seemed worthy to the Liberals.

The bicycle as a metaphor for the dictator's policy of modernism remained a safe target of criticism. The Liberals at times left restraint behind, with a parody of specific Porfirian policies. One that drew their ire was the program to dress Mexico in Western clothes. Again the cartoonist's pen came into play. One series attacked the mandatory dress of streetcar conductors as "uniforms brought by Yankee enterprise," showing even the mules that pulled the cars wearing caps and jackets and, in the last frame, picturing the conductors and mules wearing obligatory sunglasses.[8] Of course, the Liberals made extensive criticism of the working arrangement that Díaz developed with the hierarchy of the Catholic church. The victory over the clergy in the War of the Reform (1858–1861) and the expulsion of the French puppet regime (1867) seemed hollow victories.[9]

Those who became bicycle riders expressed an ambivalence toward modernization. Their machine seemed to be the miracle of technology; it also offered them the means to escape the crowded, dirty, congested, and dangerous modern city. The bicycle became a vehicle to flee progress and its consequences.[10] The Cyclist Union Club and other bicycle groups sponsored excursions into the country. Individuals often pedaled into the countryside, either consciously or subsconsciously escaping to bucolic surroundings. A few riders found more adventure than they wanted outside town. T. Philip Terry and a companion, in 1897, took a bicycle trip from Mexico City to Acapulco. As they neared Guerrero, a bandit gang galloped after them and attempted to lasso the cyclists. Both riders crouched low over the handlebars so the lasso would not fit over them; still Terry felt one lariat "as hot as any live electric-light wire" hit his forehead, burn its way down his back taking his cap with it, and ring his camara that was hooked behind his seat. The bandit got away with the camera.[11] But most Mexicans found the calm, restful country that they sought on their excursions. These escapes from the city may represent the first stirrings of a critique of modern life and what it was doing to Mexico.

Doubts about modernity did not modify the conclusion to push traditional culture out of sight, if not out of existence. From the time of independence in 1821, the political and social leaders had determined the kinds of public celebrations that would be allowed. Emperor Iturbide's congress had Mariano José Zúñiga y Ontiveros make a study of appropriate religious and civil holidays. As a result of his inquiry, the Congress issued a decree August 16, 1822, that identified ecclesiastical holidays, including the celebration in honor of both the Virgin of Remedies and the Virgin of Guadalupe, and established civic holidays—in honor of the nation's patriotic dead, the first day of the empire, the triumphal entry of Iturbide's army into Mexico City, and other imperial anniversaries.[12] Antonio López de Santa Anna when he became president established a holiday of national sacrifice on the anniversary of the day he lost his lower leg to a French cannon shell.[13] The Liberals, led by Juárez, altered the calendar of public celebrations and the Porfirians continued the practice. The latter moved against popular festivals such as passion plays and Judas burnings as threats to public order. Then the Porfirians occupied the sites of these festivities with celebrations of their own. In the case of the burnings, the elite outlawed them in the Zócalo and then forced them away from the main streets of the center of the capital by laws against fire hazards. Moreover, the Porfirians undermined the sacred character of Holy Week, which diminished the contrast provided by the Judases. The elite sponsored fiestas of flowers on Holy Friday, making one of the most sorrowful days in the Catholic religion a happy day of amusement. By the 1890s this Flowery Parade seized the major streets of the capital.[14] Other cities in Mexico followed, and one report specifically explained the purpose of such parades. The better citizens of Mazatlán in 1896 decided to sponsor an exhibition similar to the Battle of Flowers in Mexico City, with the object of weaning "the natives from the coarser sports."[15] Deprived of the sacred celebrations that provided the solemnity that called forth the hilarity of the Judas burnings, the folk tradition became trivial.

Nevertheless, all these events—Judas burnings, flowery parades, and Carnival—provided an opportunity to express the attitudes of the people and to mobilize them as well. Celebrations such as these, called two-dimensional events by anthropologist Abner Cohen, register changes in the culture in response to political developments. In the absence of other populist organizations, traditional celebrations establish social boundaries, communicate group consciousness, and challenge or endorse authority; thus they serve as the seedbed for populist political campaigns. The events remain pleasurable because they remain ambiguous, both political and cultural expressions at the same instant; they serve as metaphors of people's mentality. The substitution of a parade for a frolic expressed the Porfirian policies of order and progress so widely accepted by Mexicans of the upper ranks.[16]

Whether people wanted parades or festivals, the Díaz government controlled the location—the Zócalo and the neighboring streets—for these displays of symbolic actions in Mexico's face-to-face, nonliterate society. Modern administrators paved these public places, controlled traffic on them, and finally directed their use during holidays. This was just one more restraint on traditional society by modernizers. Curiously, and actually quite deliberately, Liberals transposed traditional oral-visual forms into printed formats, such as cartoon Judas burnings, while the Porfirians, on the other hand, wanted to eliminate what they regarded as retrograde behavior.[17] And modernity seemed to succeed.

The ground swell of modernity tossed up a few elite Mexicans who became increasingly troubled by their modern Mexico and began seeking alternatives. Several flirted with the Liberals, who trailed after Ricardo Flores Magón down the blind alley that ended in the fiasco of an anarchist revolt in Baja California.[18] Others toyed with church-sponsored reform efforts through Catholic social action.[19] Only piecemeal critiques and solutions appeared until after the fall of the Díaz government in 1911. Andrés Molina Enríquez, who swelled with pride at his country's progress, nevertheless wrote *Los grandes problemas nacionales* (The Great

National Problems) in the last decade of the dictatorship to call for a widespread program of reform altering the landholding patterns of the countryside. He recognized that agrarian troubles threatened to sweep away the other results of progress. José Limantour, the brilliant Porfirian minister of finance, understood at least dimly that foreign ownership of the nation's industry and transport threatened political autonomy and he initiated a program to bring about Mexican ownership of the railroad system.[20]

Unrest blunted criticism of the dictatorship from most members of the elite. Agrarian disturbances served as a constant preview of the countryside without the iron fist of order. Striking workers at the Cananea Copper Mines and the Rio Branco textile Mills received some sympathy when the troops fired into their demonstrations, but it was sympathy mixed with fear of these everyday Mexicans. To frock-coat Mexicans it seemed laughable to discuss democracy for workers and peasants who for centuries had been considered backward, vile, drunken, and, in the first decade of the new century more than ever, violent.[21]

And yet — a dreamer appeared.

The Porfirian persuasion that made French culture and philosophies fashionable sent the sons of elite families to Paris for education. The stunning achievements of American industry in the United States and Mexico lured other young Mexicans to universities north of the border. Neither industrial progress nor Positivism in its numerous guises stood unchallenged in either France or the United States in the last decade of the century. Mexico's neighbor had a host of reformers who turned to the government to exorcise the evils of modern society. An even greater variety of challengers to progress appeared in France, proposing solutions that ranged from workers' revolution to prayer. The Christian Humanism movement drew on the writings of Karl Christian Friedrich Krause, who opposed the social homogenization that resulted from the centralization of government, the growth of the city, and the rise of the factory. Krause's precepts contradicted the visions of Auguste Comte[22] and they became the framework of the thinking of the young Sorbonne student from Coahuila, Mexico, Francisco I. Madero.

Perhaps the vastness of the arid expanse of his native Coahuila stretched the imagination of this short man with towering visions. The emptiness of the Mexican North makes man seem smaller, but cast a longer shadow. This served perhaps as a visual parable for Francisco—as small a man as he might have great influence. So he dreamed: preserve Porfirian progress by reversing political centralization, restoring regional differences through state sovereignty and local autonomy; bring peace to the countryside and the factory by recognizing the grievances of peasants and workers, admitting their properly elected representatives to serve in government. Restitution of lost land and reforms for labor could be accomplished—and none need fear these ordinary Mexicans who would benefit—if only authorities would awaken the dignity of everyday Mexicans by counting their votes.

To Madero democracy meant honest balloting and no reelection of officeholders. In grander terms, he believed that it promised the salvation of Porfirian economic gains, the expression of the popular will, and the end of the traditional strongmen who held office until unseated by revolution. Madero penned his political views in a treatise that fell just short of hagiography of the dictator. Madero's *La Sucesión presidencial en 1910* (The Presidential Succession in 1910) praised the economic development of the nation, the modernization of the transportation system, the spectacular success of exports, and the new international reputation achieved under Díaz. The author explained Mexico's cycles of progress and regression by the failure to develop any peaceful means of presidential transition—only twice before Díaz had the office of the chief executive been transferred without revolution. The solution, so easily overlooked because of its simplicity, Madero argued, was the installation of a genuine system of democracy.[23]

Porfirio Díaz and his counselors scoffed at Madero and his visions, and encouraged him in a back-handed way by doing nothing to suppress his activity until July 1910, when it had become too late. Madero seemed to be another court jester from the mold of Nicolás Zúñiga y Miranda, a harmless eccentric, who unsuccessfully predicted comets, earthquakes, floods, and other cataclysms. Tall and thin with a drooping moustache, he always dressed in a frock coat and a sombrero with a tall crown. When he announced his campaign for the presidency in 1896, he immediately became the choice of university students, who demonstrated in rallies throughout the city. Díaz responded without humor to this mock campaign and had the candidate jailed for inciting public disorder. The dictator reversed himself four years later, deciding that a fool as an opponent contributed to the fiction of democracy, and allowed Zúñiga y Miranda to campaign. Thus he became the classic jester, deflecting genuine criticism of the regime through laughter. The Porfirians did not see that with all his exaggerated posturing and puffery he caricatured the regime's politicians.[24] Thus Díaz allowed Madero, whom he saw as a second don Nicolás, to campaign across Mexico, organize a network of local political clubs and gain the admiration of his fellow Mexicans. When the dictator finally took him seriously, the organization that would drive him from office in less than a year had already been created. This dreamer encouraged the dreams of the Mexicans who still gathered at the bull ring, some to sit in the sun and some to sit in the shade.

Both the traditional society on the sunny side of the ring, those who customarily burned Judases, and the elite society on the shady side, who arrived at the ring by bicycle, hack, or perhaps even automobiles, came forward to push their interests during the opening created by the Madero revolution of 1910–1911. A bewildering number of revolutionary causes flourished under Francisco Madero, many of them contradictory and antagonistic, so that when the old dictator fled to Paris, the revolutionaries turned on each other. Madero's dream released the creative and the violent impulses of both the traditional and the modern cultures that shared Mexico, people who had once brushed shoulders on the street when Judas appeared at the Jockey Club.

Notes

Preface

1. Kurt Vonnegut, *Palm Sunday: An Autobiographical Collage* (New York: Dell, 1981), 299.
2. On fun as the inspiration of the arts, including history, see Ray Bradbury, "Day after Tomorrow: Why Science Fiction?" *Nation* (May 2, 1953): 366. He describes the kind of enjoyable literary life he lives, careening from one unexpected event to another, as "drunk, and in charge of a bicycle." (See the introduction to *The Stories of Ray Bradbury* (New York: Alfred A. Knopf, 1981.) This good fun led him to a fanciful Mars and me to Porfirian Mexico; no telling where it will beguile the reader.
3. Rhys Isaac, *The Transformation of Virginia* (Chapel Hill: University of North Carolina Press, 1982). Eugen Weber also made excellent use of outsiders' observations in *Peasants into Frenchmen: The Modernization of Rural France, 1870–1914* (Stanford: Stanford University Press, 1976).

Introduction

1. *Siglo XIX*, April 5, 1890.
2. Carlos Fuentes, *The Death of Artemio Cruz*, trans. Sam Hileman (New York: Farrar, Straus and Giroux, 1964), 122.

3. C. Bertie-Marriott, *Un Parisien au Mexique* (Paris: E. Dentu, Editeur, 1886), 65–69.

4. Frederick Billings, *Letters from Mexico 1859* (Woodstock, Vt.: Elm Tree Press, 1936), 20, 1–2.

5. December 22, 1876, cited in Donald F. Roberts, "Mining and Modernization: The Mexican Border States during the Porfiriato, 1876–1911" (Ph.D. dissertation, University of Pittsburgh, 1974), 1.

6. *New York Times,* Sept. 17, 1897.

7. David A. Wells, *Study of Mexico* (New York: D. Appleton and Company, 1887), 82.

8. Alfred Oscar Coffin, *Land without Chimneys; or, The Byways of Mexico* (Cincinnati: Editor Publishing Co., 1898), 124–25; *Mexican Herald,* Oct. 13, 1895.

9. The metaphor "the car of Mexican prosperity rolls along on silver dollar wheels" appeared frequently in the newspapers of the day; see, for example, *Mexican Herald,* Oct. 9, 1895.

10. A sampling of the discussion about the "wooden pavement" crisis can be found in *The Two Republics,* April 16 and August 16, 1888, and February 6, 1889, where the issues were summarized.

11. Laurence John Rohlfes, "Police and Penal Correction in Mexico City, 1876–1911: A Study of Order and Progress in Porfirian Mexico" (Ph.D. dissertation, Tulane University, 1983). This is an excellent study; see especially pp. 5–6, 19–26; the quotation is found on p. 126, and the discussion of the Arroyo case, pp. 59–64.

12. *Two Republics,* Dec. 15, 1874; May 5, 1886; Aug. 12, 1887; Jan. 5, 1888.

13. E. H. Blichfeldt, *A Mexican Journey* (New York: Thomas Y. Crowell Company, 1919), 114–15; Stanton Davis Kirkham, *Mexican Trails* (New York: G. P. Putnam's Sons, 1909), 30–31; see photograph "Mexico City, Dec. 1921," in Rudolf Schuller Collection, Latin American Library, Tulane University, Box 360.

14. Mexico. Dirección General de Estadística. *Estadísticas Sociales del Porfiriato, 1887–1910* (Mexico: Secretaría de Economía, 1956), 9.

The Porfirian Persuasion: Sport
and Recreation in Modern Mexico

1. Jacqueline A. Rice attempted to study the *Científicos* as the group of intellectuals who favored scientific development. She soon discovered that no discrete

group of positivists in Mexico could be precisely identified. Her research confirms my hunch that we might best call this plan for progress a persuasion. See Rice, "The Porfirian Political Elite: Life Patterns of the Delegates to the 1892 Union Liberal Convention" (Ph.D. dissertation, University of California, Los Angeles, 1979), 1–2.

2. Trans. Peter G. Earle (Austin: University of Texas Press, 1962), 15–44.

3. Enrique Guarner, *Historia del torreo en Mexico* (Mexico: Editorial Diana, 1979), 31–34; Irving A. Leonard, *Baroque Times in Old Mexico* (Ann Arbor: University of Michigan Press, 1959), 14–17.

4. Louis A. Zurcher, Jr., and Arnold Meadow, "On Bullfights and Baseball: An Example of Interaction of Social Institutions," in *Sport in the Sociocultural Process*, ed. Marie Hart and Susan Birrell (3rd ed.; Dubuque, Iowa: Wm. C. Brown Company, 1981), 654–68; Alfred R. Conkling, *Appleton's Guide to Mexico* (New York: D. Appleton & Co., 1891), 125–26.

5. Zurcher and Meadow, "On Bullfights," 660–68.

6. For a discussion of the way in which athletes display cultural values, see Susan Birrell, "Sport as Ritual: Interpretations from Durkheim to Goffman," *Social Forces* 60, no. 2 (Dec., 1981), 354–76.

7. J. R. Flippin, *Sketches from the Mountains of Mexico* (Cincinnati: Standard Publishing Company, 1889), 260; Thomas A. Janvier, *The Mexican Guide* (New York: Scribner's, 1888), xviii; William Seymour Edwards, *On the Mexican Highlands, with a Passing Glimpse of Cuba* (Cincinnati: Press of Jennings and Graham, 1906), 76.

8. *Mexican Herald,* Oct. 2, 1895.

9. Charles M. Flandrau, *Viva Mexico!* (Urbana: University of Illinois Press, 1964), 69n; E. H. Blichfeldt, *A Mexican Journey* (New York: Thomas Y. Crowell Company, 1919), 97; *Two Republics,* June 1, 1890.

10. On the "flowery war," see: Bertram Grosvenor Goodhue, *Mexican Memories: The Record of a Slight Sojourn below the Yellow Rio Grande* (New York: George M. Allen Co., 1892), 96; *Mexican Herald,* Sept. 14, 1895; on the Cuauhtémotzin monument, unveiled on August 21, 1887, in honor of Cuauhtémoc, see, Janvier, *Guide,* xviii–xix.

11. Clifford Geertz, "Deep Play: Notes on the Balinese Cockfight," in *Sport in the Sociocultural Process,* ed. Marie Hart and Susan Birrell (3rd ed.; Dubuque, Iowa: Wm. C. Brown Company, 1981), 624–53; Birrell, "Sport as Ritual," 354–76.

12. For the Doubleday myth, see Harold Peterson, *The Man Who Invented Base-*

ball (New York: Scribner's, 1969); for Doubleday in Mexico, see *Terry's Guide to Mexico*, 8th ed. (New York: Scribner's, 1972), 145n.

13. *Two Republics,* Oct. 16, 1869. Cricket was firmly established in England by this time. The first recorded match was played in 1697; the most famous club, at Hambleton, was founded in 1719; and the English championships between seventeen counties were first contested in 1864. (See "Cricket," in *The Official Associated Press Sports Almanac 1975* [New York: Dell, 1975], 234).

14. Harry Wright, *A Short History of Golf in Mexico and the Mexico City Country Club* (New York: Privately printed, 1938), 23.

15. *Two Republics,* Oct. 17, 31, 1868; Jan. 1, 1869.

16. *Two Republics,* Nov. 7, 1868.

17. *Two Republics,* Nov. 26, Dec. 12, 1869; Feb. 12, 1870.

18. Clarke first issued this warning in *Two Republics,* Oct. 16, 1869.

19. *Mexican Herald,* Sept. 29, 1895. For the origin of soccer in Mexico, see Juan Cid y Mullet, *Libro de oro del futbol mexicano* (Mexico, 1982), and for the British domination in the town of Pachuca, see Robert W. Randall, *Real del Monte: A British Mining Venture in Mexico* (Austin: University of Texas Press, 1972).

20. *Two Republics,* Oct. 5, 22, Nov. 3, 1889.

21. *Mexican Herald,* Sept. 17, 29, Oct. 6, Nov. 4, 1895.

22. Charles C. Cumberland, *Mexico: The Struggle for Modernity* (New York: Oxford University Press, 1968), 227–29.

23. *Two Republics,* Aug. 3, 1882.

24. *Two Republics,* Feb. 18 and Aug. 5, 1883. The elder Clarke relinquished editorship to his son and his son's partner two years earlier.

25. *Two Republics,* Feb. 3, 20, 1886.

26. *Two Republics,* July 1, 23, 1887; also see report, July 13, 1888. Nemesio Guillot, a Cuban who had studied abroad, brought the game to his home in 1864, and two years later United States merchant marines challenged dockworkers in Matanzas to a contest. Baseball spread quickly throughout the island. See Eric Wagner, "Baseball in Cuba," *Journal of Popular Culture* 18, no. 1 (Summer 1984), 113–20.

27. *Two Republics,* July 26, 1887.

28. *Two Republics,* Aug. 5, 11, 13, 1887.

29. *Two Republics,* Aug. 2, 9, 16, 30, Sept. 7, Nov. 22, Oct. 18, 25, 1887; Oct. 24, 30, 1888.

30. *Two Republics,* Oct. 12, 1888.

31. *Two Republics,* Oct. 26, 29, Nov. 1, 2, 5, 10, 12, 19, 26, Dec. 3, 17, 18, 24, 31, 1889; Jan. 7, 21; Feb. 4, 1890.

32. Ramon Eduardo Ruiz, "The People of Sonora and Yankee Capitalists," unpublished manuscript, chapter 12, pp. 24–25, citing Teodoro O. Paz, *Guaymas de ayer* (Guaymas, 1974), 42 and 77, and Fernando A. Galaz, *Dejaron huella en el Hermosillo de ayer y hoy* (Hermosillo, 1971), 630.

33. Interview with Victor Niemeyer, former United States consul, Monterrey, Nuevo León, Feb. 24, 1982; Norman S. Hayner, "Mexicans at Play—A Revolution," *Sociology and Social Research* 38 (1953): 80; obituary of Glenn, stationed at Guanajuato, 1912–1917, *New York Times,* Dec. 9, 1962.

34. *Mexican Herald,* Sept. 30, Oct. 13, Nov. 25, and Dec. 21, 1895; Gonzalez Navarro, *Vida social,* 713.

35. *Mexican Herald,* Oct. 7, Dec. 21 and 30, 1895.

36. *Mexican Herald,* Sept. 29, Oct. 7, Nov. 16, and Dec. 30, 1895.

37. *Mexican Herald,* Sept. 12, 1895; William Henry Bishop, *Old Mexico and Her Lost Provinces: A Journey in Mexico, Southern California, and Arizona by Way of Cuba* (New York: Harper and Brothers, 1883), 20.

38. *El Imparcial* (Mexico City), Nov. 16, 1903.

39. Juan José Gonzáles F., "Aportaciónes para la historia de Veracruz," *El Dictamen* (Veracruz), Feb. 15, 1963; "Un Viejo aguilista en mala situación," ibid., Sept. 4, 1959.

40. Moisés González Navarro, *El Porfiriato: La vida social,* vol. 4 of *Historia moderna de Mexico,* ed. Daniel Cosío Villegas (Mexico: Editorial Hermes, 1955–1970), 713–14.

41. Hy Turkin and S. C. Thompson, *The Official Encyclopedia of Baseball* (7th ed.; New York: A. S. Barnes and Company, 1974), 503.

42. The trip was covered with daily special reports in the *Chicago Tribune,* March 3–18, 1907.

43. *Chicago Tribune,* March 15, 1907.

44. Mary Kay Vaughan, *The State, Education, and Social Class in Mexico, 1880–1928* (DeKalb: Northern Illinois University Press, 1982), 89, 258–59. The statutes of the Universidad Popular defined its purpose as developing the culture of the Mexican people and indicated several methods (e.g., lectures) to accomplish it. Sport was not specifically identified, but was promoted by several faculty. See John S. Innes, "The Universidad Popular Mexicana," *The Americas* 30, no. 1 (July 1973): 110–23; Raymond S. Portillo, "Here's How Mexico

Shows Its Kinship for the Rest of Us," *Sporting News,* Dec. 25, 1919, p. 7.

45. Eugene C. Murdock, *Ban Johnson: Czar of Baseball* (Westport, Conn: Green-wood Press, 1982), 193–97.

46. Raul Carnica, "Chalo Cordero es el auténtico pionero del softbol Mexicano," *La Prensa* (Mexico City), Dec. 6, 1959.

47. José Álvarez del Villar, *Men and Horses of Mexico: History and Practice of "Charrería"* (Mexico: Ediciones Lara, S.A., 1979), 21; Eduardo Muhlenfordt, *Versuch einer getreuen Schilderung der Republik Mexiko,* ed. Ferdinand Anders (1844; reprint, Graz, Austria: Akademische Druck u. Verlagsanstal, 1969), 1:312–13.

48. *Two Republics,* Dec. 4, 1869.

49. *Two Republics,* June 7, 1876.

50. Robert S. Barrett, *The Standard Guide to the City of Mexico and Vicinity* (City of Mexico: Modern Mexico Publishing Company, 1901), 65–66. In the United States, as a comparison, the South Carolina Jockey Club, the first, was formed in 1735.

51. *Two Republics,* Jan. 12, April 6, 1882.

52. *Two Republics,* April 16, 1869.

53. *Diccionario Porrúa,* 2:1756, 1763; *Two Republics,* April 30, May 4, 1882.

54. *Two Republics,* April 30, May 7, 11, 14, 1882.

55. *Two Republics,* Nov. 2, 5, 9, 12, 19, 1882.

56. *Two Republics,* Jan. 28, 1883.

57. *Two Republics,* May 25, 1883.

58. *Diccionario Porrúa,* 1:67, 715, 963, and 1155.

59. *Two Republics,* Mar. 8, 1883.

60. *Two Republics,* May 12, 1882; Nov. 8, 23, and Dec. 10, 1883; April 20, 1884; *El Siglo XIX,* April 18, 1892.

61. Leaflet, "La Casa de los Azulejos," distributed by Sanborns, throughout Mexico City.

62. González Navarro, *Vida social,* 711.

63. Matt W. Ransom Collection, Southern Historical Collection, University of North Carolina, Box 39, file 465, E. C. Butler to M. W. Ransom, June 17, 1895; Wallace Gillpatrick, *The Man Who Likes Mexico* (New York: Century Co., 1911), 284; *Mexican Herald,* Nov. 1, 4, 10, 11, 17, and Dec. 12, 1895.

64. *Mexican Herald,* Oct. 2, 6, 15, 16, Nov. 12 and 16, 1895.

65. González Navarro, *Vida social,* 711; *Mexican Herald,* April 17, 1896.

66. For a discussion of horse racing and gambling, see T. H. Breen, "Horses and

Gentlemen: The Cultural Significance of Gambling among the Gentry of Virginia," *William and Mary Quarterly* 3rd Ser., 34, no. 2 (April 1974), 239–57; *Mexican Herald,* Nov. 11, 17, 20, Dec. 2 and 9, 1895.

67. Celso Enríquez, *El deporte antiguo mexicano y el deporte de nuestro tiempo* (Mexico: Litográfica Machado, S.A., n.d.), 19–21.

68. Ralph Hancock, *The Magic Land: Mexico* (New York: Coward-McCann, Inc., 1948), 227–28.

69. *Mexican Herald,* Sept. 23, 1895.

70. *Two Republics,* Feb. 14, Mar. 4, 1868; "Spectator to Editor," Mar. 7, 1868. Another fencing academy opened in 1874; see *ibid.,* May 24, 1874. Pompard continued his academy until his death in 1896 (see *Mexican Herald,* Jan. 28, 1896).

71. Norbert Elias and Eric Dunning, "The Quest for Excitement in Unexciting Societies," in *The Cross-Cultural Analysis of Sport and Games,* ed. Gunther Lüschen (Champaign, Ill.: Stipies Publishing Co., 1978), 31–51.

72. David A. Wells, *Study of Mexico* (New York: D. Appleton and Company, 1887), 69.

73. The outstanding general history of Mexico is Michael C. Meyer and William L. Sherman, *The Course of Mexican History,* 2nd ed. (New York: Oxford University Press, 1982). See pages 313–402 for Mexico's nineteenth-century problems.

74. *Two Republics,* April 23, 1887, and Feb. 3, 1891.

75. *Mexican Herald,* Nov. 25, 1895; Roberto Berdecio and Stanley Appelbaum, *Posada's Popular Mexican Prints* (New York: Dover Publishing, 1972), 90, print #154. The Posada is not identified, but internal evidence, e.g., a black vs. a white boxer, makes it apparent that it refers to the Clarke-Smith fight.

76. *Mexican Herald,* Oct. 31, Nov. 6, 30, Dec. 3 and 6, 1895.

77. *Two Republics,* Mar. 31, 1896; see cartoon of Billy Clark (*sic*) making everyone else look like weaklings in *El Hijo del Ahuizote,* Jan. 16, 1898.

78. Jack London, "The Mexican," in *Sporting Blood: Selections from Jack London's Greatest Sports Writings,* ed. Howard Lochtman (Novato, Calif.: Presidio Press, 1981), 173–91.

79. *Diccionario Porrúa,* 2:1660–61.

80. T. Philip Terry, *Terry's Mexico: Handbook for Travellers,* 2nd ed. (London: Gay and Hancock, Ltd., 1909), 463–64.

81. *Diccionario Porrúa,* 2:1913.

82. Howard Conkling, *Mexico and the Mexicans; or, Notes of Travel in the Winter*

and Spring of 1883 (New York: Taintor Brothers, Merrill & Co., 1883), 178.

83. *New York Times,* August 20, 1894.

84. Conkling, *Mexico and the Mexicans,* 180–88; the quotations respectively come from p. 182 and p. 180.

85. Bishop, *Old Mexico,* 175.

86. Ibid., 176–83.

87. Janvier, *The Mexican Guide* (New York: Scribner's, 1888), 384–85.

88. *Mexican Herald,* Nov. 1, 4, 5, 1895. Admiral Carey Brenton of the Mexican navy also made the trip.

89. Blichfeldt, *A Mexican Journey,* 200–201.

90. *Terry's Mexico,* 463.

91. Edmund Otis Harvey, "Mountain Climbing in Mexico," *Outing* 52, no. 1 (April 1908), 85–95.

92. *New York Times,* Aug. 20, 1894.

93. Michael Ritchie, "Scaling the Heights—Then and Now: The Passage to Popocatépetl," *Americas* (Sept.–Oct., 1983), 23–31.

94. *Two Republics,* Mar. 24, 1875. For a discussion of this interest in the Canadian Rockies, see Edward Carrell and Jon Whyte, *Rocky Mountain Madness: A Bittersweet Romance* (Banff: Altitude Publishing, 1982), esp. p. 7.

95. "Velocipede Notes," *Scientific American* 20 (May 1869), 343; Norman L. Dunham, "The Bicycle Era in American History" (Ph.D. dissertation, Harvard University, 1956), 159; *Two Republics,* April 21, July 3, 1869. Silvestre Terrazas, *El Ciclismo: Manual de velocipedia* (Chihuahua: Tip. de Silvestre Terrazas, [1896]), 22.

96. Terrazas, *El Cyclismo,* 24; *New York Times,* Jan. 25 and Feb. 29, 1880.

97. Terrazas, *El Cyclismo,* 24; *New York Times,* Jan. 25 and Feb. 29, 1880; *Two Republics,* Mar. 18, 1884; May 1, Aug. 5, Sept. 22, Oct. 4, 1888; *Mexican Herald,* Sept. 29, 1895; *El Financiero,* Mar. 21, 1885.

98. *Mexican Herald,* Sept. 23, 29, Nov. 13, 21, and Dec. 1, 1895; González Navarro, *Vida social,* 717.

99. *Mexican Herald,* Oct. 18, 1895.

100. *Mexican Herald,* April 16, 1896; *New York Times,* Jan. 9, 1895. "Dute" Cabanne endured a two-year suspension (reduced from a life-time ban) when he was discovered conspiring with Fred Titus and Charles Murphy to fix the three premier races on the U.S. professional circuit in the summer of 1895. E. F. Leonart rode a mile in 1 minute 35 seconds, beating the time of the champion race horse Salvator, settling the question of speed in favor of the

machine. See Robert A. Smith, *A Social History of the Bicycle: Its Early Life and Times in America* (New York: American Heritage Press, 1975), 143, 157–58.

101. *New York Times,* Mar. 6, 1895.

102. *New York Times,* Mar. 9, 11, 1895.

103. Terrazas, *El Cyclismo,* 29.

104. "Cyclist to Editor," *Mexican Herald,* Oct. 26, 1895.

105. Allen Guttmann, *From Ritual to Record: The Nature of Modern Sports* (New York: Columbia University Press, 1978), 15–55, discusses these attributes of modern society and sport. A discussion of some of these characteristics in Mexico is the substance of Hugo Hiriart, *El universo de Posada: Estética de la obsolescencia,* vol. 8 of *Memoria y olvido: Imagenes de Mexico* (Mexico: Secretaría de Educación Publica, 1982).

106. *Mexican Herald,* Oct. 15, Nov. 5, 13, Dec. 2, 9, 18, 1895. On U.S. bicycle exports to Mexico, see *U.S. Census Report, X, 12th Census, 1900: Manufactures,* Part IV: *Special Reports on Selected Industries* (Washington, D.C.: Government Printing Office, 1900), 335. For a comparison of the impact of the bicycle in the United States, see Dunham, "The Bicycle Era in American History"; Smith, *Social History of the Bicycle; Mexican Herald,* Dec. 8, 10, 1895.

107. *Mexican Herald,* Dec. 23, 1895; Terrazas, *El Ciclismo,* 29, 31.

108. Smith, *Social History of the Bicycle,* 19.

109. Pope was one of the fathers of the American bicycle industry; see Smith, *Social History of the Bicycle,* 8–12, 18–19, 36–40, 207–9; *Mexican Herald,* Nov. 24, 1895.

110. *Mexican Herald,* Oct. 20 and Nov. 20, 1895.

111. *Mexican Herald,* editorial, Dec. 9, 1895.

112. *Mexican Herald,* Dec. 8, 1895.

113. *Mexican Herald,* Sept. 20, 1895.

114. *Mexican Herald,* Nov. 7, 1895. There was also an international curiosity about bicycling in Mexico that was satisfied in part with articles such as T. Philip Terry, "In Aztec Land Awheel," *Outing* 23, no. 6 (Mar. 1894), 461–63, and Terry's "My Ride to Acapulco: A Cycling Adventure in Mexico," *Outing* 29, no. 6 (Mar. 1897), 593–96.

115. *Mexican Herald,* Sept. 29, 1895.

116. *Mexican Herald,* Nov. 16, 1895.

117. *Mexican Herald,* Oct. 15, 1895; *Mexican Financier,* Oct. 15, 1895.

118. *Mexican Herald,* Oct. 20, 1895; Sept. 28, 1895; "Editorial," Dec. 9, 1895; Oct. 15, 1895.

119. *Two Republics,* Jan. 21, 1891.

120. *Mexican Herald,* Dec. 7 and 8, 1895.

121. *Mexican Herald,* Dec. 19, 1895.

122. *Siglo XIX,* April 14, 1892. These rules were reissued; see *Mexican Herald,* Sept. 28, 1895.

123. *Mexican Herald,* Sept. 28, 1895.

124. Terrazas, *El Cyclismo,* 39–40, 49, 51.

125. *Ibid.,* 32–38, esp. 39.

126. *Ibid.,* 44.

127. *Mexican Herald,* Sept. 22 and Oct. 5, 1895.

128. *Mexican Herald,* Jan. 19, Feb. 19, 1896.

129. *Mexican Herald,* Feb. 5, 1896.

130. Fernando Rosenzweig, "La Industria," in *La Vida económica,* vol. 1 of *Historia moderna,* ed. Daniel Cosío Villegas (Mexico: Editorial Hermes, 1955–1970), 1: 467.

131. Information on the 1896 season comes from the Sport Information Directors, University of Missouri and University of Texas. The Missouri information includes a story by Joe Pollack of the *St. Louis Post-Dispatch* written for the September 15, 1879, Mizzou football program.

132. On the restrictions against Sunday athletics in the United States, see J. Thomas Jable, "Sunday Sport Comes to Pennsylvania: Professional Baseball and Football Triumph over the Commonwealth's Archaic Blue Laws," *Research Quarterly* 47 (Oct. 1976), 357–65; *Mexican Herald,* Dec. 26, 1896. The Texas Sport Information Office incorrectly recorded the score as 18 to 4 for the game in Monterrey.

133. *Mexican Herald,* Dec. 16, 17, 24, 1896.

134. *Mexican Herald,* Dec. 28, 1896. Neither the University of Texas nor the University of Missouri records indicated that two football games were played in Mexico City. But the game was reported in the *News & Observer* (Raleigh, NC), Dec. 30, 1896.

135. *Mexican Herald,* Dec. 29, 30, 1896.

136. White is quoted in the Pollack article, and the Texas fan in the information from the University of Texas sport information office.

137. *Mexican Herald,* Dec. 30, 1896.

138. Sport Information Office, University of Missouri.

139. González Navarro, *Vida social*, 714.

140. *Mexican Herald*, Dec. 28, 30, 1896.

141. *Mexican Herald*, Dec. 29, 30, 1896, carried reports from the Mexico City press; *El Hijo del Ahuizote*, Dec. 12, 1897.

142. Bishop, *Old Mexico*, 112.

143. *Mexican Herald*, Nov. 17, 20 and Dec. 9, 1895. Vogel Beer was brewed by the Germania brewery. The *Herald* published a weekly Puebla letter on sporting activities there. A British merchant imported the first Clydesdales in 1825 to make a grand appearance in the promenade on the Paseo de Bucareli. His intentions were frustrated for several months because Mexicans wanted to stone the horses, a foot taller and a hundred pounds heavier than their animals, as heretic beasts. The merchant kept them at the Hacienda San Antonio (present-day community of Tlalpán) until January 17, 1826, when he had them blessed on Saint Anthony's Day. As Christian horses, they then began to draw the merchant's ostentatious coach on his drives down Bucareli. See Alan Probert, "The Heretic Horses: The Introduction of the Clydesdale Breed into Mexico," *Journal of the West* 9, no. 4 (Oct. 1970), 519–36.

144. The comment on Spanish occupations comes from Charles M. Flandrau, *Viva Mexico!* (Urbana: University of Illinois Press, 1964), 153. The fronton was located near the Cuauhtemoc statue and the Café Colón. See *Mexican Herald*, Nov. 10, Dec. 12, 15, 26, and 30, 1895.

145. *Mexican Herald*, Sept. 13, 17, 29, 30, Oct. 6, and Nov. 4, 1895.

146. *Mexican Herald*, Dec. 3, 9, 16, 20, and 28, 1895. Ross's activities in the United States before coming to Mexico can be found in "World-Renowned Champion Amazon: Jaguarina," paper presented at the North American Society for Sport History, Monte Alto, Penn., May 30, 1983, by Lynne Emery of California State Polytechnic University, Pomona. See her abstract in *Proceedings, 1983*, North American Society for Sport History, p. 33.

147. Blichfeldt, *A Mexican Journey*, 110; Conkling, *Mexico and the Mexicans*, 72; Mary Barton, *Impressions of Mexico with Brush and Pen* (New York: Macmillan, 1911), 61; *Mexican Herald*, Oct. 2, 14, 28, Dec. 9, and 23, 1895.

148. C. Howard Hopkins, *History of the Y.M.C.A. in North America* (New York: Association Press, 1951), 236, 349, 512–13, 675, 678, and 697; *News & Observer* (Raleigh, N.C.), Jan., 1902.

149. Leopoldo Salazar Viniégra, "Cuarenta y cinco años exemplares de la Y.M.C.A." *Excelsior*, Nov. 1, 1947. The YMCA established its International Training School in Springfield, Mass., in 1885. See John Richards Betts,

America's Sporting Heritage, 1850–1950 (Reading, Mass.: Addison-Wesley Publishing Company, 1974), 110; and Hopkins, *YMCA*, 251–70.

150. *Mexican Herald,* Sept. 23, 25, and Oct. 6, 1895.

151. *Two Republics,* Dec. 20, 1886; Jan. 1, 15, and Feb. 20, 1887.

152. Joanna Richardson, *Sarah Bernhardt and Her World* (New York: G. P. Putnam's Sons, 1977), 117–18; J. H. Bates, *Notes of a Tour in Mexico and California* (New York: Burr Printing House, 1887), 45–66. For Mexican theater in general and criticism of it, see Stanton Davis Kirkham, *Mexican Trails* (New York: G. P. Putnam's Sons, 1909), 44–45; H. H. Bancroft, *History of Mexico* (San Francisco: History Company, Publishers, 1888), 6: 624–25; Flandrau, *Viva Mexico,* 3–4, 221, and 285–86; *Mexican Herald,* Nov. 17, 24, and Dec. 20, 1895.

153. Susan E. Bryan, "Teatro popular y sociedad durante el porfiriato," *Histora Mexicana* 33, no. 129 (1983), 63–84; and, "The Commercialization of the Theater in Mexico and the rise of the Teatro Frívolo," paper presented at the American Historical Association, Chicago, 1984.

154. *Two Republics,* Oct. 20, 1886; June 21, 1888; July 1, 1890.

155. Arthur Inkersley, "A Winter Regatta in Aztec Land," *Outing* 23, no. 4 (Jan. 1894), 302–8; *Mexican Herald,* Sept. 16, 29, Nov. 4, and Dec. 27, 1895; González Navarro, *Vida social,* 712.

156. J. B. MacMahan, "Polo in the West," *Outing* 27, no. 6 (Mar. 1897), 593–96; *Two Republics,* Feb. 25, Sept. 20, 1888; Mar. 24, 26, and Oct. 30, 1889. For information on Carden, see Peter Calvert, *The Mexican Revolution: The Diplomacy of Anglo-American Conflict* (Cambridge: Cambridge University Press, 1968), 216, 218–19, 279–81.

157. *Two Republics,* Mar. 18, 1871; Dec. 16, 1876; Nov. 17, 1877.

158. *Two Republics,* Feb. 9, 1878; April 8, and May 24, 1883; González Navarro, *Vida social,* 711.

159. *Two Republics,* Sept. 25, 30, Oct. 13, 17, and 27, 1889.

160. *Two Republics,* Jan. 23, 26, 1886; *Siglo XIX,* Mar. 31, 1893; *Mexican Herald,* Oct. 10, Nov. 1, 6, Dec. 15, 18, 24, 27, and 31, 1895; Jan. 20, 1896; González Navarro, *Vida social,* 711.

161. *Two Republics,* April 19, 1883; *Mexican Herald,* Jan. 26, 1896.

162. "Espacios Libres y Reservas forestrales de la ciudades: Su adaptación a Jardines, Parques y Lugares de juegos. Aplicación a la Ciudad de Mexico." Conferencia dada en la Exposición de Higiene por Ing. Miguel Quevedo, vocal del Consejo Superior de Salubridad, Jefe del Departimiento de Bosques (Mexico:

Gomar y Bussón, 1911). This pamphlet, inscribed to Luis Montes de Oca by the author, is preserved in the Bancroft Library, University of California, Berkeley. The Plan de Texcoco called for reforestation and the creation of artificial lakes to reduce the terrible dust storms that contribute to Mexico City's choking air pollution. (See *Times of the Americas,* Nov. 24, 1971.)

163. For the playground movement in the United States, see Betts, *America's Sporting Heritage,* 179–85; and for Boston in particular, "Playgrounds for Children," in Stephen Hardy, *How Boston Played: Sport, Recreation, and Community, 1865–1915* (Boston: Northeastern University Press, 1982), 85–106.

164. Alfred Oscar Coffin, *Land Without Chimneys: or, the Byways of Mexico* (Cincinnati: Editor Publishing Co., 1898), 297–98.

165. Hiriart, *Universo de Posada,* 17.

Rocks and Rawhide in Rural Society:
Tools and Technology in Porfirian Mexico

1. Mary Elizabeth Blake and Margaret F. Sullivan, *Mexico: Picturesque, Political, and Progressive* (Boston: Lee and Shepard, Publishers, 1888), 80.

2. J. R. Flippin, *Sketches from the Mountains of Mexico* (Cincinnati: Standard Publishing Company, 1889), 7.

3. Alfred Oscar Coffin, *Land without Chimneys; or, The Byways of Mexico* (Cincinnati: Editor Publishing Co., 1898), 300; J. H. Bates, *Notes of a Tour in Mexico and California* (New York: Burr Printing House, 1887), 57–58.

4. David A. Wells, *Study of Mexico* (New York: D. Appleton and Company, 1887), 35.

5. Coffin, *Without Chimneys,* 300–301, 71.

6. A. A. Graham, *Mexico with Comparisons and Conclusions* (Topeka, Kan.: Crane & Company, 1:907), 16.; Robert C. West, "The Flat-Roofed Folk Dwelling in Rural Mexico," *Geoscience and Man* 5 (June 1964), 111–32.

7. John J. Winberry, "The Log House in Mexico," *Annals* of the Association of American Geographers, 64, no. 1 (Mar. 1974), 54–69; and "Ecology and Etymology of the Rural Folk House: Example of the Log House in Mexico," in *Man, Culture, and Settlement,* ed. Robert C. Eidt, Kashi N. Singh, and Rana P. B. Singh (New Delhi, 1977), 170–75.

8. Solomon Bulkley Griffin, *Mexico of To-Day* (New York: Harper and Brothers, 1886), 91–92.

9. William Seymour Edwards, *On the Mexican Highlands, with a Passing Glimpse of Cuba,* 2nd ed. (Cincinnati: Press of Jennings and Graham, 1906), 129.

10. Flippin, *Sketches,* 292–93.

11. Stanton Davis Kirkham, *Mexican Trails* (New York: G. P. Putnam's Sons, 1909), 108–9.

12. *Ibid.,* 42.

13. Coffin, *Without Chimneys,* 14; William Bullock, *Six Months Residence and Travels in Mexico* (London: John Murray, 1824), 230.

14. H. H. Bancroft, *History of Mexico* (San Francisco: History Company, Publishers, 1888), 6: 615.

15. T. J. Jackson Lears, *No Place of Grace: Antimodernism and the Transformation of American Culture, 1880–1920* (New York: Pantheon Books, 1981), 15–16.

16. Wells, *Mexico,* 26.

17. Nancy M. Farriss, *Maya Society under Colonial Rule: The Collective Enterprise of Survival* (Princeton: Princeton University Press, 1984), 94; Coffin, *Without Chimneys,* 51. On the hat and pants laws, see Charles M. Flandrau, *Viva Mexico!* (Urbana: University of Illinois Press, 1964), 69, and the footnote on pp. 69–70; E. H. Blichfeldt, *A Mexican Journey* (New York: Thomas Y. Crowell Company, 1919), 97; *Two Republics,* June 1, 1890.

18. See Wallace Gillpatrick, *The Man Who Likes Mexico* (New York: Century Co., 1911), photographs, pp. 67 and 335.

19. Flippin, *Sketches,* 176. For a general discussion of clothing as an expression of cultural attitudes and social standing, see Alison Lurie, *The Language of Clothes* (New York: Random House, 1981).

20. Maturin M. Ballou, *Aztec Land* (Boston and New York: Houghton Mifflin, 1890), 88.

21. Flippin, *Sketches,* 174.

22. Edwards, *Highlands,* 176.

23. Wells, *Mexico,* 25.

24. Coffin, *Without Chimneys,* 50.

25. *Ibid.,* 36–37; Patty Guthrie, *Eliza and Etheldreda in Mexico: Notes of Travel* (New York: Broadway Publishing Co., 1911), 103.

26. Guthrie, *Eliza,* 103.

27. Griffin, *To-Day,* 91.

28. William Bullock, *Six Months,* 227.

29. *New York Times,* Mar. 13, 1892.

30. Griffin, *To-Day,* 45. This book was originally written as a series of articles for the *Springfield* (Mass.) *Republican.*

31. Flippin, *Sketches,* 7–8; Coffin, *Without Chimneys,* 297–98.

32. Wells, *Mexico,* 126.

33. Norman S. Hayner, *New Patterns in Old Mexico* (New Haven: College and University Press, 1966), 28.

34. Coffin, *Without Chimneys,* 298; Graham, *Mexico,* 62.

35. Ballou, *Aztec Land,* 38–39.

36. Cora Haywood Crawford, *The Land of the Montezumas* (New York: John B. Alden, 1889), 104–5.

37. Wells, *Mexico,* 126–27.

38. William Henry Bishop, *Old Mexico and Her Lost Provinces: A Journey in Mexico, Southern California, and Arizona by Way of Cuba* (New York: Harper & Brothers, 1883), 248.

39. Coffin, *Without Chimneys,* 287.

40. Flippin, *Sketches,* 34–35.

41. Thomas L. Rogers, *Mexico? Sí, Señor* (Boston: Mexican Central Railway Co., 1893), 61.

42. Wells, *Mexico,* 23; Ballou, *Aztec Land,* 93.

43. Ballou, *Aztec Land,* 92.

44. Flippin, *Sketches,* 43.

45. Edwards, *Highlands,* 137–38.

46. Gillpatrick, *Who Likes Mexico,* 50.

47. Edwards, *Highlands,* 137–38.

48. Flippin, *Sketches,* 67.

49. Edwards, *Highlands,* 137–38.

50. Flippin, *Sketches,* 71–73.

51. Ballou, *Aztec Land,* 101.

52. Flippin, *Sketches,* 78.

53. Alan Probert, "Mules, Men, and Mining Machinery: Transport on the Veracruz Road," *Silver Quest: Episodes of Mining in New Spain: Nine Readings, Journal of the West* 14, no. 2 (April 1975), 104.

54. Flippin, *Sketches,* 291.

55. Wells, *Mexico,* 127.

56. Rural civilization has been most closely studied in the French countryside from 1330 to 1730. See Emmanuel LeRoy Ladurie, "The Quantitative Revo-

lution and the French Historians: Record of a Generation (1932–1968)," in *The Territory of the Historian*, trans. Ben and Siân Reynolds (Sussex: Harvester Press, Ltd., 1979), 12.

57. I have taken "balance mechanisms" from LeRoy Ladurie. See his "Rural Civilization," *ibid.*, 79–110, esp. p. 93.

58. See chapters 3 "The Equilibrium of Poverty," and 4 "Accommodation," in John Kenneth Galbraith, *The Nature of Mass Poverty* (Cambridge: Harvard University Press, 1979), esp. pp. 44–52 and 61–63.

59. *Ibid.*, 62–63.

60. T. Philip Terry, *Terry's Mexico: Handbook for Travellers*, 2nd ed. (London: Gay and Hancock, Ltd., 1909), xlvi–xlvii.

61. Keith Thomas, "Work and Leisure in Pre-Industrial Society," *Past and Present*, no. 29 (Jan. 1965), 50–62; Herbert Applebaum, ed., *Work in Non-Market & Transitorial Societies* (Albany: State University of New York Press, 1984), 1–39. For an introduction to the literature on village and neighborhood sponsorship of formal celebrations, see Judith Friedlander, "The Secularization of the Cargo System: An Example from Postrevolutionary Central Mexico," *Latin American Research Review* 15, No. 2 (1981), 132–43; John D. Early, "Some Ethnographic Implications of an Ethnohistorical Perspective on the Civil-Religious Heirarchy among the Highland Maya," *Ethnohistory* 30, no. 4 (1983), 185–202; John K. Chance and William B. Taylor, "Cofradías and Cargos: An Historical Perspective on the Mesoamerican Civil-Religious Hierarchy," *American Ethnologist* 12, no. 1 (Feb. 1985), 1–26.

62. See the discussion revising this approach by Farriss in *Maya Society*, 49–51.

63. *New York Times*, March 13, 1892.

64. Flippin, *Sketches*, 7.

65. Griffin, *To-Day*, 45; Henry Howard Harper, *A Journey in Southeastern Mexico: Narrative of Experiences and Observations on Agricultural and Industrial Experiences* (Boston: Privately printed, 1910), 65.

66. *Ibid.*

67. See John H. Coatsworth, "Obstacles to Economic Growth in Nineteenth-Century Mexico," *American Historical Review* 83, no. 1 (Feb. 1978), 80–100, esp. 82–90.

68. *Ibid.*, 91–92.

69. Sidney George Fisher, *The Laws of Race, as Connected with Slavery* (Philadelphia: William P. Hazard, 1860), 39–40.

70. Blichfeldt, *Mexican Journey,* 226.

71. Flippin, *Sketches,* 294.

72. Gillpatrick, *Who Likes Mexico,* 212.

73. Dean Harris, *Days and Nights in the Tropics* (Toronto: Morang & Co., 1905), 86.

74. Bishop, *Old Mexico,* 34.

75. Kirkham, *Trails,* 31; Coffin, *Without Chimneys,* 224.

76. Coffin, *Without Chimneys,* 225.

77. Bates, *Notes,* 71.

78. Howard Conkling, *Mexico and the Mexicans: or, Notes of Travel in the Winter and Spring of 1883* (New York: Taintor Brothers, Merrill & Co., 1883), 74.

79. Blake and Sullivan, *Mexico,* 56.

80. Flippin, *Sketches,* 266.

81. Bancroft, *Mexico,* 6: 613; Flippin, *Sketches,* 160, 162; Terry, *Mexico* (1909), lxvii–lxviii.

82. See excellent discussion of this theme in S. H. Alatas, *The Myth of the Lazy Native* (London: Frank Cass, 1977), 2, 213–14, and ch. 7.

83. Flippin, *Sketches,* 167.

84. *Ibid.,* 169.

85. Renato I. Rosaldo, Jr., "The Rhetoric of Control: Ilongots Viewed as Natural Bandits and Wild Indians," in *The Reversible World: Symbolic Inversion in Art and Society,* Barbara A. Babcock, ed. (Ithaca: Cornell University Press, 1978), 240–57; see esp. 242, 255.

86. H. G. Ward, *Mexico* (London: Henry Colburn, 1829), 1: iii–iv, v, 414.

87. Galbraith, *Mass Poverty,* vi.

88. *Profile of Man and Culture in Mexico,* trans. Peter G. Earle (Austin: University of Texas Press, 1962), 15–44.

89. Galbraith, *Mass Poverty,* 55–56.

90. Griffin, *To-Day,* 46.

91. Harper, *Journey,* 79–80.

92. Edwards, *Highlands,* 109.

93. Blichfeldt, *Mexican Journey,* 249–50.

94. Wells, *Mexico,* 26.

95. Coffin, *Without Chimneys,* 209; Ballou, *Aztec Land,* 138.

96. Peter Farb and George Armelagos, *Consuming Passions: The Anthropology of Eating* (Boston: Houghton Mifflin, 1980), 10, 12, and 174.

97. Ballou, *Aztec Land,* 63.

98. Thomas Rees, *Spain's Lost Jewels: Cuba and Mexico* (Springfield: Illinois State Register, 1906), 157–59.

99. Harper, *Journey,* 65.

100. Flippin, *Sketches,* 63; Harper, *Journey,* 65; Rees, *Lost Jewels,* 332.

101. Blake, *Mexico,* 24–25.

102. Victor Turner and Edith Turner, *Image and Pilgrimage in Christian Culture: Anthropological Perspectives* (New York: Columbia University Press, 1978), p. 7 and Ch. 2; Kirkham, *Trails,* 120.

103. Paul Stoller, "Horrific Comedy: Cultural Resistance and the Hauka Movement in Niger," *Ethos* 12, no. 2 (Summer 1984), 167–68. Also see the valuable discussion in Roger Bastide, *The African Religions of Brazil: Toward a Sociology of the Interpenetration of Civilizations,* trans. Helen Sebba (Baltimore: Johns Hopkins University Press, 1978), 156 and *passim;* and William H. Beezley, "Recent Mexican Political Humor," *Journal of Latin American Lore* 11, no. 2 (1985), 195–223.

Judas at the Jockey Club

1. Makhail Bakhtin, *Rabelais and His World,* trans. Helene Iswolsky (Cambridge: M.I.T. Press, 1965), 8; *Mexican Herald,* April 18, 1908.

2. See *Encyclopedia Americana,* 1985, s.v. "Carnival"; Bakhtin, *Rabelais,* 5.

3. *Funk and Wagnalls Standard Dictionary of Folklore, Mythology, and Legend* (New York, Funk and Wagnalls, 1972), s.v. "Judas."

4. Dorothy Gladys Spicer, *Festivals of Western Europe* (New York: H. W. Wilson Company, 1958), 94–95.

5. Roger Bastide, *The African Religions of Brazil: Toward a Sociology of the Interpenetration of Civilizations,* trans. Helen Sebba (Baltimore: Johns Hopkins University Press, 1978), 80, 424n.

6. Funk and Wagnalls, *Standard Dictionary of Folklore,* s.v. "Judas"; Florence H. and Robert M. Pettit, *Mexican Folk Toys: Festival Decorations and Ritual Objects* (New York: Hastings House Publishers, 1978), 123.

7. José de J. Núñez y Domínguez, "Judases en Mexico," *Mexican Folkways* 5, no. 2 (April 1929), 92–93.

8. Efraín Subero, *Origen y expansión de la Quema de Judas: Aporte a la investigación del Folklore literario de Venezuela* (Caracas: Universidad Católica "Andres Bello," 1974); F. Villanueva Berrizbeitía, *Deiciseis Cancilleres de*

Venezuela (Caracas: Ediciones de la Cancilleria Venezolana, 1960), 193; Dorothy Kamen-Kaye, *Venezuelan Folkways* (Detroit: Blaine-Ethridge, 1976; reprint of 1947 edition published by the *Caracas Journal*), 228–29; Carlos Miguel Suárez Radillo, *Trece Autores del Nuevo Teatro Venezolano* (Caracas: Monte Avila Editores, C.A., 1971), 108; the play was published by the Sección Teatro, Universidad Central de Venezuela, 1965.

9. Thomas Ewbank, *Life in Brazil: A Journal of a Visit to the Land of the Cocoa and the Palm* (New York: N.p. 1856); Associated Press report, Mar. 3, 1929; discussion of the Brazilian customs can be found in Bastide, *Religions of Brazil,* 80–81 and footnotes 20 and 21, pp. 424–25.

10. Celso A. Lara F., "La Quema del Diablo en Guatemala," *Latin American Lore* 1, no. 2 (1975), 199–209; Dario Guevara, "La Quema del Año Viejo en Quito," *Folklor Americano* 14 (1966), 164–84.

11. O. L., "Holy Week in Mexico," *Lippincott's Magazine* 57 (1896), 525.

12. Erna Fergusson, quoting Icazbálceta, in *Fiesta in Mexico* (New York: Alfred A. Knopf, 1934), 12–13.

13. Victor Inzúa Canales, *Artesanías en papel y cartón* (Mexico: Fondo Nacional para el Fomento de la Artesanías, 1982), 13; M. O. Mendízabal, "Powder That Kills and Powder That Amuses," *Mexican Folkways* 3, no. 1 (Feb. 1927), 5–18.

14. Núñez y Domínguez, "Judases," 92, 93.

15. C. C. Becher, *Cartas sobre Mexico: La República Mexicana durante los años Decisivos de 1832 y 1833,* trans. Juan A. Ortega y Medina (Mexico: Universidad Nacional Autónoma de Mexico, 1959), 98–99.

16. Guillermo Prieto, *Memorias de mís tiempos,* vol. 2, and Marcos Arróniz, *Manual del viajero de Mexico,* are both cited in Núñez y Domínguez, "Judases," p. 7; Erle Stanley Gardner, *Neighborhood Frontiers* (New York: William Morrow Company, 1954), 234–61; Paul Vanderwood to the author, April 3, 1983.

17. Frederick Starr, *Catalogue of a Collection of Objects Illustrating the Folklore of Mexico* (London: Folk-Lore Society of London, 1899), 81.

18. Howard T. and Marion Hall Fisher, eds., *Life in Mexico: The Letters of Fanny Calderón de la Barca* (Garden City, N.Y.: Doubleday, 1966), 203–4.

19. Carl Sartorius, *Mexico about 1850* (1858; reprint, Stuttgart: F. A. Brockhause Dom.-Gesch. G. M. B. H., Abt. Antigarium, 1961), 159; Guillermo Prieto, quoted in Núñez y Domínguez, "Judases," 94.

20. See announcement of best locations to watch the Judas burnings in *The Two*

Republics, April 23, 1886; April 8, 1887; March 30, 1888; April 19, 1889; April 5, 1890; March 27, 1891.

21. Frederick Starr, "Holy Week in Mexico," *Journal of American Folk-Lore* 12, no. 46 (July–September 1899), 164–65.

22. William Seymour Edwards, *On the Mexican Highlands, with a Passing Glimpse of Cuba* (Cincinnati: Press of Jennings and Graham, 1906), 186.

23. Howard Conkling, *Mexico and the Mexicans; or, Notes of Travel in the Winter and Spring of 1883* (New York: Traintor Brothers, Merrill & Co., 1883), 81–82.

24. "Matracas Oficiales," *El Hijo del Ahuizote,* March 25, 1894. The card-size paper matracas, of course, are ephemeral; for an example, see "mí matraca," from the early 1920s, a tissue paper request for a handout, reading, "The Holy Church orders us to fast during Lent, which I won't have to get used to, since I'm already accustomed to fasting every day" (Rudolf Schuller Collection, Latin American Library, Tulane University, Box 29, folder 7). Pictures of matracas appear in Pettit and Pettit, *Mexican Folk Toys,* 121. Folklorist Frederick Starr collected several matracas in the 1890s. See descriptions, Starr, *Catalogue,* 81.

25. For a discussion of fireworks in Mexico, see Evon Z. Vogt, "On the Symbolic Meaning of Percussion in Zinacanteco Ritual," *Journal of Anthropological Research* 33, no. 3 (Fall 1977), 231–44; Mendízabal, "Powder That Kills," 5–18; Stanley H. Brandes, "Fireworks and Fiestas: The Case from Tzintzuntzán," *Journal of Latin American Lore* 7, no. 2 (1981), 171–90. For a discussion of fireworks in general, see George Plimpton, *Fireworks: A History and Celebration* (Garden City, N.Y.: Doubleday, 1984).

26. John K. Chance and William B. Taylor, "Cofradías and Cargos: An Historical Perspective on the Mesoamerican Civil-religious Hierarchy," *American Ethnologist* 12, no. 1 (Feb. 1985), 1–26, is a stimulating analysis of the evolution of the cargo and cofradía system in Mexico during the 350 years from the Spanish conquest to the establishment of the Porfirian regime.

27. Bakhtin, *Rabelais,* 11–12. A brief effort to explain this tradition by a Mexican sarvant is Octavio Paz, "The Eye of Mexico: Todos Santos, Día de Muertos," *Evergreen Review* no. 7 (1959), 22–37.

28. Moisés González Navarro, *El Porfiriato: La vida social,* vol. 4 of *Historia moderna de Mexico,* ed. Daniel Cosío Villegas (Mexico: Editorial Hermes, 1955–1970), 461.

29. O. L., "Holy Week," 525.

30. Paz, "Eye of Mexico," 26.

31. Edward Larocque Tinker, *Corridos and Calaveras* (Austin: University of Texas Press, 1961), 21, 25–26.

32. Victor Turner, *Dramas, Fields, and Metaphors: Symbolic Action in Human Society* (Ithaca: Cornell University Press, 1976).

33. Robert H. Lavenda, book review, *Studies of Latin American Popular Culture,* 1 (1982), 278; Roberto Da Matta, "Constraint and License: A Preliminary Study of Two Brazilian National Rituals," in *Secular Ritual,* ed. Sally F. Moore and Barbara G. Myerhoff (Amsterdam: Van Gorcum, 1977), 244–66.

34. Barbara A. Babcock, ed., *The Reversible World: Symbolic Inversion in Art and Society* (Ithaca: Cornell University Press, 1978), 15, 25; Louis A. Hieb, "Meaning and Mismeaning: Toward an Understanding of the Ritual Clown," in *New Perspectives on the Pueblos,* ed. Alfonso Ortiz (Albuquerque: University of New Mexico Press, 1972), 163–96.

35. See Proclamations, March 23, 1790, and April 16, 1791, "Con la justa mira de corregir el desordén con que muchas individuos de ambos sexos concurran a las procesiónes de Semana Santa," Bandos de Revilla Gigedo, part 2, numbers 4 and 14, Bancroft Library, University of California, Berkeley.

36. Julia Newell Jackson, *A Winter Holiday in Summer Lands* (Chicago: A. C. McClurg and Company, 1890), 156, 161.

37. *Ibid.,* 160.

38. *Ibid.,* 164–65.

39. William Bullock, *Six Months Residence and Travels in Mexico* (London: Jon Murray, 1824), 103.

40. Jackson, *Summer Lands,* 164–65.

41. *Ibid.,* 165, 166.

42. Becher, *Cartas,* 98.

43. Starr, "Holy Week," 165; Starr, *Catalogue,* 81.

44. Patty Guthrie, *Eliza and Etheldreda in Mexico: Notes of Travel* (New York: Broadway Publishing Co., 1911), 64–65.

45. E. H. Blichfeldt, *A Mexican Journey* (New York: Thomas Y. Crowell Company, 1919), 254.

46. Núñez y Domínguez, "Judases," 29.

47. Alfredo Ramos Espinosa, "Piñatas," *Anuario de la Sociedad Folklórica de Mexico,* No. 3 (1942), 33–36.

48. David Kunzle, "World Upside Down: The Iconography of a European Broadsheet Type," in *The Reversible World,* ed. Barbara A. Babcock (Ithaca: Cor-

nell University Press, 1978), 39–94, esp. p. 76.

49. LeRoy Ladurie argues that identifying trends is often all we can achieve because of the inaccuracy of records in preindustrial societies. See Emmanuel LeRoy Ladurie, *The Peasants of Languedoc*, trans. John Day (Urbana: University of Illinois Press, 1974), 26.

50. Becher, *Cartas*, 98.

51. Quoted in Núñez y Domínguez, "Judases," 97–99.

52. *Two Republics*, Nov. 6, 1867, Feb. 26, 1870, Mar. 4, 1870.

53. *Ibid.*, Feb. 18, 1870.

54. *Ibid.*, Aug. 18, 1871; Jan. 13, 1872.

55. Harriott Wright Sherratt, *Mexican Vistas Seen from Highways and Byways of Travel* (Chicago: Rand McNally & Company, 1896), 120; William Henry Bishop, *Old Mexico and Her Lost Provinces: A Journey in Mexico, Southern California, and Arizona by Way of Cuba* (New York: Harper and Brothers, 1883), 64, 152, 154; Thomas Unett Brocklehurst, *Mexico To-Day: A Country with a Great Future* (London: John Murray, 1883), 74; Salvador Novo, *Los paseos de la ciudad de Mexico* (Mexico: Fondo de la cultura económica, 1974), 30–35.

56. *Two Republics*, Mar. 8, 1876.

57. *Two Republics*, June 28, 1876.

58. Natalie Zemon Davis, "Women on Top: Symbolic Inversions and Political Disorder in Early Modern Europe," in *The Reversible World*, ed. Barbara Babcock (Ithaca: Cornell University Press, 1978), 183.

59. John H. Coatsworth, *Growth against Development: The Economic Impact of Railroads in Porfirian Mexico* (DeKalb: Northern Illinois University Press, 1981), 149–74.

60. Bishop, *Old Mexico*, 32.

61. Merle E. Simmons, *The Mexican Corrido as a Source for Interpretive Study of Modern Mexico* (Bloomington: Indiana University Press, 1957), 422.

62. *Two Republics*, May 9, 1886; Charles C. Cumberland, "The Sonora Chinese and the Mexican Revolution," *Hispanic American Historical Review* 40 (1960), 191–211.

63. Bakhtin, *Rabelais*, 6; Paz, "Eye of Mexico," 25.

64. Paz, "Eye of Mexico," 7, 11–12.

65. Sartorius, *About 1850*, 159.

66. Jackson, *Summer Lands*, 167–68.

67. Maturin M. Ballou, *Aztec Land* (Boston and New York: Houghton Mifflin,

1890), 341–42.

68. Núñez y Domínguez, "Judases," 96.

69. Sartorius, *About 1850,* 153–54. Sartorius reported similar events at the bullfights in the 1850s. After the last bull, banquet tables were prepared in the arena for the masses. As soon as the crowd collected around the tables, a bull, with covered horns, was released.

70. *Mexican Herald,* April 17, 1897; April 18, 1897.

71. Sartorius, *About 1850,* 145; Mary J. Jacques, *Texan Ranch Life with Three Months through Mexico in a "Prairie Schooner"* (London: Horace Cox, 1894), 345. Also see Solomon Bulkey Griffin, *Mexico of To-Day* (New York: Harper and Brothers, 1886), 95, and Stanton Davis Kirkham, *Mexican Trails* (New York: G. P. Putnam's Sons, 1909), 104, for discussion of the aguador.

72. Dr. Alt [Gerardo Murrilo], *Las artes populares en Mexico* (Mexico: Instituto Nacional Indígenista, 1980), 191.

73. Victor Turner and Edith Turner, *Image and Pilgrimage in Christian Culture: Anthropolitical Perspectives* (New York: Columbia University Press, 1978), ch. 2.

74. Evelyn P. Stephens, "Marianismo: The Other Face of Machismo in Latin America," in *Female and Male in Latin American,* ed. Anne Pescatello (Pittsburgh: University of Pittsburgh Press, 1973), 89–102; Jane H. Hill and Carole Browner, "Gender Ambiguity and Class Stereotyping in the Mexican Fotonovela," *Studies in Latin American Popular Culture* 1 (1981), 43–64.

75. González Navarro, *Vida social,* 469–70.

76. *Mexican Herald,* Oct. 13, 1895.

77. Blichfeldt, *Journey,* 255.

78. González Navarro, *Vida social,* 461.

79. Bakhtin, *Rabelais,* 33, 34–35.

80. *Two Republics,* April 16, 1890.

81. *Two Republics,* March 29, 1891.

82. *Two Republics,* April 17, 1892.

83. *Siglo XIX,* April 1, 1893.

84. *El Universal,* April 3, 1893; *Siglo XIX,* April 3, 1893.

85. *Two Republics,* April 10, 1892; April 2, 3, 1893.

86. Stith Thompson, *Motif-Index of Folk-Literature,* 6 vols. (Bloomington: Indiana University Press, 1955–1958), K498.

87. Beryl Rowland, *Animals with Human Faces: A Guide to Animal Symbolism* (Kι.ᴑxville: University of Tennessee Press, 1973), 38–39.

88. See Francisco Javier Santamaría, *Diccionario de Mexicánismos* (Mexico: Editorial Porrúa, 1978).

89. Alfred Oscar Coffin, *Land without Chimneys: or, The Byways of Mexico* (Cincinnati: Editor Publishing Co., 1898), 205–6; *Mexican Herald,* Feb. 19, 1886.

90. *Mexican Herald,* Feb. 19, 1896; April 17, 1908.

91. Laurence John Rohlfes, "Police and Penal Correction in Mexico City, 1876–1911: A Study of Order and Progress in Porfirian Mexico (Ph.D. dissertation, Tulane University, 1983), 87.

92. *Mexican Herald,* April 17, 1908.

93. J. A. Pérez-Rioja, *Diccionario de símbolos y mitos* (Madrid: Editorial Tecnos, s.a., 1980), 163, 381.

94. Folklore Archives, University of California, Berkeley (hereinafter cited as FA/UCB), "Mexico: Proverbs," S2, "Más sabe el diablo."

95. Rowland, *Animals with Human Faces,* 37–43; Pérez-Rioja, *Diccionario,* 251.

96. FA/UCB, Mexico, Proverbs IV, J. L. Torres-Hernández, Nov. 5, 1971.

97. Núñez y Domínguez, "Judases," 99.

98. Fedérico C. Aguilar, *Ultimo año de residencia en Mexico* (Bogotá: Imprenta de Ignacio Borda, 1885), 74–75.

99. Pettit, *Mexican Folk Toys,* 121.

100. Inzúa Canales, *Artesanías,* 19.

101. *Uno Más Uno* (Mexico City), April 19, 1984.

102. *El Heraldo de Mexico,* April 19, 1984.

103. Kunzle, "World Upside Down," 89–90.

104. One outstanding study is Francisco Xavier Hernández, *El juguete popular en Mexico* (Mexico: Editorial Mexicana, S.A., 1950); another is Dr. Alt, *Las artes populares en Mexico,* who discusses the Judas figures in the section on toys, pp. 190–91.

105. Frances Toor, *A Treasury of Mexican Folkways* (New York: Crown, 1947), 65–67, sketch on p. 66.

106. *Ibid.,* 216, 3.

107. Fergusson, *Fiesta in Mexico,* 194–95.

108. Letter to the author from Cayuquí Estage Noel, Head of the Taller de Investigación de Teatro Indígena de la Escuela de Bellas Artes, Universidad Autónoma Benito Juárez de Oaxaca, Nov. 9, 1983.

109. Gardner, *Neighborhood Frontiers* 235–61; Martínez quote, p. 234. Paul Vanderwood of San Diego State University witnessed this ceremony and described it in a letter to the author, April 3, 1983.

110. John G. Kennedy and Paul A. López, *Semana Santa in the Sierra Tarahumana: A Comparative Study in Three Villages* (Los Angeles: Los Angeles County Museum, 1984).

111. *El Hijo de Ahuizote,* April 10, 1898.

112. *Ibid.,* April 7, 1901, April 12, 1903.

113. "Testamento de Judas Iscariote," folder 6, Box 29, Schuller Papers, Tulane University.

114. For a stimulating and suggestive article, see Iu. M. Lotman, "Theater and Theatricality in the Order of Early Nineteenth Century Culture," in *Semiotics and Structuralism: Readings from the Soviet Union,* ed. Henryk Baran (White Plains, N.Y.: International Arts and Sciences Press, 1974), 33–63, esp. 48–49.

Afterword

1. *El Hijo del Ahuizote,* Nov. 27, 1898.

2. *Ibid.,* Aug. 12, 1984.

3. *Ibid.,* Oct. 31, 1897.

4. *Ibid.,* Nov. 14, 1897.

5. *Ibid.,* Feb. 27, 1898.

6. *Ibid.,* Jan. 30, 1898.

7. *Ibid.,* Jan. 23, 1898.

8. *Ibid.,* July 17, 1898.

9. See *ibid.,* Nov. 27, 1897, for an example of the biting cartoons about the relationship between the church and state that appeared in virtually every issue of the newspaper.

10. For this explanation of the bicycle, I have drawn on Richard Harmond, "Progress and Flight: An Interpretation of the American Cycle Craze of the 1890s," *Journal of Social History* 5 (Winter 1971), 235–57, especially p. 236.

11. T. Philip Terry, "My Ride to Acapulco: A Cycling Adventure in Mexico," *Outing* 29, no. 6 (Mar. 1897), 593–96.

12. Decrees of Aug. 16, 1822, are contained in the Viceregal and Ecclesiastical Mexican Collection, Legato 39, expediente 20, 1822, Tulane University.

13. Lesley Byrd Simpson, *Many Mexicos,* 4th ed. (Berkeley: University of California Press, 1971), 248–49.

14. Coffin, *Land without Chimneys; or, The Byways of Mexico* (Cincinnati: Editor Publishing Co., 1898), 248–49.

15. *Mexican Herald,* Jan. 8, 1896.

16. Abner Cohen, "Drama and Politics in the Development of a London Carnival," *Man* n.s. 15, No. 1 (Mar. 1980), 66–67, 79, 81, 83; Michael L. Conniff, ed. *Latin American Populism in Comparative Perspective* (Albuquerque: University of New Mexico Press, 1982), offers the best available introduction to this topic.

17. A brilliant discussion of a nonliterate society undergoing change is Rhys Isaac, *The Transformation of Virginia, 1740–1790* (Chapel Hill: University of North Carolina Press, 1982).

18. See the following volumes for a discussion of the Flores Magón brothers: Lyle C. Brown, *The Mexican Liberals and Their Struggle against the Díaz Dictatorship, 1900–1906* (Mexico: Mexico City College Press, 1956); W. Dirk Raat, *Revoltosos: Mexico's Rebels in the United States, 1902–1923* (College Station: Texas A & M University Press, 1981); and, for the episode in Baja California in particular, Lowell L. Blaisdell, *The Desert Revolution: Baja California, 1911* (Madison: University of Wisconsin Press, 1962).

19. See Laurence John Rholfes, "Mexican Catholic Social Action during the Porfiriato, 1903–1911 (M.A. thesis, Tulane University, 1977).

20. Andrés Molina Enríquez, *Los grandes problemas nacionales* (Mexico: Imprenta de A. Carranza e Hijos, 1909).

21. Three excellent monographs dealing with agrarian troubles and labor disturbances are John M. Hart, *Anarchism and the Mexican Working Class, 1860–1931* (Austin: University of Texas Press, 1978); Rodney D. Anderson, *Outcasts in Their Own Land: Mexican Industrial Workers, 1906–1911* (DeKalb: Northern Illinois University Press, 1976); Leticia Reina, *Las rebeliones campesinas en Mexico, 1819–1906* (Mexico: Siglo Ventiuno, 1980).

22. William D. Raat, "Ideas and Society in Don Porfirio's Mexico," *The Americas* 30, no. 1 (July 1973), 32–53, especially 50–53; Fredrick B. Pike, *Spanish America, 1900–1970: Tradition and Social Innovation* (New York: W. W. Norton, 1973), 15–28. See Charles Hale, "The Great Textbook Debate of 1880 and the Influence of Spanish Krausism in Mexico," lecture given on induction into the Mexican Historical Academy, 1985; it offers an excellent discussion of the challenges to Positivism.

23. Francisco I. Madero, *La sucesión presidencial en 1910* (San Pedro, Coahuila: N.p., 1908).

24. *Diccionario Porrúa,* 2:2354; also see Arlene K. Daniels and Richard R. Daniels, "The Social Function of the Career Fool," *Psychiatry* 27, no. 3 (1964), 219–29, for a discussion of the fool in rigid or oppressive social situations.

Bibliography

The recent appearance of a number of monographs investigating the years of the Porfirian dictatorship and the society created by the dictator have given a new vigor to the study of this era of Mexican history. A discussion of the new directions indicated by these volumes goes well beyond the intention of this study. Readers interested in this scholarship should consult the excellent essay by Thomas Benjamin in the volume he edited with William McNellie, *Other Mexicos: Essays on Regional Mexican History* (Albuquerque: University of New Mexico Press, 1984). Benjamin gives a thoughtful and provocative evaluation of the literature of the Porfirian era.

What follows is a list of the sources cited in the notes to this volume.

Aguilar, Federico C. *Ultimo año de residencia en Mexico.* Bogotá: Imprenta de Ignacio Borda, 1885.

Alatas, S. H. *The Myth of the Lazy Native.* London: Frank Cass, 1977.

Alt, Dr. [Gerardo Murrillo]. *Las artes populares en Mexico.* Mexico: Instituto Nacional Indigenista, 1980.

Álvarez del Villar, José. *Men and Horses of Mexico: History and Practice of "Charrería."* Mexico: Ediciones Lara, S.A., 1979.

Anderson, Rodney D. *Outcasts in Their Own Land: Mexican Industrial Workers, 1906–1911.* DeKalb: Northern Illinois University Press, 1976.

Applebaum, Herbert, ed. *Work in Non-market & Transitional Societies.* Albany: State University of New York Press, 1984.

Babcock, Barbara A., ed. *The Reversible World: Symbolic Inversion in Art and Society.* Ithaca: Cornell University Press, 1978.

Bakhtin, Makhail. *Rabelais and His World.* Translated by Helene Iswolsky. Cambridge: M.I.T. Press, 1965.

Ballou, Maturin M. *Aztec Land.* Boston and New York: Houghton Mifflin, 1890.

Bancroft, H. H. *History of Mexico,* Vol. 6. San Francisco: History Company, Publishers, 1888.

Bandos de Revilla Gigedo. Bancroft Library, University of California, Berkeley.

Barrett, Robert S. *The Standard Guide to the City of Mexico and Vicinity.* City of Mexico: Modern Mexico Publishing Company, 1901.

Barton, Mary. *Impressions of Mexico with Brush and Pen.* New York: Macmillan, 1911.

Bastide, Roger. *The African Religions of Brazil: Toward a Sociology of the Interpenetration of Civilizations.* Translated by Helen Sebba. Baltimore: Johns Hopkins University Press, 1978.

Bates, J. H. *Notes of a Tour in Mexico and California.* New York: Burr Printing House, 1887.

Becher, C. C. *Cartas sobre Mexico: La República Mexicana durante los años decisivos de 1832 y 1833.* Trans. Juan A. Ortega y Medina. Mexico: Universidad Nacional Autónoma de Mexico, 1959.

Beezley, William H. "Mexican Political Humor." *Journal of Latin American Lore* 11, no. 2 (1985): 195–223.

Berdecio, Roberto, and Stanley Appelbaum. *Posada's Popular Mexican Prints.* New York: Dover Publishing, 1972.

Bertie-Marriott, C. *Un Parisien au Mexique.* Paris: E. Dentu, Editeur, 1886.

Betts, John Richards. *America's Sporting Heritage, 1850–1950.* Reading, Mass.: Addison-Wesley Publishing Company, 1974.

Billings, Frederick. *Letters from Mexico 1859.* Woodstock, Vt.: Elm Tree Press, 1936.

Birrell, Susan. "Sport as Ritual: Interpretations from Durkheim to Goffman." *Social Forces* 60, no. 2 (December 1981): 354–76.

Bishop, William Henry. *Old Mexico and Her Lost Provinces: A Journey in Mexico, Southern California, and Arizona by Way of Cuba.* New York: Harper and Brothers, 1883.

Blaisdell, Lowell L. *The Desert Revolution: Baja California, 1911.* Madison: University of Wisconsin Press, 1962.

Blake, Mary Elizabeth, and Margaret F. Sullivan. *Mexico: Picturesque, Political, and Progressive.* Boston: Lee and Shepard, Publishers, 1888.

Blichfeldt, E. H. *A Mexican Journey.* New York: Thomas Y. Crowell Company, 1919.

Bradbury, Ray. *The Stories of Ray Bradbury.* New York: Alfred A. Knopf, 1981.

———. "Day after Tomorrow: Why Science Fiction?" *Nation,* May 2, 1953, 366.

Brandes, Stanley H. "Fireworks and Fiestas: The Case from Tzintzuntzán." *Journal of Latin American Lore* 7, no. 2 (1981): 171–90.

Breen, T. H. "Horses and Gentlemen: The Cultural Significance of Gambling among the Gentry of Virginia." *William and Mary Quarterly* 3rd Ser., 34, no. 2 (April 1974), 239–57.

Brocklehurst, Thomas Unett. *Mexico To-Day: A Country with a Great Future.* London: John Murray, 1883.

Brown, Lyle C. *The Mexican Liberals and Their Struggle against the Díaz Dictatorship, 1900–1906.* Mexico: Mexico City College Press, 1956.

Bryan, Susan E. "Teatro popular y sociedad durante el porfiriato." *Historia Mexicana* 33, no. 129 (1983): 63–84.

———. "The Commercialization of the Theater in Mexico and the Rise of the Teatro Frívolo." Paper presented at the American Historical Association meeting, Chicago, 1984.

Bullock, William. *Six Months Residence and Travels in Mexico.* London: John Murray, 1824.

Calvert, Peter. *The Mexican Revolution: The Diplomacy of Anglo-American Conflict.* Cambridge: Cambridge University Press, 1968.

Carnica, Raul. "Chalo Cordero es el auténtico píonero del softbol Mexicano," *La Prensa* (Mexico City), December 6, 1959.

Carrell, Edward, and Jon Whyte. *Rocky Mountain Madness: A Bittersweet Romance.* Banff: Altitude Publishing, 1982.

Chance, John K., and William B. Taylor, "Cofradías and Cargos: An Historical Perspective on the Mesoamerican Civil-Religious Hierarchy," *American Ethnologist* 12, no. 1 (February 1985): 1–26.

Chicago Tribune, March 3–18, 1907.

Cid y Mullet, Juan. *Libro de Oro del Futbol Mexicano.* Mexico, N.p., 1982.

Coatsworth, John H. *Growth against Development: The Economic Impact of Rail-*

roads in Porfirian Mexico. DeKalb: Northern Illinois University Press, 1981.

———. "Obstacles to Economic Growth in Nineteenth-Century Mexico." *American Historical Review* 83, no. 1 (February 1978): 80–100.

Coffin, Alfred Oscar. *Land without Chimneys; or, The Byways of Mexico.* Cincinnati: Editor Publishing Co., 1898.

Cohen, Abner. "Drama and Politics in the Development of a London Carnival." *Man* n.s. 15, no. 1 (March 1980): 65–87.

Conkling, Alfred R. *Appleton's Guide to Mexico.* New York: D. Appleton & Co., 1891.

Conkling, Howard. *Mexico and the Mexicans; or, Notes of Travel in the Winter and Spring of 1883.* New York: Traintor Brothers, Merrill & Co., 1883.

Conniff, Michael L., ed. *Latin American Populism in Comparative Perspective.* Albuquerque: University of New Mexico Press, 1982.

Crawford, Cora Haywood. *The Land of the Montezumas.* New York: John B. Alden, 1889.

Cumberland, Charles C. *Mexico: The Struggle for Modernity.* New York: Oxford University Press, 1968.

———. "The Sonora Chinese and the Mexican Revolution." *Hispanic American Historical Review* 40 (1960): 191–211.

Daniels, Arlene K., and Richard R. Daniels. "The Social Function of the Career Fool." *Psychiatry* 27, no. 3 (1964): 219–29.

Davis, Natalie Zemon. "Women on Top: Symbolic Inversions and Political Disorder in Early Modern Europe." In *The Reversible World: Symbolic Inversion in Art and Society,* edited by Barbara Babcock. Ithaca: Cornell University Press, 1978.

Da Matta, Roberto. "Constraint and License: A Preliminary Study of Two Brazilian National Rituals." In *Secular Ritual,* edited by Sally F. Moore and Barbara G. Myerhoff. Amsterdam: Van Gorcum, 1977.

Diccionario Porrúa. 3rd ed. 2 vols. Mexico: Editorial Porrúa, S.A., 1970.

Dunham, Norman L. "The Bicycle Era in American History." Ph.D. dissertation, Harvard University, 1956.

Early, John D. "Some Ethnographic Implications of an Ethnohistorical Perspective on the Civil-Religious Hierarchy among the Highland Maya." *Ethnohistory* 30, No. 4 (1983): 185–202.

Edwards, William Seymour. *On the Mexican Highlands, with a Passing Glimpse of Cuba.* Cincinnati: Press of Jennings and Graham, 1906.

Elias, Norbert, and Eric Dunning. "The Quest for Excitement in Unexciting Societies." In *The Cross-Cultural Analysis of Sport and Games,* edited by Gunther Lüschen. Champaign, Ill.: Stipes Publishing Co., 1978.

Emery, Lynne. "World-Renowned Champion Amazon: Jaguarina." Paper presented at the North American Society for Sport History, Monte Alto, Penn. May 30, 1983.

Encyclopedia Americana, 1985 ed. S.v. "Carnival."

Enríquez, Celso. *El deporte antiguo mexicano y el deporte de nuestro tiempo.* Mexico: Litográfica Machado, S. A., n.d.

Ewbank, Thomas. *Life in Brazil: A Journal of a Visit to the Land of the Cocoa and the Palm.* New York: N.p., 1856.

Farb, Peter, and George Armelagos. *Consuming Passions: The Anthropology of Eating.* Boston: Houghton Mifflin, 1980.

Farriss, Nancy M. *Maya Society under Colonial Rule: The Collective Enterprise of Survival.* Princeton: Princeton University Press, 1984.

Fergusson, Erna. *Fiesta in Mexico.* New York: Alfred A. Knopf, 1934.

El Financiero. (Mexico City)

Fisher, Howard T., and Marion Hall Fisher, eds. *Life in Mexico: The Letters of Fanny Calderón de la Barca.* Garden City, N.Y.: Doubleday, 1966.

Fisher, Sidney George. *The Laws of Race, as Connected with Slavery.* Philadelphia: Willis P. Hazard, 1860.

Flandrau, Charles M. *Viva Mexico!* Urbana: University of Illinois Press, 1964.

Flippin, J. R. *Sketches from the Mountains of Mexico.* Cincinnati: Standard Publishing Company, 1889.

Folklore Archives. University of California. Berkeley.

Friedlander, Judith. "The Secularization of the Cargo System: An Example from Postrevolutionary Central Mexico." *Latin American Research Review* 15, no. 2 (1981): 132–43.

Fuentes, Carlos. *The Death of Artemio Cruz.* Translated by Sam Hileman. New York: Farrar, Straus and Giroux, 1964.

Funk and Wagnalls Standard Dictionary of Folklore, Mythology, and Legend (New York: Funk and Wagnalls, 1972), s.v. "Judas Iscariot."

Galbraith, John Kenneth. *The Nature of Mass Poverty.* Cambridge: Harvard University Press, 1979.

Gardner, Erle Stanley. *Neighborhood Frontiers.* New York: William Morrow Company, 1954.

Geertz, Clifford. "Deep Play: Notes on the Balinese Cockfight." In *Sport in the Sociocultural Process,* edited by Marie Hart and Susan Birrell. 3rd ed. Dubuque, Iowa: Wm. C. Brown Company, 1981.

Gillpatrick, Wallace. *The Man Who Likes Mexico.* New York: Century Co., 1911.

Gonzáles F., Juan José. "Un viejo aguilista en mala situación." *El Dictamén* (Veracruz), September 4, 1959.

———. "Aportaciones para la historia de Veracruz," *El Dictamén* (Veracruz), February 15, 1963.

González Navarro, Moisés. *El Porfiriato: La vida social.* Vol. 4 of *Historia moderna de Mexico,* edited by Daniel Cosío Villegas. Mexico: Editorial Hermes, 1955–1970.

Goodhue, Bertram Grosvenor. *Mexican Memories: The Record of a Slight Sojourn below the Yellow Rio Grande.* New York: George M. Allen Co., 1892.

Graham, A. A. *Mexico with Comparisons and Conclusions.* Topeka, Kan.: Crane and Company, 1907.

Griffin, Solomon Bulkey. *Mexico of To-Day.* New York: Harper and Brothers, 1886.

Guarner, Enrique. *Historia del torreo en Mexico.* Mexico: Editorial Diana, 1979.

Guevara, Darío. "La Quema del Año Viejo en Quito." *Folklor Americano* 14 (1966): 164–84.

Guthrie, Patty. *Eliza and Etheldreda in Mexico: Notes of Travel.* New York: Broadway Publishing Co., 1911.

Guttmann, Allen. *From Ritual to Record: The Nature of Modern Sports.* New York: Columbia University Press, 1978.

Hale, Charles. "The Great Textbook Debate of 1880 and the Influence of Spanish Krausism in Mexico." Lecture given on induction into the Mexican Historical Academy, Mexico City, 1985.

Hancock, Ralph. *The Magic Land: Mexico.* New York: Coward-McCann, Inc., 1948.

Hardy, Stephen. *How Boston Played: Sport, Recreation, and Community, 1865–1915.* Boston: Northeastern University Press, 1982.

Harmond, Richard. "Progress and Flight: An Interpretation of the American Cycle Craze of the 1890s." *Journal of Social History* 5 (Winter 1971): 593–96.

Harper, Henry Howard. *A Journey in Southeastern Mexico: Narrative of Experiences and Observations on Agricultural and Industrial Experiences.* Boston: Privately printed, 1910.

Harris, Dean. *Days and Nights in the Tropics.* Toronto: Morang & Co., 1905.

Hart, John M. *Anarchism and the Mexican Working Class, 1860–1931.* Austin: University of Texas Press, 1978.

Harvey, Edmund Otis. "Mountain Climbing in Mexico." *Outing* 52, no. 1 (April 1908), 85–95.

Hayner, Norman S. *New Patterns in Old Mexico.* New Haven: College and University Press, 1966.

———. "Mexicans at Play—A Revolution." *Sociology and Social Research* 38 (1953): 80–86.

El Heraldo de Mexico. Mexico City.

Hernández, Francisco Xavier. *El Juguete popular en Mexico.* Mexico: Editorial Mexicana, S.A., 1950.

Hieb, Louis A. "Meaning and Mismeaning: Toward an Understanding of the Ritual Clown." In *New Perspectives on the Pueblos,* edited by Alfonso Ortiz. Albuquerque: University of New Mexico Press, 1972.

Hill, Jane H., and Carole Browner. "Gender Ambiguity and Class Stereotyping in the Mexican Fotonovela." *Studies in Latin America Popular Culture* 1 (1981): 43–64.

Hiriart, Hugo. *El universo de Posada: Estética de la obsolescencia.* Vol. 8 of *Memoria y Olvido: Imágenes de Mexico.* Mexico: Secretaría de Educación Pública, 1982.

Hopkins, C. Howard. *History of the Y.M.C.A. in North America.* New York: Association Press, 1951.

El Imparcial (Mexico City), November 16, 1903.

Inkersley, Arthur. "A Winter Regatta in Aztec Land." *Outing* 23, no. 4 (January 1894): 302–8.

Innes, John S. "The Universidad Popular Mexicana." *The Americas* 30, no. 1 (July 1973): 110–23.

Inzúa Canales, Victor. *Artesanías en papel y cartón.* Mexico: Fondo Nacional para el Fomento de la Artesanías, 1982.

Isaac, Rhys. *The Transformation of Virginia, 1740–1790.* Chapel Hill: University of North Carolina Press, 1982.

Jable, J. Thomas. "Sunday Sport Comes to Pennsylvania: Professional Baseball and Football Triumph over the Commonwealth's Archaic Blue Laws." *Research Quarterly* 47 (October 1976), 357–65.

Jackson, Julia Newell. *A Winter Holiday in Summer Lands.* Chicago: A. C. McClurg and Company, 1890.

Jacques, Mary J. *Texas Ranch Life with Three Months through Mexico in a "Prairie Schooner."* London: Horace Cox, 1894.

Janvier, Thomas A. *The Mexican Guide.* New York: Scribner's, 1888.

Kamen-Kaye, Dorothy. *Venezuelan Folkways.* Detroit: Blaine-Ethridge, 1976. Reprint of 1947 edition published by the *Caracas Journal.*

Kennedy, John G., and Paul A Lopez. *Semana Santa in the Sierra Tarahumana: A Comparative Study in Three Villages.* Los Angeles: Los Angeles County Museum, 1984.

Kirkham, Stanton Davis. *Mexican Trials.* New York: G. P. Putnam's Sons, 1909.

Kunzle, David. "World Upside Down: The Iconography of a European Broadsheet Type." In *The Reversible World: Symbolic Inversion in Art and Society,* edited by Barbara A. Babcock. Ithaca: Cornell University Press, 1978.

"La Casa de los Azulejos." Leaflet distributed by Sanborns, Mexico City.

Lara F., Celso A. "La Quema del Diablo en Guatemala." *Latin American Lore* 1, no. 2 (1975): 199–209.

Lavenda, Robert H. Book review. *Studies of Latin American Popular Culture* 1 (1982): 278.

Lears, T. J. Jackson. *No Place of Grace: Antimodernism and the Transformation of American Culture, 1880–1920.* New York: Pantheon Books, 1981.

Leonard, Irving A. *Baroque Times in Old Mexico.* Ann Arbor: University of Michigan Press, 1959.

LeRoy Ladurie, Emmanuel. *The Peasants of Languedoc.* Translated by John Day. Urbana: University of Illinois Press, 1974.

———. *The Territory of the Historian.* Translated by Ben and Siân Reynolds. Sussex: Harvester Press, 1979.

London, Jack. "The Mexican." In *Sporting Blood: Selections from Jack London's Greatest Sports Writings,* edited by Howard Lochtman. Novato, Calif.: Presidio Press, 1981.

Lotman, Iu. M. "Theater and Theatricality in the Order of Early Nineteenth Century Culture." In *Semiotics and Structuralism: Readings from the Soviet Union,* edited by Henryk Baran. White Plains, N.Y.: International Arts and Sciences Press, 1974.

Lurie, Alison. *The Language of Clothes.* New York: Random House, 1981.

MacMahan, J. B. "Polo in the West." *Outing* 27, no. 6 (March 1897): 593–96.

Madero, Francisco I. *La sucesión presidencial en 1910.* San Pedro, Coahuila: N.p., 1908.

Mendizabal, M. O. "Powder That Kills and Powder That Amuses." *Mexican Folkways* 3, no. 1 (February 1927): 5–18.

Meyer, Michael C., and William L. Sherman. *The Course of Mexican History*. 2nd ed. New York: Oxford University Press, 1982.

Mexico. Dirección General de Estadística. *Estadísticas Sociales del Porfiriato, 1887–1910*. Mexico: Secretaría de Economía, 1956.

Molina Enríquez, Andrés. *Los grandes problemas nacionales*. Mexico: Imprenta de A. Carranza e Hijos, 1909.

Mühlenfordt, Eduardo. *Versuch einter getreuen Schilderung der Republik Mexiko*. Edited by Ferdinand Anders. Vol. 1. 1844. Reprint. Graz, Austria: Akademische Druck u. Verlagsanstal, 1969.

Murdock, Eugene C. *Ban Johnson: Czar of Baseball*. Westport, Conn.: Greenwood Press, 1982.

News and Observer (Raleigh, N.C.), January, 1902.

New York Times

Noel, Cayuquí Estage. Letter to Author, November 9, 1983.

Novo, Salvador. *Los paseos de la ciudad de Mexico*. Mexico: Fondo de la cultura económica, 1984.

Núñez y Domínguez, José de J. "Judases en Mexico." *Mexican Folkways* 5, no. 2 (April 1929): 90–104.

O. L. "Holy Week in Mexico." *Lippincott's Magazine* 57 (1896): 525.

Official Associated Press Sports Almanac 1975. New York: Dell Publishing Company, 1975.

Paz, Octavio. "The Eye of Mexico: Todos Santos, Día de Muertos." *Evergreen Review* no. 7 (1959): 22–37.

Pérez-Rioja, J. A. *Diccionario de símbolos y mitos*. Madrid: Editorial Tecnos, s.a., 1980.

Peterson, Harold. *The Man Who Invented Baseball*. New York: Scribner's, 1969.

Pettit, Florence H., and Robert M. Pettit. *Mexican Folk Toys: Festival Decorations and Ritual Objects*. New York: Hastings House Publishers, 1978.

Pike, Fredrick B. *Spanish America, 1900–1970: Tradition and Social Innovation*. New York: W. W. Norton, 1973.

Plimpton, George. *Fireworks: A History and Celebration*. Garden City, N.Y.: Doubleday, 1984.

Portillo, Raymond S. "Here's How Mexico Shows Its Kinship for the Rest of Us." *Sporting News*, December 25, 1919.

Probert, Alan. "The Heretic Horses: The Introduction of the Clydesdale Breed into Mexico." *Journal of the West* 9, no. 4 (October 1970): 519–36.

———. "Mules, Men, and Mining Machinery: Transport and the Veracruz Road." *Silver Quest: Episodes of Mining in New Spain: Nine Readings. Journal of the West* 14, no. 2 (April 1975): 104–24.

Quevedo, Miguel. "Espacios libres y reservas forestrales de la ciudades: su adaptación a jardines, parques, y lugares de juegos. Aplicación a la Ciudad de Mexico." Conferencia dada en la Exposición de Higine por Ing. Miguel Quevedo, vocal del Consejo Superior de Salubridad, Jefe del Departimiento de Bosques. Mexico: Gomar y Bussón, 1911. Pamphlet in Bancroft Library, University of California, Berkeley.

Raat, W. Dirk. *Revoltosos: Mexico's Rebels in the United States, 1902–1923.* College Station: Texas A & M University Press, 1981.

———. "Ideas and Society in Don Porfirio's Mexico." *The Americas* 30, no. 1 (July 1973): 32–53.

Rabelais, François. *Garantua and Pantagruel.* Translated by Jacques LeClercq. New York: Heritage Press, 1936.

Ramos, Samuel. *Profile of Man and Culture in Mexico.* Translated by Peter G. Earle. Austin: University of Texas Press, 1962.

Ramos Espinosa, Alfredo. "Piñatas." *Anuario de la Sociedad Folklórica de Mexico,* No. 3 (1942): 33–36.

Randall, Robert W. *Real del Monte: A British Mining Venture in Mexico.* Austin: University of Texas Press, 1972.

Matt W. Ransom Collection. Southern Historical Collection. University of North Carolina.

Rees, Thomas. *Spain's Lost Jewels: Cuba and Mexico.* Springfield: Illinois State Register, 1906.

Reina, Leticia. *Las rebeliones campesinas en Mexico, 1819–1906.* Mexico: Siglo Ventiuno, 1980.

Rice, Jacqueline A. "The Porfirian Political Elite: Life Patterns of the Delegates to the 1892 Union Liberal Convention." Ph.D. dissertation, University of California, Los Angeles, 1979.

Richardson, Joanna. *Sarah Bernhardt and Her World.* New York: G. P. Putnam's Sons, 1977.

Ritchie, Michael. "Scaling the Heights—Then and Now: The Passage to Popocatépetl." *Americas* (September–October 1983): 23–31.

Roberts, Donald F. "Mining and Modernization: The Mexican Border States during the Porfiriato, 1876–1911." Ph.D. dissertation, University of Pittsburgh, 1974.

Rogers, Thomas L. *Mexico? Sí, Señor.* Boston: Mexican Central Railway Co., 1893.

Rohlfes, Laurence John. "Mexican Catholic Social Action during the *Porfiriato,* 1903–1911." Master's thesis, Tulane University, 1977.

———. "Police and Penal Correction in Mexico City, 1876–1911: A Study of Order and Progress in Porfirian Mexico." Ph.D. dissertation, Tulane University, 1983.

Rosaldo, Renato I., Jr. "The Rhetoric of Control: Ilongots Viewed as Natural Bandits and Wild Indians." In *The Reversible World: Symbolic Inversion in Art and Society,* edited by Barbara A. Babcock. Ithaca: Cornell University Press, 1978.

Rosenzweig, Fernando. "La Industria." In *La Vida económica.* Vol. 1 of *Historia moderna de Mexico.* Edited by Daniel Cosío Villegas. Mexico: Editorial Hermes, 1955–1970.

Rowland, Beryl. *Animals with Human Faces: A Guide to Animal Symbolism.* Knoxville: University of Tennessee Press, 1973.

Ruiz, Ramón Eduardo. "The People of Sonora and Yankee Capitalists." Unpublished manuscript.

Salazar Viniégra, Leopoldo. "Cuarenta y cinco años exemplares de la Y.M.C.A." *Excelsior,* November 1, 1947.

Santamaria, Francisco Javier. *Diccionario de Mexicanismos.* Mexico: Editorial Porrúa, 1978.

Sartorius, Carl. *Mexico about 1850.* 1858. Reprint. Stuttgart: F. A. Brockhause Dom.-Gesch. G. M. B. H. Abt. Antigarium, 1961.

Stephens, Evelyn P. "Marianismo: The Other Face of Machismo in Latin America." In *Female and Male in Latin America,* edited by Anne Pescatello. Pittsburgh: University of Pittsburgh Press, 1973.

Rudolf Schuller Collection. Latin American Library. Tulane University. 36 boxes.

Sherratt, Harriott Wright. *Mexican Vistas Seen from Highways and Byways of Travel.* Chicago: Rand McNally & Company, 1896.

El Siglo XIX

Simmons, Merle E. *The Mexican Corrido as a Source for Interpretive Study of Modern Mexico.* Bloomington: Indiana University Press, 1957.

Simpson, Lesley Byrd. *Many Mexicos.* 4th ed. Berkeley: University of California Press, 1971.

Smith, Robert A. *A Social History of the Bicycle: Its Early Life and Times in America.* New York: American Heritage Press, 1972.

Spicer, Dorothy Gladys. *Festivals of Western Europe.* New York: H. W. Wilson Company, 1958.

Sports Information Office. University of Missouri, Columbia, Missouri.

Sports Information Office. University of Texas, Austin, Texas.

Starr, Frederick. *Catalogue of a Collection of Objects Illustrating the Folklore of Mexico.* London: Folk-Lore Society of London, 1899.

———. "Holy Week in Mexico." *Journal of American Folk-Lore* 12, no. 46 (1899): 164–65.

Stoller, Paul. "Horrific Comedy: Cultural Resistance and the Hauka Movement in Niger." *Ethos* 12, no. 2 (Summer 1984): 165–88.

Suárez Radillo, Carlos Miguel. *Trece Autores del Nuevo Teatro Venezolano.* Caracas: Monte Avila Editores, C.A., 1971.

Subero, Efraín. *Origen y expansión de la Quema de Judas: Aporte a la investigación del folklore literario de Venezuela.* Caracas: Universidad Católica "Andres Bello," 1974.

Terrazas, Silvestre. *El Ciclismo: Manual de velocipedia.* Chihuahua: Tip. de Silvestre Terrazas, [1896].

Terry's Guide to Mexico. 8th ed. New York: Scribner's, 1972.

Terry, T. Philip. *Terry's Mexico: Handbook for Travellers.* 2nd ed. London: Gay and Hancock, Ltd., 1909.

———. "In Aztec Land Awheel." *Outing* 23, no. 6 (March 1894): 461–63.

———. "My Ride to Acapulco: A Cycling Adventure in Mexico." *Outing* 29, no. 6 (March 1897): 593–94.

Thomas, Keith. "Work and Leisure in Pre-Industrial Society." *Past and Present,* no. 29 (January 1965): 50–62.

Thompson, Stith. *Motif-Index of Folk-Literature.* 6 vols. Bloomington: Indiana University Press, 1955–1958.

Times of the Americas, November 24, 1971.

Tinker, Edward Larocque. *Corridos and Calaveras.* Austin: University of Texas Press, 1961.

Toor, Frances. *A Treasury of Mexican Folkways.* New York: Crown, 1947.

Turkin, Hy, and S. C. Thompson. *The Official Encyclopedia of Baseball.* 7th ed. New York: A. S. Barnes and Company, 1974.

Turner, Victor. *Dramas, Fields, and Metaphors: Symbolic Action in Human Society.* Ithaca: Cornell University Press, 1976.

Turner, Victor, and Edith Turner. *Image and Pilgrimage in Christian Culture: Anthropological Perspectives*. New York: Columbia University Press, 1978.

The Two Republics

United States Census Report, X, 12th Census, 1900: Manufactures. Part IV: Special Reports on Selected Industries. Washington, D.C.: Government Printing Office, 1900.

Uno Más Uno. Mexico City.

Vanderwood, Paul. Letter to the author, April 3, 1983.

Vaughan, Mary Kay. *The State, Education, and Social Class in Mexico, 1880–1928*. DeKalb: Northern Illinois University Press, 1982.

"Velocipede Notes." *Scientific American* 20 (May 1869): 343.

Viceregal and Ecclesiastical Mexican Collection. Tulane University.

Villanueva Barrizbeitía, F. *Deiciseis Cancilleres de Venezuela*. Caracas: Ediciones de la Cancilleria Venezolana, 1960.

Vogt, Evon Z. "On the Symbolic Meaning of Percussion in Zinacanteco Ritual." *Journal of Anthropological Research* 33, no. 3 (Fall 1977): 231–44.

Vonnegut, Kurt. *Palm Sunday: An Autobiographical College*. New York: Dell, 1981.

Wagner, Eric. "Baseball in Cuba." *Journal of Popular Culture* 18, no. 1 (Summer 1984): 113–20.

Ward, H. G. *Mexico*. 2 vols. London: Henry Colburn, 1829.

Weber, Eugen. *Peasants into Frenchmen: The Modernization of Rural France, 1870–1914*. Stanford: Stanford University Press, 1976.

Wells, David A. *Study of Mexico*. New York: D. Appleton and Company, 1887.

West, Robert C. "The Flat-Roofed Folk Dwelling in Rural Mexico." *Geoscience and Man* 5 (June 1964): 111–32.

Winberry, John J. "Ecology and Etymology of the Rural Folk House: Example of the Log House in Mexico." In *Man, Culture, and Settlement*, edited by Robert C. Eidt, Kashi N. Singh, and Rana P. B. Singh. New Delhi: N.p., 1977.

———. "The Log House in Mexico." *Annals* of the Association of American Geographers 64, no. 1 (March 1974): 54–69.

Wright, Harry. *A Short History of Golf in Mexico and the Mexico City Country Club*. New York: Privately printed, 1938.

Zurcher, Louis A., Jr., and Arnold Meadow. "On Bullfights and Baseball: An Example of Interaction of Social Institutions." In *Sport in the Sociocultural Process*, edited by Marie Hart and Susan Birrell. 3rd. ed. Dubuque, Iowa: Wm. C. Brown Company, 1981.

Index

31; and household, 68–69; in Porfirian Mexico, 6; and roller skating, 63; wardrobe, 71

Work and leisure, 78–79

Yaquis, 119–20

YMCA, 56, 58–59